T0305944

The Rural-Urban Nexus in India's Economic Transformation

This book describes and analyzes the transformation of Indian economy taking into account historical changes and present dynamics of the rural–urban nexus.

India has recently experienced a period as a high-performing economy, with the great improvement of indices of human development, including literacy rates, life expectancy, child mortality rates, and others. In contrast to this bright outlook, features such as the retarded growth of women's average height, the noticeable gap between male and female population, the overwhelming proportion of informal employment in the manufacturing sector, or increasing pollution overshadow India's future, in some cases pose a threat to lifestyle and environment.

Examining the rural–urban nexus where the new transformative dynamics of Indian socio-economy is most conspicuous, the contributors to this book shed light on the actual changes taking place at the bottom of Indian society through regional comparisons and spatial differentiation. The book offers unique perspectives on the topic produced mostly by Japanese scholars, including analysis of original data that have hitherto been unavailable and inaccessible to an international audience.

As the first book published on the rural–urban nexus in India, this book will be of interest to researchers studying South Asian History, Economics, Politics, Geography, Sociology and Anthropology, Development Studies, and Economic History.

Tsukasa Mizushima is a historian in the fields of Indian economic history and global history and Professor Emeritus of the University of Tokyo, Japan. His recent publications include *Sustainable Development in India: Groundwater Irrigation, Energy Use, and Food Production*, co-edited with Koichi Fujita (Routledge, 2020), and *Hinterlands and Commodities: Place, Space, Time and the Political Economic Development of Asia over the Long Eighteenth Century*, co-edited with George Bryan Souza and Dennis O. Flynn (2014).

Routledge New Horizons in South Asian Studies

Series Editors: Crispin Bates, *Edinburgh University*; Akio Tanabe, *Kyoto University*; Minoru Mio, *National Museum of Ethnology, Japan*

Modernity and Spirit Worship in India
An Anthropology of the Umwelt
Miho Ishii

Sustainable Development in India
Groundwater Irrigation, Energy Use, and Food Production
Edited by Koichi Fujita and Tsukasa Mizushima

The Dynamics of Conflict and Peace in Contemporary South Asia
The State, Democracy and Social Movements
Edited by and Minoru Mio, Kazuya Nakamizo and Tatsuro Fujikura

Caste and Equality in India
A Historical Anthropology of Diverse Society and Vernacular Democracy
Akio Tanabe

Language, Identity, and Power in Modern India
Gujarat, c. 1850–1960
Riho Isaka

Indian Economic Growth in Historical Perspective
The Roots of Development
Late Prof. Haruka Yanagisawa (ed. Tsukasa Mizushima)

The Rural-Urban Nexus in India's Economic Transformation
Tsukasa Mizushima

Inclusive Development in South Asia
Toshie Awaya and Kazuo Tomozawa

The Rural-Urban Nexus in India's Economic Transformation

**Edited by
Tsukasa Mizushima**

Routledge
Taylor & Francis Group

LONDON AND NEW YORK

First published 2023
by Routledge
4 Park Square, Milton Park, Abingdon, Oxon OX14 4RN

and by Routledge
605 Third Avenue, New York, NY 10158

Routledge is an imprint of the Taylor & Francis Group, an informa business

British Library Cataloguing-in-Publication Data
A catalogue record for this book is available from the British Library

ISBN: 978-1-032-31891-2 (hbk)
ISBN: 978-1-032-31889-9 (pbk)
ISBN: 978-1-003-31189-8 (ebk)

DOI: 10.4324/9781003311898

Typeset in Times New Roman
by KnowledgeWorks Global Ltd.

Contents

Figures

Tables

Maps

Preface

Starting from 2010, the National Institute for the Humanities (NIHU) in Japan organized the Contemporary India Area Studies (INDAS) program. Around the same time, the Japan Society of Promotion of Sciences granted a generous fund to a research program titled "Long-term trends of Indian villages" (Grant-in-Aid for Scientific Research (S): 21221010) organized by Tsukasa Mizushima for five years between 2009 and 2014. This volume is one of the outcomes of these two programs funded by the two national academic agencies.

A few dozen other South Asian specialists, both from Japan and India, participated more actively in the programs than the contributors of this volume, and the discussions in a number of meetings among all the members are reflected here. I am grateful to Fumiko Oshikawa, Koichi Fujita, Masahiko Togawa, Hiroyuki Kawashima, Junko Shindo, Katsuo Okamoto, Akiko Takahashi, Azusa Fujimori, Yuri Kitamura, Atsuko Kamiike, Etsuro Ishigami, and all others who were heavily committed to these programs.

Special thanks go to the series editors, Crispin Bates, Akio Tanabe, and Minoru Mio, without whose assistance and encouragement this publication would never have been possible. I would also like to thank Dorothea Schaefter and Saraswathy Narayan for their support and to the reviewers at Routledge for their valuable comments and for putting the product on the market.

Lastly, we, the authors, hope that this book can contribute to the understanding of South Asia, which is emerging strongly as one of the most important players in changing the world.

Tsukasa Mizushima

Contributors

Hideki Esho is an economist in the field of development economics and Indian economy. He is currently a Professor Emeritus at Hosei University, Japan. His publications include *India's Globalizing Political Economy: New Challenges and Opportunities in the 21st Century*, co-editor (Sasakawa Peace Foundation, 2009), *Industrialization of China and India: Their Impacts on the World Economy*, co-author (Routledge, 2013), and "Modinomics 1.0 and the Indian Economy", *Journal of Interdisciplinary Economics*, 1–11, 2019.

Atsushi Fukumi is a Professor of Economic Development at the Institute for Policy Analysis and Social Innovation, University of Hyogo. He received his PhD in Economics at Kobe University in 2002. His research interests are in Political Economy, Power Sector Reform, and State Finance in India. His publications include "Issues in the Development of the Energy Distribution Sector in India: The Cases of the Electricity and Gas Industries" in *Privatization of Public City Gas Utilities* (2020), and "Political Economy of Agricultural Electricity Tariffs: Rural Politics of Indian States", co-authored with Atsushi Kato, *Energy Policy*, 2020, Vol. 145.

Takashi Kurosaki is a Professor at the Institute of Economic Research, Hitotsubashi University, Tokyo, Japan. He holds a PhD from Stanford University (1995) in applied economics. He has been conducting theoretical and empirical work from a microeconomic perspective on questions of economic development and poverty reduction in South Asia. He has published numerous articles in international journals such as *Journal of Development Economics*, *American Journal of Agricultural Economics*, and *World Development*. His books in English include *Risk and Household Behavior in Pakistan's Agriculture* (Tokyo: Institute of Developing Economies, 1998), which won the 1999 Award for the Promotion of Studies on Developing Countries, and *Comparative Economic Development in India, Pakistan, and Bangladesh: Agriculture in the 20th Century* (2017).

Tsukasa Mizushima is a historian in the fields of Indian economic history and in global history. He is currently a Professor Emeritus at the University of Tokyo, Japan. His publication includes *Hinterlands and Commodities: Place, Space, Time and the Political Economic Development of Asia over the Long Eighteenth Century*, co-editor (Brill, 2014), *Concise History of South India: Issues and Interpretations*, co-editor (2014), *Nattar and the Socio-Economic Change in South India in the 18th–19th Centuries*, Study of Languages and Cultures of Asia and Africa, Monograph Series, no. 19, ILCAA, Tokyo University of Foreign Studies, 1986, "Did India experience Rapid Population Growth in the Pre-Census Period?: A Village-level Study from South India", *International Journal of South Asian Studies*, 6, 2014.

Vikas Rawal is a Professor of Economics at the Centre for Economic Studies and Planning, Jawaharlal Nehru University, New Delhi. His research focuses mainly on agrarian development in India. His featured methodology lies in combining detailed village studies with empirical analysis of agrarian change using large-scale statistical data. In recent years, he has also been working on international issues of food and agriculture. His publications include *Ending Malnutrition: From Commitment to Action* (co-authored) (FAO, 2014), *Socio-Economic Surveys of Two Villages in Rajasthan: A Study of Agrarian Relations* (co-edited) (2014), "The Global Economy of Pulses" (co-edited) (FAO, 2019), and *When Governments Fail: A Pandemic and Its Aftermath* (co-edited).

Takahiro Sato is a Professor at the Research Institute for Economics and Business Administration (RIEB) at Kobe University. His areas of research are development economics and studies on the Indian economy. He has authored numerous books and articles, which appeared in *Journal of Policy Modeling, Economics of Governance, Oxford Development Studies, Economic and Political Weekly*, and *European Journal of Development Research*. In 2007, he received the first JASAS Award from the Japanese Association for South Asian Studies.

Ippei Sekido is a Project Researcher at the Graduate School of Arts and Sciences, the University of Tokyo, and a Research Fellow at National Institutes for the Humanities. He was a Research Fellow (2016) at the Graduate School of Humanities and Sociology, the University of Tokyo. His areas of research are environmental sciences, environmental economics, agricultural economics, and historical GIS. He studies long-term environmental and economic change of South Asian counties and Japan with an emphasis on nitrogen cycle, food supply, water pollution, demographic change, and land use. His publications include "The Nitrogen Cycle and Fertilizer Subsidy in India" in *Sustainable Development in India* (Routledge, 2021).

Daizo Sugimoto is an agro-economist specializing in agriculture and food consumption in India. He is currently a Professor at Meijo University, Japan. His publications include "Impact of Non-Farm Employment on Landholding Structures in Punjab: Comparison of Three Villages",

Industrial Clusters, Migrant Workers, and Labour Markets in India (2014), and "Groundwater Depletion Effects on Punjab Agriculture", *Structural Transformation in Globalizing South Asia: Comprehensive Area Studies for Sustainable, Inclusive, and Peaceful Development* (National Museum of Ethnology, 2017).

Yoshifumi Usami taught for many years at the University of Osaka Prefecture and is currently a research fellow at the Center for South Asian Studies, the University of Tokyo. He is interested in the study of labor market in rural India. His publications include "A Note on Recent Trends in Wages in Rural India", *Review of Agrarian Studies*, 1(1), 2011, "Wage Rates in Rural India, 1998–99 to 2016–17" (co-authored), *Review of Agrarian Studies* 7(2), (2017), and "An Augmented Definition of Work Participation in Rural India" (co-authored), in V.K. Ramachandran et al. (eds) *Women and Work in Rural India* (New Delhi, Tulika Books, 2020).

Kazuya Wada is an Associate Professor at College of Human and Social Science at Kanazawa University. He specializes in development economics, with an emphasis on health, education, gender, and environmental problems in rural areas. His publications include "Spatial Characteristics of Long-term Changes in Indian Agricultural Production: District-Level Analysis, 1965–2007", *Review of Agrarian Studies* 5(1) (with T. Kurosaki), "Demographic Change and Women's Status in India", *Senri Ethnological Studies* 96, and "Impacts of Instream Water Rights on River Water Conservation in Oregon", *Regional Environmental Change* 19(8).

Haruka Yanagisawa, who passed away in 2015, was a Professor Emeritus of the University of Tokyo, Japan. He was much loved and respected for his kindness and academic commitment. His publications include *A Century of Change: Caste and Irrigated Lands in Tamilnadu 1860s–1970s,* Manohar, 1996, *Towards a History of Consumption in South Asia,* co-editor (2010), *Local Agrarian Societies in Colonial India: Japanese Perspectives,* co-editor (1996) (reprinted 2013), *Community, Commons and Natural Resource Management in Asia,* editor (2015). His articles have been published in *Indian Economic and Social History Review, Conservation and Society,* and *Review of Agrarian Studies.* He has also published many books and articles in Japanese.

Introduction[1]

Tsukasa Mizushima

A few decades after the start of its liberalization policy, India entered a period of high economic performance. The Green Revolution, from its beginning in the mid-1960s, has shaped India into one of the most important exporters of agricultural commodities. The change in lifestyle symbolized by the mushrooming of shopping centres, the enormous number of mobile phone users, the tremendous increase of car and motorcycle users on the road and other developments indicate a new image of India following several decades of the "Hindu Growth Rate". Although the growth rate dropped radically between 2019 and 2020 due to the COVID-19 pandemic, many expect a rebound. Her share in the world GDP started increasing from 3% in 1980 to around 7% in 2020. With an expected annual growth rate of 7% or more after the pandemic, this figure will continue to increase in the coming years. Though the poverty headcount ratio at $1.90 a day (2011 PPP) still remains at 21.2% in 2011, this actually represents a sharp drop from 31.1% in 2009 (The World Bank, http://povertydata.worldbank.org/poverty/country/IND). Literacy rates, life expectancy, child mortality rates, and other indices of human development indicate great improvement in recent decades, too. Such factors seemingly convince us that India has entered a new phase. In contrast to this bright outlook, features such as the retarded growth of women's average height, the noticeable gap between male and female population, the overwhelming proportion of informal employment in the manufacturing sector, and increasing pollution overshadow India's future, in some cases posing a threat to lifestyle and environment. The chapters collected in this book aim to clarify what is actually changing at the bottom of Indian society.

The ten chapters contained here discuss economic development in India. One of the specific features common to all is the situating of short-term or micro-level information in a long-term and macro-level historical development. They also seek to integrate findings by utilizing GIS (Geographical Information System) tools. This approach, for which a five-year grant from the Japan Society for Promotion of Sciences was awarded, enabled us to focus more on regional differences across India over long periods. The chapters in this book aim to highlight spatial variations not only at a district

DOI: 10.4324/9781003311898-1

level but at a village or even hamlet level. This priority was intentionally decided upon in the initial stages of the research project as all members were conscious of its importance. Each contributor has a specific field in relation to India. Mizushima, Yanagisawa, and Wada have conducted field studies mainly in Tamil Nadu, South India, while Usami, Sugimoto, and Kurosaki have spent years in Punjab and other areas in North India. During discussions with the other specialists working in different parts of India, the members seized upon the importance of highlighting not only decadal but also regional differences. Therefore, throughout this book, each author has tried to include spatial aspects in his argument as much as possible.

In Chapter 1, Mizushima deals with the long-term agricultural development of the past two centuries. From the position of being one of the least populated and least cultivated regions at the beginning of the 19th century, with a high potential for developing huge "cultivable waste", Tamil Nadu has made rapid progress in agricultural development, going through a number of quantitative and qualitative changes. Along with Punjab, Tamil Nadu stands ahead of the rest of the states. Currently occurring, however, is the conversion of agricultural land to non-agricultural land or the desertion of agriculture. After centuries of effort toward agricultural development, Tamil Nadu seems to have entered a new stage. By using hamlet level historical sources and clarifying the structural changes observed there, Mizushima situates the Indian rural society of today within a long-term historical context.

Chapter 2 also takes up long-term trends in agricultural production by focusing on crop specialization across regions. By tracing the trends in crop production at a district level over a hundred years, starting from the beginning of the 20th century, Kurosaki explores the importance of the main breakthrough in the early 1950s or pre-Green Revolution period. Investigations into spatial concentration indices of a number of crops in the past several decades also reveal important changes. For instance, there occurred not only a substantial inter-district heterogeneity in the share of non-food grain and the share of rice and wheat but also a rise of spatial concentration in some crops like pearl millets and cotton. Another finding is that the speed of concentration was much faster at the district level than at the national level. Kurosaki's conclusions, based upon a large quantity of district-level data, verify the hypothesis that while food consumption patterns become more homogeneous across regions, urbanization with its integrated markets makes some local regions specialize more in agricultural production.

Yanagisawa, in Chapter 3, approaches the issue from his intensive village studies conducted in Tamil Nadu in 1979/81 and 2007. It is widely observed that the increasing opportunities in non-farm economic activities like construction work and the resultant tightening of the labour market in favour of employees in rural areas has strengthened the bargaining position of lower class villagers. Their socioeconomic status has been greatly improved.

In contrast, the control of rural elites over them has seriously decreased. Yanagisawa describes this change in class relations as a "social revolution". It is, however, known that the lower classes, who are generally less educated than the elite classes, even if their economic position has been improved, find it impossible to get well-paid jobs in the formal sector. There is a gap between their expectations and reality. They usually end up working in a range of precarious small-scale and informal sectors in both agrarian and non-agrarian job markets. As a result, they have to maintain their livings by finding lowly paid jobs – like construction work, which is created on a large scale in urban and rural areas – without leaving their villages permanently. The close proximity of the rural and urban areas has thus emerged as a product of this temporary movement of the lower classes of the rural societies.

Economic development in the non-agrarian sector has been occurring not only in urban areas but also in rural areas in recent decades. People and commodities incessantly cross the rural–urban boundaries from both sides, and the boundaries are increasingly melting down. However, the way people cross boundaries and the way boundaries stand differs from person to person. Usami and Rawal, in Chapter 4, analyze the changing employment structure, especially for youth, by differentiating the trends between men and women, between rural and urban workers, and across different sectors. By focusing on the period between 2004/05 and 2011/12, when there was a significant contraction of employment and a shift from agriculture to construction was observed, and by adopting a detailed age-cohort-wise analysis among young workers, Usami and Rawal investigate how educational attainments influence employment. The authors found that there was still a substantial number of less educated young workers even after the conspicuous improvement of their educational attainment in recent years and that these less educated rural males were absorbed increasingly into construction work. Even among rural men with more than ten years of education, it becomes hardly possible to find employment in the non-agrarian sectors unless they possess technical diplomas or college education. Further, rural females with limited educational attainments dropped out of the labour force altogether during the same period. On the other hand, educated urban men and women are largely incorporated into non-agrarian sectors as regular workers. Usami and Rawal conclude that on account of the large contraction of employment in agriculture, all age-cohorts except the youngest (15–21 years) saw a massive decline in the number of workers and that the less educated were edged out, even from agricultural works. As Yanagisawa points out, the choice for these people is to enter construction and similarly precarious jobs. Yanagisawa's argument of the emancipation of lower classes needs to be carefully read in this context.

If the employment situation for many of the less educated rural mass remains low and precarious, how can they maintain their lives? What is the key behind their survival? Sugimoto approaches this problem in Chapter 5 by examining how low-income households managed to maintain their diets after the inception of economic liberalization in the 1990s. He offers comprehensive statistical analysis on food consumption covering all states of India taking into account inter-regional variation. His analysis is based upon unit-level data of three National Sample Survey (NSS) conducted from 1993/93 to 2009/10 and covers food policies like the Public Distribution System (PDS) and regional differences in people's food preferences. It demonstrates that the PDS cereals played an important role in cereal consumption of poor households. This chapter reveals that food consumption among the poor is maintained by the distribution of the PDS cereals supplied at extremely low prices, by the substitution of traditional oil (groundnut) with cheaper non-traditional imported oil (palm), and by abundantly consumed home-produced milk. Sugimoto argues that these three factors function to keep the wage rates in both rural and urban areas extremely low.

Milk, the crucial food for maintaining a poorer section of the society, is the subject of Esho's study in Chapter 6. For Esho, the dairy industry presents a symbolic case for advancing a new approach to Indian society from the perspective of "from urban to rural" or "from consumption to production". The development of the dairy industry, "a representative case of demand-driven growth", was closely related to the economic liberalization policy. Findings such as a sudden jump of the proportion of female cattle in total bovines between 2007 and 2012, a complete withdrawal of the landless from milk husbandry, an aggressive entry of large and medium farmers into commercial dairy farming, a double increase of the share of livestock sector GDP in agricultural GDP between 1980/81 and 2012/13, a conspicuous growth of milk production since the Independence, the increase of the milk and milk products in total food expenditure, and the higher growth rates of milk price since 2010/11, are all related to the policy change from protection to liberalization. Esho also traces the case of the leaping cooperative dairy society but stresses that private companies, including foreign capital, have become much more prevalent. The competition between the cooperatives and the private has become acute. However, some cooperatives have responded very aggressively and successfully. Along with the development of dairy companies, there also emerged in many states the commercial dairy farms run by the so-called "progressive dairy farmers" who came from outside of agriculture. Esho concludes that various changes of lifestyle in recent decades have caused a big change in consumption patterns, in which milk occupies an important share, and predicts that a "consumption revolution" affecting milk production will eventually break the mixed crop-livestock system that Indian agriculture has maintained for centuries.

If the level of merger between rural and urban areas regarding employment, consumption, and other ways of life has become so high, what type of differences can we observe in the quality of life between rural and urban? Wada, in Chapter 7, takes up the issue of child welfare and examines the changing situation between the rural and urban areas. Though the socioeconomic improvements in India in recent years are quite apparent, Wada thinks the issue of regional and/or rural–urban differences needs further clarification. By comparing two National Family Health Surveys (NFHS) conducted in 1992/93 and 2005/06, he finds the environment for child survival to have improved greatly during the period at an all-India level. However, the inter-state as well as rural–urban variation continues. In order to clarify what factors generate differences in child welfare, he explores several separate variables for rural and urban areas and finds contrastive trends between the two, even though their differences have decreased on average. While the inter-state differences become gradually ameliorated in rural areas, the urban areas intensified diversity among the states. Interpretation of these trends presents difficulties, as situation from state to state is complicated. Other findings also reject simple interpretations. For instance, the effect of a mother's schooling years on child survival differed from state to state, and the child survival rate in non-slums was significantly worse than that in slums in Kolkata. Wada attempts to give interpretations for these complex problems but also stresses the need for further exploration. Overridingly, his arguments emphasize the importance of identifying rural–urban and regional differences.

When large-scale development occurs in a short period of time, it becomes hardly possible to avoid some environmental problems. Air and water become polluted and rubbish is produced, affecting environments. Sekido approaches, in Chapter 8, this issue in relation to nitrogen flow at a district level across India. He uses the nitrogen inflow and outflow around farmland as an index of the impact of food production on the rural environment, whereas the nitrogen load from humans is used to assess the urban impact of food consumption. As to the former, he finds that heavy use of nitrogen fertilizer is found in the rice and wheat producing regions like Punjab and Ganges Basin, while some districts near big cities have decreased their use due to the conversion of land from agriculture to other purposes. What is conspicuously increasing is the poultry farms near big cities, and Sekido warns that they will pose serious local problems in coming years unless an effective measure to use excrement as fertilizer is taken. On the other hand, the nitrogen load from humans very much depends upon population increase and its spatial concentration. After investigating factors such as total fertility rate, scale of migration, district-level future population, trends of cereal production, and patterns of protein consumption, Sekido finds that the per-capita protein consumption does not have either regional variance or rural–urban differences. Because of the unique food habit in India, the consumption of animal protein remains very much limited and is predicted to continue to be so. Population concentration in the big cities and their surroundings, therefore, is the only potential factor posing an environmental problem. This problem, according to Sekido, is controllable via the development of sewerage treatment facilities. Sekido urges government initiatives for the solution of the problem. The future of environmental problems in India very much depends upon the performances of the central and state governments.

Another important issue concerning the future of Indian economy is the fragile power infrastructure. Compared with China, India lags far behind in terms of per-capita power consumption. The poor power infrastructure, which causes outages and voltage fluctuations in different degrees from state to state, is the highest hurdle hindering foreign investment and economic development. Improving it must become a top priority for India. Fukumi deals with the electricity problem in Chapter 9 and tries to explore the roots of the problem. Toward this, he assesses the effects of governance reform on the private sector by using firm-level data regarding commercial losses caused by power outages. The solution, however, seems difficult to find; issues like distorted tariff structure and state subsidies are heavily involved with state-specific economic and political factors. Fukumi argues that the corporate and regulatory governance in the respective states critically decides the quality of the power supply. The future of the performance of the Indian power structure and economy looks very much dependent upon the streamlining of irrational political and economic factors.

The previous chapters deal with India's economic development by paying attention to regional and rural–urban differences within India. In Chapter 10, Sato attempts to locate India in comparative perspectives. This is done through cross-country regression studies covering around 100 countries, with a particular focus on China. While posing "absolute convergence" and "conditional convergence" in the neoclassical growth model as a theoretical framework, Sato investigates the relation of growth rate to such variables as urbanization rates, initial GDP, educational attainment, life expectancy, population growth, total fertility rates, government consumption, investment rates, inflation rates, terms of trade, external openness, qualities of governing authority, and the democracy index. By controlling the country-fixed effect, he tries to identify which variables work positively and which negatively. Among other factors, he argues that the improvement of people's well-being itself is the most important for higher economic growth.

Thus, the ten chapters deal with various aspects of Indian economic development over the past two centuries by utilizing data of the lowest possible unit. It would be the authors' honour if they receive comments from the readers and active debates occur after this publication.

Note

1 This work was supported by Japan Society for the Promotion of Science (JSPS) KAKENHI (Grant-in-Aid for Scientific Research(S)), Grant Number JP21221010.

1 A Long-Term Trend of Rural India

Tsukasa Mizushima

Compared with the Gangetic Plains, which were thickly populated before the start of the colonial period, the population density of South India was much lower except in the Cauvery delta. One of the earliest colonial records, *Zamindari Statement*, prepared at the introduction of the zamindari settlement in 1801, gives us information of around 2,000 villages in the Jagir (later renamed as Chingleput). A calculation of the record shows that the average number of houses and the population in a village were 29 and 136, respectively, and the population density was just 95 persons per km^2. It is also surprising to find that 80 per cent of the villages had less than 30 houses (Table 1.1). The *2011 Census* of the same locality shows that the population density came to be as high as 981 persons per km^2.

We do not have the same level of information in other parts of India at the beginning of the 19th century so that it is difficult to judge the general situation of population change in other parts of India from the beginning of the 19th century till the first Census of 1871. What attracts attention, however, is the regional difference. Table 1.2, produced by Guha, shows the population change of four major regions in the period between 1800 and 1881. According to it, South India had the highest increase rate at 113 per cent. This contrasts sharply with North India, which showed only a 26 per cent increase. As Guha himself admits, these figures are "guesstimates," not even "estimates," as the information necessary to verify the trend is insubstantial. However, the higher increase rates of East India and South India compared with North India is understandable if we take the longer historical background of the Gangetic Plain into consideration. Map 1.1 indicates the district-level population density across India in 1872. As is clearly indicated, the Gangetic Plain was much more densely populated than South India (with the exception of the Cauvery delta). To put it in other way, South India had much more potential for land and agricultural development than the already saturated area in the Gangetic Plain at the beginning of the colonial rule. If we pay attention to such regional variances in the past, it will produce hints to understand the roots of wide variance of developmental speed among the states today.

DOI: 10.4324/9781003311898-2

Table 1.1 Size of the hamlets in Chingleput, 1801

No. of houses	No. of hamlets	Accumulated percentage
1	529	30%
10	465	56%
20	283	72%
30	170	81%
40	96	87%
50	52	90%
60	38	92%
70	28	93%
80	23	95%
90	13	95%
100	11	96%
110	12	97%
120	10	97%
130	5	97%
140	6	98%
150	4	98%
160	5	98%
170	0	98%
180	0	98%
190	5	99%
200	13	99%
300	6	100%
400	2	100%
500	1	100%
600	2	100%
700	1	100%

Source: Zamindari Statement (1801).

Note: Out of 2,315 hamlets in Chingleput, there were 441 hamlets without any houses. In addition, there were 94 hamlets whose statistics were included in other hamlets. The figures in the table cover the remaining 1,780 hamlets.

This chapter mainly examines long-term trends of rural development in Tamil Nadu to highlight such regional variances of economic development in India. Tamil Nadu is well known to have attained a higher level of agricultural growth and, together with Punjab, has moved ahead of other states

Table 1.2 Regional variance of population increase, 1800–1881

	1800	*1881*	*Increase*
East	39.00	76.42	96%
West	16.43	25.96	58%
Central	21.70	32.87	51%
North	64.45	80.20	26%
South	18.34	39.06	113%
Total	158.92	254.51	60%

Source: Guha (2001: 58 (Table 1.4)).

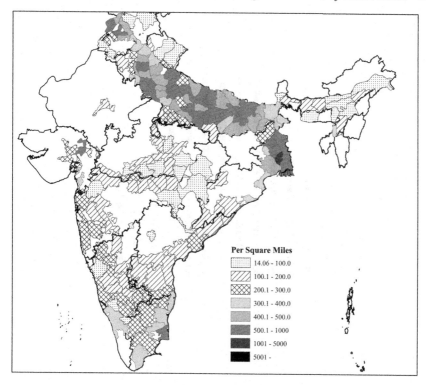

Map 1.1 Population density in districts in British India, 1872.

Source: Prepared from Memorandum on the Census of British India 1871–72, Appendices,
Table 1 (British India), Tables 2–14 (Provinces) http://piketty.pse.ens.fr/files/ideologie/data/
CensusIndia/CensusIndia1871/CensusBritishIndia (downloaded on November 28, 2021).

in recent decades. By using village-level information to periodize historical
development over the past two centuries and by clarifying the structural
changes observed therein, it attempts to situate the Indian rural society of
today within the long-term historical context. This chapter also sets the
baseline of the arguments taken up in the following chapters.

Late Pre-Colonial

Pre-colonial South Indian society had several specific features besides lower
population density and the smaller size of villages as mentioned above.
A low percentage of cultivated area in the total village area (32 per cent)
and a high percentage of irrigated area in the total cultivable area (76 per
cent) were the two distinctive features of the period. Land development was
concentrated in the limited area irrigated by water tanks or river channels
that enabled comparatively stable agriculture. In other words, only such a
stable area could accommodate the population to settle.

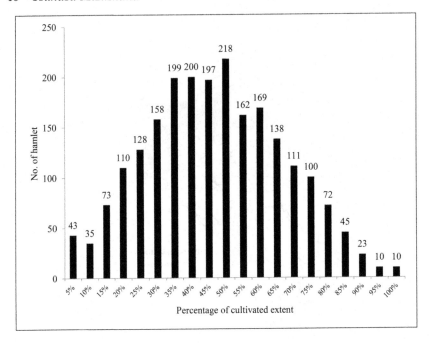

Figure 1.1 Percentage of cultivated extent in Chingleput, 1801.

Source: Zamindari Statement (1801).

Note: Percentage of cultivated extent = (cultivated land in the State land + Inam land)/all the land.

Potentiality for further land development, however, varied widely, as Figure 1.1 indicates. While some villages had little room for extending land, some had ample potential. What was pursued as much as possible by the people was to develop uncultivated areas either within their villages or in the frontiers. The previously untouched peripheral area started to be zealously developed from the beginning of the 19th century.

Somewhat unexpected but very important finding concerning the late precolonial period was the very high percentage of people engaged in non-agricultural sectors. *Barnard Records* are the detailed village accounts compiled in the late 1770s. The records, covering 62,529 households in around 2,000 villages in Chingleput, reveal that the peasantry comprised 53 per cent of the population and the non-agriculturists 45 per cent (Table 1.3). The latter's high percentage indicates in a way high productivity of agriculture in the period. The main factor explaining it must be the concentration of cultivation in the irrigated land.

Lastly, an extensive existence of a share-distribution system, called *mirasi* system in the contemporary records, should be mentioned to understand the nature of the rural society in the period. In the *mirasi* system, everyone in the locality, including temples, priests, peasants, artisans, etc., was entitled to some proportional share in the whole local produce. In exchange for

Table 1.3 Occupational structure in the Jagir (Chingleput), 1770s

Occupation/others	No. of houses	Percentage
Administration	2,107	4.0%
Cotton manufacturer	3,333	6.4%
Crafts & industry	2,621	5.0%
Merchant	4,840	9.3%
Military	1,056	2.0%
Miscellaneous	180	0.3%
Muslim	657	1.3%
Peasantry	27,737	53.1%
Ritual, culture	7,685	14.7%
Service	1,586	3.0%
Unclarified	418	0.8%
Total	52,220	100.0%

Source: Compiled from Barnard Records (1770s).

Note: Muslims were summarily included in the occupational list in the original record. Many lived in towns and were most probably engaged in non-agricultural occupations.

the share, they performed some specific role for the local society. Though we cannot go into the details here, the system had lasted for centuries since the Chola period. What is to be noted is that the early colonial records in the Madras Presidency are full of evidence about the operation of the system. Similar system existed in other parts of India as well, including the *vatan* system in Deccan (Kotani et al., 2008).

While the *mirasi* system can be basically characterized as one in the subsistence economy, there emerged a new economy outside the *mirasi* system. It was none but the market economy that had developed to the extent of having periodic markets in the countryside as well as the overseas markets spreading across the Indian Ocean. The driving force was the cotton industry, facilitated by the activities of European commercial powers from the 17th century and also by the colonial urban development along coasts. A gradual shift from the *mirasi* system to the market economy was observed during the period. For instance, some of the *Mirasi* shares, which had functioned within the subsistence economy of the local society, came to be transacted in cash across different localities (Mizushima, 2015). The centuries-old *mirasi* system had come to be deeply shaken in the late pre-colonial period.

From the Beginning of the 19th Century to the 1870s

The turn of the century and the start of full-scale colonial rule marked a clear shift in rural society. Firstly, the introduction of the *raiyatwari* system dissolved the *mirasi* system and converted the society from a share-based to the land-based one.[1] Resources in the local society were now divided and incorporated into the respective land lots in the *raiyatwari* system.

Local society came to be composed of hundreds of independent land lots owned by a number of landholders called *pattadar*. The removal of land from under the sway of local society eventually released land as independent property, thus laying the foundations for the land market. Secondly, the pace of land development and population increase accelerated. Not only the uncultivated land on the periphery inside the village area but also the forest and other types of lands previously thought unfit for cultivation in the virgin area came to be newly developed. This, on the other hand, signified the start of a process that amplified the instability of cultivation on a large scale.

It is interesting to investigate who played the leading role in such land development during the first half of the 19th century, when the economy is said to have suffered from deflation (Raju, 1941: Chapter XV). Though we do not have space to discuss this issue in detail, the merchants and other non-agriculturists, who were more or less deprived of the preexistent economic interests in the course of colonial development, and some European entrepreneurs who found business chances under the British colonial rule, were most probably involved in new land development through agricultural financing within the deepening monetizing process. This issue will be taken up later.

These developments converted South India into a densely populated agricultural society by 1871, when the first Census was conducted. Demographic studies on India generally understand that India entered a period of rapid population growth only in the 1920s after decades of stagnation with a high mortality rate. Due to the lack of information in the pre-Census period, the information contained in the late 16th century *Ain-i-Akbari* has been utilized to reach population figures at the beginning of the 19th century.[2] This chapter, instead, utilizes the village-level data between 1801 and 1871. After making village-to-village comparisons of all the villages in Chingleput with the Geographic Information System (GIS) tools,[3] a conclusion was reached that the period experience a great population increase. Some of the key summary figures showing the changes between 1801 and 1871 are indicated in Table 1.4.

The increase rate of population, that is, 384 per cent over 70 years, looks quite high in the modern sense. There is some possibility of a temporal

Table 1.4 Demographic changes between 1801 and 1871 in the Jagir (Chingleput)

	1801–1871	*Increase*
Hamlets	2,315(1,856) → 2,395 (2,166)	117%
Houses	52,785 → 135,985	258%
Population	244,845 → 941,047	384%
Density (per km²)	95 → 178	187%

Source: Zamindari Statement (1801), and Census of India, 1871.

Note: The number of inhabited villages is indicated in brackets.

population drop in the concerned area from the late 18th century till 1801 because of the Mysore Wars.[4] A high increase rate as observed in South India, however, was not unusual in some countries in Southeast Asia with similar developmental stages. If we examine the global situation, the 19th century was a period of agricultural development (Williams, 2006: 228). Led by the global development of transactions in many types of agricultural commodities, South and Southeast Asian countries did experience rapid land development and population growth during the period.[5]

The third aspect of societal change between the turn of the century and the 1870s was the development of an infrastructure of transport and communication linked to the growing global economy. South India was an active participant in this process. Railway construction started from the 1850s and made progress across the country. Many other parts of India came to be incorporated in the global economy, too. India offered a market for British manufactured goods, but she also produced commodities for global markets. This process was accompanied by extensive land development and population growth in many parts of Asia. It signified the expansion of a consumer market in Asia and constituted the base of intra-Asian trade as well (Sugihara, 2010). The agricultural development of India and the related changes in rural society were the products of these factors.

From the 1870s to the 1910s

The 1870s was the starting point of the new phase of development in India. As a result of rapid and hasty land development, the degree of land scarcity and instability of agricultural production was deepened. The population growth was hindered during the period, though South India could continue to have a moderate population increase even with the big casualties from two great famines and the epidemic during the period. This inertia necessitated a breakthrough in industrial development and the increase in non-agrarian employment. Colonial India, however, could not find much in these spheres.

Features of Indian agriculture and rural society in the period can be summarized as follows. First, a saturation of land development occurred in many parts. Unlike in the previous period, the process of extension of agriculture from favorable land to inferior land came to a standstill by the end of the 19th century. South India was losing an important choice she had possessed until then. What progressed instead was the exploitation of underground water for irrigation. South India gradually shifted toward intensive agriculture by digging wells across the country (see Figure 1.2 for the changes in irrigated extent of various sources in the Madras Presidency between 1884/85 and 1942/43). A village study conducted by the author in the 1980s in RM village in Lalgudi sub-district, Tiruchirappalli district, for instance, found that well digging started in the 1890s and increased almost 10 times in the next 100 years (Table 1.5). While being affected by the price

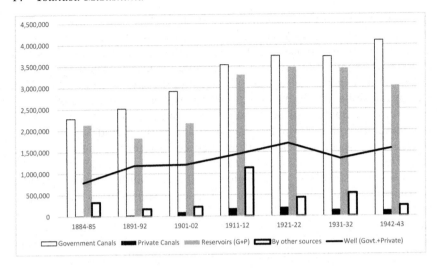

Figure 1.2 Changes in the irrigated extent of various sources in the Madras Presidency, 1884/85–1942/43.

Source: Compiled from the Agricultural Statistics of British India of various years.

fluctuation of the global market, South Indian rural society intensified the cultivation of cash crops, including rice, by employing more stable irrigation sources.

The period also saw the rising price of agricultural products (see Figure 1.3 for the increase in prices from the late 19th century). A gradually lowered proportional share of land tax in the gross produce made agriculture profitable in some years. This was especially so when there occurred an economic boom like the one after the American Civil War, though the price

Table 1.5 Increase in number of wells in RM village from the late 19th century

Year of construction	Number of wells
Before 1892	23
1893–1914	41
1915–1939	24
1940–1949	29
1950–1959	33
1960–1969	34
1970–1979	32
1980–1984	6
Year unidentified (after 1914)	5
Unidentified	3
Total	230

Source: Settlement Registers of various years, village survey maps of various years, and the author's field study conducted in 1983/84.

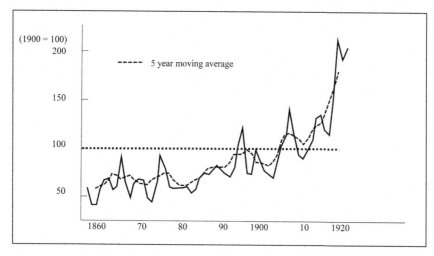

Figure 1.3 Upward trend of prices of agricultural commodities in North India from the late 19th century.

Source: Matsui (1977: Figure I-1).

fluctuations occasionally hit farmers severely, taking away instantly all the profit previously saved. The progress of intensive agriculture facilitated by the development of irrigational facilities meant that land productivity also increased. However, the irrigational attainments still heavily depended on the natural environment at this stage.

It is to be noted that the changes in rural society had activated agricultural finances and established an extensive land market by the late 19th century. Merchant-cum-moneylenders invested in the land market and became absentee landlords or controlled transactions through advances. Map 1.2 indicates the landholding ratio of the Chettiyars, the well-known merchant-cum-moneylender community in South India, in Ponneri villages located to the north of Madras. Their landholding was widely found in the late 19th century. Farmers, on the other hand, became indebted in the waves of price fluctuations. Many cases of land transfer started to be recorded (see Table 1.6 for the increase of land mortgage and transfer cases in the late 19th century). The colonial government noticed this problem, and it is interesting to know that *1901 Census* counted and recorded the number of moneylenders in every village. Map 1.3 indicates the distribution of moneylenders in Lalgudi sub-district in 1901. They were widely spread across the irrigated villages along the Coleroon River, where the land was rich and its productivity was high. Growing rice market and the development of moneylending business went hand in hand in the period.

During this unstable transition period, there occurred two great famines, as mentioned above. The famines, one in the late 1870s and another in the

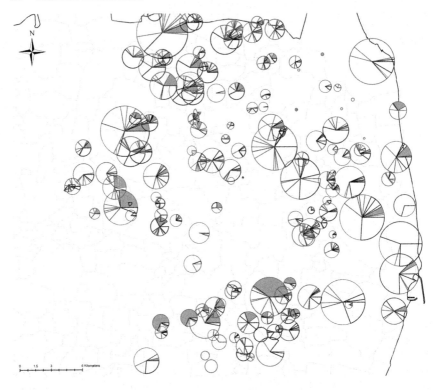

Map 1.2 Chettiyars' landholding in Ponneri villages, 1877.

Source: Prepared from Settlement Registers of Ponneri villages, 1877.

late 1890s, were caused by severe droughts. However, what should be noted are the impacts from the excessive land exploitation in the inferior area and from the rapid population growth that had continued from the beginning of the 19th century to this period. The extensive development of less favorable land had lowered resilience against severe climatic fluctuations. It may be added that the dissolution of the local society with the collapse of the *mirasi*

Table 1.6 Increase in the number of mortgage cases in the late 19th century

Year	Annual average of sale		Annual average of mortgage		Annual average of land value (Rs./acre)
	Compulsive	Arbitrary	Compulsive	Arbitrary	
1878–83	60,130	50,259	1,03,987	74,808	1,007
1883–88	94,154	84,181	1,23,516	1,19,603	1,089
1888–93	2,28,999		1,71,074	1,70,948	1,399

Source: Report Regarding the Possibility of Introducing Land and Agricultural Banks into the Madras Presidency, Madras, Government Press, 1895: 239.

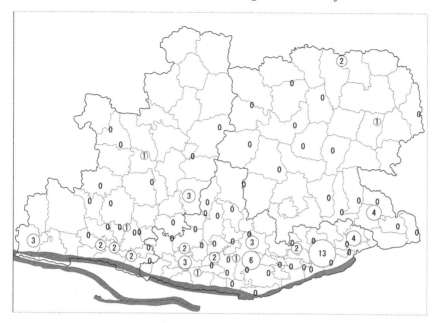

Map 1.3 Distribution of moneylenders in Lalgudi Taluk, Trichinopoly District, 1901.

Source: Prepared from *Census of India, 1901*.

Note: The Coleroon River runs on the southern edge of the Lalgudi Taluk.

system in the previous period had greatly shaken the society. One of the notable results was the loosening of ties between the upper and lower classes in the village. During the famines the lower classes, who could not secure the support from the upper classes, left their villages in great numbers and joined the relief works organized by the colonial government (*Famine Commission, 1879*: 15). Such experience further loosened the ties Migration to outside worlds was another characteristic of the period. Agricultural developments in Ceylon, Burma, the Malay Peninsula, and East Africa from the late 19th century attracted many South Indians to migrate either as indentured laborers, Kangani-type coolies, or free migrants. Totally around 30 million Indians experienced migration to abroad between the 1830s and 1930s (Table 1.7). The Nattukottai Chettiyars from the Pudukottai State facilitated this movement and played a very important role in developing land and agriculture in Southeast Asia through financing (Mizushima, 1997; Rudner, 1994; Mahadevan, 1978). However, those who left villages were not necessarily the lower classes. Unlike in Bihar and other northern Indian states, the upper classes in South India also left their villages to find employment outside their villages. The development of colonial establishments and the growth of urban centers were creating non-agrarian job opportunities, first for Brahmins and later for upper agrarian castes like Vellalas.[6]

Table 1.7 Estimated total migration to and from India, 1834–1937 (In thousands)

Year	Emigrants	Returned migrants	Net
1834–35	62	52	10
1836–40	188	142	46
1841–45	240	167	72
1846–50	247	189	58
1851–55	357	249	108
1856–60	618	431	187
1861–65	793	594	199
1866–70	976	778	197
1871–75	1,235	958	277
1876–80	1,505	1,233	272
1881–85	1,545	1,208	337
1886–90	1,461	1,204	256
1891–95	2,326	1,536	790
1896–1900	1,962	1,268	694
1901–05	1,428	957	471
1906–10	1,864	1,482	383
1911–15	2,483	1,868	615
1916–20	2,087	1,867	220
1921–25	2,762	2,216	547
1926–30	3,298	2,857	441
1931–35	1,940	2,093	−162
1936–37	815	755	59
Total	30,191	23,941	6,250

Source: Davis (1951: 99).

Note: The totals are original.

It is to be noted that the mobility of these upper classes to urban places enabled some lower classes to acquire land left behind and transformed landholding structure greatly. As indicated in Table 1.8, the Reddiyar caste, who dominated landholding in RM in 1864, steadily and greatly reduced their holding to one-quarter in 1982. On the other hand, the Gounder and others, including scheduled castes, increased their share proportionally. This was never an isolated case. Similar changes are found in many other villages in Tamil Nadu.

This was also the period when the manufacturing industries slowly developed. A dual economy in which the upper market was dominated by European goods whereas the lower market was occupied with Indian goods progressed. It may be mentioned that the South Indian weaving industry escaped from total bankruptcy and survived by diversifying its production toward the top market, producing handmade high-end textiles with imported high-count yarn. For the bottom market, they produced coarse cloth with a lower yarn count. Local factories started spinning, and their products were widely used by local weavers who produced textiles for both

Table 1.8 Changes of landholding by castes in RM village between 1864 and 1982

	1864		1898		1924		1982	
	Acs.	*%*	*Acs.*	*%*	*Acs.*	*%*	*Acs.*	*%*
Total extent	3,707.43	100.0	4,044.00	100.0	4,046.94	100.0	4,046.94	100.0
Cultivated or occupied land	1,071.09	28.9	1,808.00	44.7	2,441.93	60.3	2,620.19	65.7
Inam (tax-exempted) land	78.25	2.1	39.00	1.0	36.90	0.9	36.90	0.9
Waste or unoccupied land	1,744.05	47.0	1,374.00	34.0	335.17	8.3	156.91	3.9
Unassessed land		0.0		0.0	11.89	0.3	11.89	0.3
Poramboke (common) land	814.04	22.0	823.00	20.4	1,221.05	30.2	1,221.05	30.2
Landholding by castes	*Acs.*	*%*	*Acs.*	*%*	*Acs.*	*%*	*Acs.*	*%*
Reddiyar	823.41	77.6	1,057.53	60.3	971.90	40.6	[539.25]	26.9
Gounder	2.33	0.2	35.56	2.0	276.28	11.5	[369.22]	18.4
Muthraja	81.57	7.7	294.58	16.8	383.33	16.0	[441.46]	22.1
Udaiyar	21.31	2.0	73.69	4.2	170.75	7.1	[149.47]	7.5
Scheduled Castes (sub-total)	8.07	0.8	148.56	8.5	406.63	17.0	[380.62]	19.0
Hindu Pariah	1.61	0.2	48.28	2.8	137.15	5.7	[118.9]	5.9
Christian Pariah	2.26	0.2	57.79	3.3	108.13	4.5	[103.8]	5.2
Pallan	2.80	0.3	22.52	1.3	84.88	3.5	[86.8]	4.3
Sakkili	1.40	0.1	19.97	1.1	76.47	3.2	[71.1]	3.6
Muslim	20.14	1.9	11.47	0.7	66.53	2.8	[39.39]	2.0
Brahmin		0.0		0.0	3.31	0.1		0.0
Pandaram	4.14	0.4	0.68	0.0	6.20	0.3	[4.65]	0.2
Chettiyar		0.0		0.0	26.94	1.1	[35.45]	1.8
Ottan Chetti		0.0	10.77	0.6		0.0	[10.94]	0.5
Kal Ottan		0.0		0.0		0.0	[0.02]	0.0
Asari	13.65	1.3	28.34	1.6	17.58	0.7	[17.64]	0.9
Vannan		0.0	8.08	0.5	7.57	0.3	[2.84]	0.1
Pariyari				0.0	9.97	0.4	[5.32]	0.3
Vanniyar				0.0	5.24	0.2	[5.7]	0.3
Nayakkan	2.66	0.3	23.18	1.3	5.99	0.3		0.0
Pillai	0.80	0.1	3.86	0.2		0.0		0.0
Konar		0.0	13.20	0.8	10.09	0.4		0.0
Kusavan		0.0	24.60	1.4	6.04	0.3		0.0
Others		0.0		0.0	13.71	0.6		0.0
Unidentified	82.78	7.8	17.82	1.0	6.57	0.3		0.0
Sub-total	1,060.86	100.0	1,753.38	100.0	2,394.63	100.0	[2,001.97]	100.0
Temple/Inam land	79.30		83.27		81.66		[83.31]	
Total	1,140.16		1,836.65		2,476.29		[2,085.28]	
Land held by outsiders							571.80	

Source: Settlement Registers of various years and the author's field study conducted in 1983/84.

Note: The figures for 1982 in brackets concern the land held by RM villagers only. The outsiders held 571.80 acres at the time of the author's field study.

domestic and overseas markets. The entrepreneurs included not only merchant communities but also agricultural classes (Damodaran, 2008; Singer, 1972; Berna, 1960; Harriss, 2003). The employment opportunities offered by factory-based industries were, however, still very much limited at this stage.

1920s–1960s

From the 1920s, a high rate of population growth was resumed at all-India level.

The first characteristic feature of the period was the stagnation of agricultural development. Agriculture production was severely hit by the great price fluctuations in the interwar period. The extension of cultivation previously pursued came almost to an end.[7] Increasing population pressure from the 1920s and the lack of a primogeniture rule for inheritance accelerated the downward trend of farm size. The average cultivated extent per household in Chingleput, for instance, went down from 6.22 hectares in 1801 to 2.58 hectares in 1871, and finally to 0.96 hectares in 2001. The development of underground water resources also stagnated in the mid-1920s, only revived decades later (see Figure 1.2 for the stagnation from the 1920s). The climatic condition where downpour of rain lasts just for a few days and long duration of dry days continues afterward, and the saturation of land availability as experienced in North India centuries ago made South Indian agriculture experience chronical food problems during the period. South India had to wait for the Green Revolution in the next period.

The second important feature of the period was the extremely slow progress of urban development and the very limited non-agrarian employment opportunities. As indicated in Table 1.9, the urban population in India remained below 20 per cent until the 1960s. The percentage of

Table 1.9 Composition of rural/urban population in India, 1901–2001

Year	Rural	Urban	Total
1901	89%	11%	23,83,96,327
1911	90%	10%	25,20,93,390
1921	89%	11%	25,13,21,213
1931	88%	12%	27,89,77,238
1941	86%	14%	31,86,60,580
1951	83%	17%	36,10,88,090
1961	82%	18%	43,92,34,771
1971	80%	20%	54,81,59,652
1981	77%	23%	68,33,29,097
1991	74%	26%	84,63,02,688
2001	72%	28%	1,02,87,37,436

Source: Census of India of various years.

non-agricultural workforce among the total workforce in India remained at 25 per cent during the period 1901–1951, and the absolute number increased from 32.9 million to 39.5 million only during the same period (Sivasubramonian, 2000: 29–30). It should be added that overseas migration opportunities greatly decreased after the Great Depression and were virtually stopped by the start of WWII.

1970s–the Present

The dominant feature of this period was the qualitative change in Indian agriculture. The Green revolution began in Punjab in the mid-1960s and had spread all over India, including Tamil Nadu, by the 1970s. The diffusion of High Yielding Varieties (HYV), an increased use of chemical fertilizer, and the intensified exploitation of underground water with tube wells and electrical pumps transformed Indian agriculture greatly. India now becomes one of the important exporters of food products in the world. Sustained by the stable agricultural production, not only the Indian economy but also Indian rural society entered a new stage of development. Problems like the lowering underground water level or the abandonment of agriculture pose some uncertainties, but Indian agriculture definitely overpassed the period of food deficiency.

Changes in rural India are occurring within the tightly knitted rural–urban nexus. The internal relationship inside rural areas has been defined by outside factors. For instance, remittances from the Gulf and other places usually far exceed the agricultural income obtainable in rural areas. Non-agrarian employments in urban areas offer much better income so that those availing themselves of such opportunities, usually the upper classes, leave their villages permanently while those who do not or cannot, mainly the lower classes, have to remain in the villages. The latter may acquire landholding but remain as small peasants while supplementing their income by finding part-time construction works in the town as Yanagisawa argues in Chapter 3. The chance of getting a highly paid job very much depends upon educational attainments as Rawal and Usami clarify in Chapter 4. In order to seek limited chances, the upper class parents often choose to move to newly emerging "towns" located between the big towns for their children's higher education while managing agriculture in their home villages. The mushrooming of the so-called "Census Town," taken up for study in Chapter 4, is often the product of these processes. To meet such a demand, a number of colleges have been founded in remote rural areas. More and more villages with an easier access to urban centers have been involved with new housing and industrial developments in their villages. Speculation in land and the resulting rise of land prices, especially in suburban villages like Census towns, has often led to a loss of interest in agriculture and to the eventual abandonment of farming. Tightly integrated rural–urban nexus has brought all these changes in rural India today.

Imminent Problems and "Possible" Solutions

This chapter attempted to periodize the economic development of rural India in the past two centuries into five stages and gave brief descriptions of the features of respective periods as a basis for arguments in the following chapters. During the investigation, several imminent issues were pointed out. Under the severe climatic conditions and in light of the absolute insufficiency of resources in contrast to the enormous population in rural India, there wait a number of problems to solve. It goes without saying that possible solutions are not only difficult to find out but also difficult to accomplish. For instance, the land development in the past centuries in the inferior area has caused fragility and instability of production. It may be solved by developing underground water resources in these areas, but the availability of underground water is never promised. Concentration of agricultural resources into a limited number of farmers or favorable areas may enrich the selected farmers and maintain the land productivity and the level of production, but how can those pushed away from these attempts survive without alternative opportunities in other economic fields?

The intensification of rural–urban nexus is bringing many new features to rural India, including migration to towns or abroad, remittances from outside, lowering the share of agricultural income, inclusion of service-exchange system to a market economy, destruction of pre-existed landowning structure, party politics to gain subsidies, disparity in educational attainments, and many others. The authors of the following chapters are basically economists and utilize large scale statistics in their analysis. However, all are aware of the necessity of making intensive observations on, for instance, how village resources like reservoirs, grazing ground, underground water, and uncultivated land are utilized, how village lives like temple festivals, sports days, and school meetings are planned and conducted, how village problems like insufficient drinking water and electricity, poor sanitary facilities, and lack of a rubbish disposal system are discussed and solved. We notice creating and maintaining a village system that maximizes the opportunities to stabilize production and enable sustainability is essential for the future of Indian villages. The rest of the chapters will explore these problems in more detail.

Notes

1 The service-exchange system called *jajmani* system in the later period may look similar to the *mirasi* system. It, however, differs fundamentally from the *mirasi* system as it is cut from the entire production system of the local society and was formed among parts of the local communities. See Kotani et al. (2008).
2 See various statistics in Visaria and Visaria (1982: 466).
3 "India Place Finder" (https://india.info-proto.com).
4 Depopulation in the Tamil area from the late precolonial to the early colonial period is discussed by Lardinois (1989). According to him, a general feature of desertion and depopulation seemed prevalent in many districts under

the Madras Presidency. So far as Chingleput was concerned, however, the situation looked "a little perplexing" as the number of deserted villages was quite small. According to the information in Zamindari Statement (1801), there was a total of 245,105 inhabitants in 52,805 houses in Chingleput. Information contained in *Barnard Record, 1770s* (a series of village accounts of Chingleput area collected and compiled by Thomas Barnard in the late 18th century) shows that there was a total of 52,279 houses (there is no information about population). Some more studies are needed to verify "depopulation" in Chingleput in the late 18th century.

5 According to Kano, the cultivated extent increased from 960 in 1832 to 2,980 in 1900 in Java, from 300 in 1850s to 2,000 in the early 20th century in Lower Burma, and from 1,000 in 1850 to 1,400 in the early 20th century in Chao Phraya delta of Thailand (figures in thousand hectares). He also cited the following population increase between 1800 and 1900: Burma (4,600–10,491), north and central Vietnam (7,000–11,409), Java (5,000–29,000), the Philippines (1,835–7,635) (figures in thousands) (Kano, 2001: 18–19, 298).

6 According to the *Census of Madras,* 1871, there were 32,979 in the military service, 19,911 in the police, 384 civil servants, 4,341 court servants, 13,507 government servants, 1,597 lawyers, 9,233 physicians and surgeons, 12,837 teachers, 579 authors, 6 engineers, and 75 surveyors, and others (*Report on the Census of the Madras Presidency, 1871 with Appendix containing the Results of the Census arranged in Standard Forms prescribed by the Government of India,* Vol. I, Madras, 1874: xlviii–liv [Appendix No. VI. General Statement of Population according to Occupation]). According to Susan Bayly, there were half a million members of the middle class in India (Bayly, 1999: 148–149).

7 In the case of RM village studied by the author, the cultivated extent increased from 1,071 acres (1864) to 1,808 acres (1898), to 2,442 acres (1924), and finally to 2,620 acres (1983). The "waste or unoccupied" land, on the other hand, decreased from 1,744 acres (1864) to 1,374 acres (1898), to 335 acres (1924), and finally to 157 acres (1983). Actually, the land categorized as "waste or unoccupied" in the year 1983 was filled with rocks removed from the surrounding fields.

References

Primary Sources

Barnard Records, 1770s, Tamil Nadu State Archives.

Famine Commission, 1878, Compilation of Replies to Questions circulated by the Famine Commission for the Madras Presidency, Madras, Govt. Press, 1879.

Zamindari Statement, 1801, Statement relating to Permanent Settlement of Jagir forwarded as Enclosures to Mr. Greenway's Letter, March 29, 1801, *Permanent Settlement Records*, vols. 20–22 (*Board's Revenue Miscellaneous Record*).

Secondary Sources

Bayly, S. (1999) *Caste Society and Politics in India from the Eighteenth Century to the Modern Age,* (The New Cambridge History of India, IV.3), Cambridge University Press.

Berna, James J. (1960) *Industrial Entrepreneurship in Madras State*, Asia Publishing House.

Damodaran, H. (2008) *India's New Capitalists: Caste, Business, and Industry in a Modern Nation*, Permanent Black.

Davis, K. (1951) *The Population of India and Pakistan*, Princeton University Press.

Guha, S. (2001) *Health and Population in South Asia: From Earliest Times to the Present*, Hurst & Company.

Harriss, J. (2003) "The Great Tradition Globalizes: Reflections on Two Studies of 'The Industrial Leaders' of Madras," *Modern Asian Studies*, 37–2: 327–362.

Kano, H. (2001) "Sosetsu," "Nouson Syakai no Saihen," *Syokuminchi Keizai no Han-ei to Cholaku, (Tonan Ajia Shi, 6)* (in Japanese, "Introduction," "Reorganization of Rural Society," *Prosperity and Decline of Colonial Economy*), (*Southeast Asian History*, vol. 6), Iwanami Shoten: 1–33: 297–314.

Kotani, H., Mita, M. and Mizushima, T. (2008) "Indian History from Medieval to Modern Periods: An Alternative to the Land-System-Centred Perspective," *International Journal of South Asian Studies*, 1: 31–49.

Lardinois, R. (1989) "Deserted Villages and Depopulation in Rural Tamil Nadu, c. 1780–c. 1830," *India's Historical demography, Studies in Famine, Disease and Society*, Tim Dyson (ed.), Curzon Press: 16–48.

Mahadevan, R. (1978) "Immigrant Entrepreneurs in Colonial Burma: An Exploratory Study of the Role of Nattukottai Chettiars of Tamil," *The Indian Economic and Social History Review*, XV–3: 329–358.

Matsui, T. (1977) *Kita-Indo Nousanbutsu Kakaku no Shiteki Kenkyu II* (in Japanese: *A Historical Study on the Prices of Agricultural Products in North India*), Institute of Oriental Culture, the University of Tokyo.

Mizushima, T. (1997) "A Historical Study on Land Transaction in a Local Town in Malaysia – Kuala Kangsar Shop Lots between 1885 and 1995," *Regional Views*, No.10: 81–111.

———. (2015) "Linking Hinterlands with Colonial Port Towns: Madras and Pondicherry in Early Modern India," *Place, Space, and Time: Asian Hinterlands and Political Economic Development in the Long Eighteenth Century*, Tsukasa Mizushima, George Bryan Souza, and Dennis O. Flynn (eds.), Brill: 126–144.

Raju, A.S. (1941) *Economic Conditions in the Madras Presidency, 1800–1850*, University of Madras.

Rudner, D.W. (1994) *Caste and Capitalism in Colonial India: the Nattukottai Chettiars*, University of California Press.

Singer, M. (1972) *When a Great Tradition Modernizes: An Anthropological Approach to Indian Civilization*, The University of Chicago Press.

Sivasubramonian, S. (2000) *The National Income of India in the Twentieth Century*, Oxford University Press.

Sugihara, K. (2010) "An Introduction," *Japan, China and the Growth of the Asian International Economy, 1850–1949*, Sugihara, K. (ed.), Oxford University Press: 1–19.

Visaria, L. and Visaria, P. (1982) "Population (1757–1947)," *The Cambridge Economic History of India, vol. II, c. 1757–1970*, Cambridge University Press: 463–532.

Williams, M. (2006) *Deforesting the Earth: From Prehistory to Global Crisis: An Abridgment*, The University of Chicago Press.

2 Crop Specialization and Long-Term Productivity Growth in Indian Agriculture

A District-Level Analysis

Takashi Kurosaki

In this chapter, the role of crop specialization[1] over space in the process of urbanization is investigated empirically using district-level production data of Indian agriculture. Such investigation enables us to characterize the nature of market development and urbanization in India.

Historical records available in South Asia have confirmed the growth of agricultural productivity as a result of the introduction of modern technologies, commercialization of agriculture, capital deepening, factor shifts from agriculture to non-agricultural sectors, and other factors. This entire process can be regarded as an "agricultural transformation," for which the contribution of each factor has been quantified in the existing literature on growth accounting using macro data (Timmer 1988). This process of agricultural transformation usually occurs concomitantly with urbanization. During the initial period of urbanization and agricultural transformation, the diversity of traditional and subsistence agriculture may decrease at both national and household levels because of crop shifts reflecting comparative advantage. The actual pattern of specialization and diversification might differ according to disaggregation levels and region- and time-specific factors.

The contrast between the diversification of national food production and that of farm-level production is presented in Figure 2.1, subtracted from Timmer (1997). Timmer (1997) speculated that, as agricultural transformation progresses, the level of national production diversification may increase again because rising demand for diversified food consumption will be associated with a higher share of service elements in the final food product, which cannot be met by imports. In this phase also, the level of diversification at the farm level is likely to fall because the principle of comparative advantage continues to be applicable.

Kurosaki (2003) presented empirical evidence in support of the idea included in Figure 2.1 through a long-term analysis of district-level panel data from West Punjab (mostly corresponding to areas under the Punjab Province of today's Pakistan) during 1903–1992. He found that shifts from low to high value crops and from low to high productivity districts contributed to agricultural growth.[2] Similar effects of crop shifts from low to high value crops at the national level in India have been described by Kurosaki

DOI: 10.4324/9781003311898-3

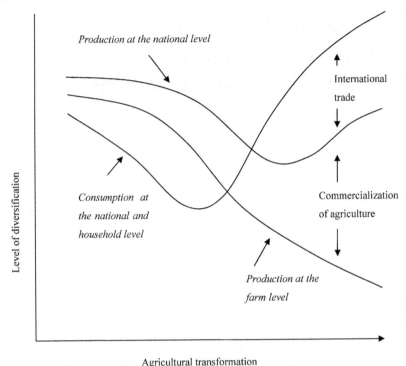

Figure 2.1 Relations among alternative measures of food crop diversification.
Source: Timmer (1997).

(2002) and Kurosaki (2015), but such evidence on the shift effects from low productivity districts to high productivity districts is not readily available for India. In a related study, Kurosaki and Wada (2015) described the spatial shifts of crops in India at the district level for 1965–2007. Using GIS maps, they addressed questions such as which districts produced which crops and how such spatial patterns changed over time. However, Kurosaki and Wada (2015) did not discuss changes in the measures of specialization across districts associated with such changes.

This chapter represents an attempt to fill that research gap, particularly addressing changes in specialization across districts in Indian agriculture. Referring again to Figure 2.1, during the initial phase of agricultural transformation, because of the absence of well-developed agricultural produce markets, diversification levels are likely to be similar between the macro and micro levels: farmers must grow crops they want to consume. As rural markets develop, however, farmers are capable of making production choices that more closely reflect their comparative advantages, contributing to productivity improvement at the aggregate level evaluated at common market prices. As this argument implies, production at a more micro level is becoming less diverse than production at a more macro level. The development of rural factor markets also enables farmers to grow more market-oriented crops through the reduction of constraints on family factor endowments. It allows them to smooth consumption more effectively (Kurosaki 2003).

No long-term data representative of India (or a state within) is available for the household level. However, if we use a district as the more micro level instead of households, and use India as the more macro level, then long-term panel data concerning production can be easily obtained. With this motivation, Figure 2.1 is redrawn as Figure 2.2 to match the motivation of this chapter more closely. In Chapter 5 of this book, Sugimoto analyzes the dynamics of regional consumption patterns. In this chapter, the degree of production similarity across districts is analyzed. As Figure 2.2 shows, the similarity level is expected to decrease as urbanization and agricultural transformation proceed. This point is examined empirically using Indian districts as the unit of investigation, as defined by district boundaries prevailing in 1965. Because agriculture is mostly conducted in rural

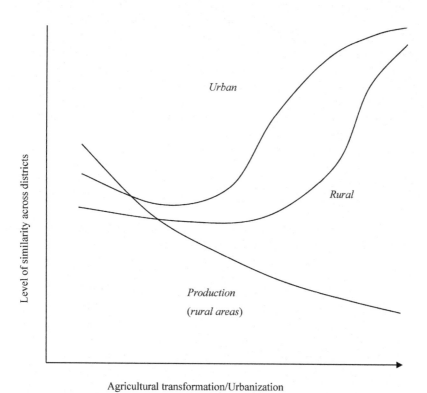

Figure 2.2 Regional similarity in food crops and economic development.

Source: Drawn by the author.

areas, the district-level analysis in this chapter is expected to shed new light on the rural–urban interaction of food production and consumption when combined with points revealed in Sugimoto's chapter. The level of similarity across districts can be measured in several ways. Following Kurosaki (2003), we use the Hirschman–Herfindahl index.

The remainder of the chapter is presented as follows. The first section presents a description of the data used. The second section characterizes long-term changes in agricultural production in India and shows that increasing intensity characterizes Indian agriculture during the twentieth century. The third section describes our investigation into whether the long-term changes were experienced homogeneously in all districts or not. The fourth section then provides empirical results related to the spatial concentration indices across Indian districts during 1965–2007. The final section concludes the chapter.

Data

The annual[3] data used in this chapter is compiled from two sources. First, as the source of background information related to very long-term changes in Indian agriculture, the time-series dataset of agricultural production for 1901–2002 (agricultural years from 1901–02 to 2001–02) corresponding to the current national boundaries of India, Pakistan, and Bangladesh is used. This dataset was analyzed by Kurosaki (2015). The data compilation procedure is described in detail by Kurosaki (2011). In this dataset, the respective areas and production of 18 major crops are compiled, together with auxiliary time-series of the ratio of these crops in the total crops sector, the value-added ratio, relative prices, etc., which enable us to estimate macroeconomic variables of the agricultural sector. The 18 crops include foodgrains[4] (rice, wheat, barley, jowar [sorghum], bajra [pearl millet], maize, ragi [finger millet], and gram [chickpea]), oilseeds (linseed, sesamum, rape and mustard, and groundnut), and other crops (sugarcane, tea, coffee, tobacco, cotton, and jute and mesta).

The second data source is the district-level study (DLS) database compiled by the International Crops Research Institute for the Semi-Arid Tropics (ICRISAT). The original data sources include government statistics such as *Agricultural Statistics of India* and related publications at the state level. The compilation procedure is reported in the DLS manual (ICRISAT 1998). Although our dataset is based on the revised version up to 2007, the DLS manual has not been revised. The analyzed period is 42 years: from the agricultural year 1965–66 through 2006–07. Smaller districts in which agricultural production is negligible and for which statistics are reported only sporadically have been dropped from analyses. Several observations with inconsistent data have also been dropped. In this chapter, we use a balanced panel dataset for 42 years, with the data of 311 districts spread over 19 major states of India (Andhra Pradesh, Assam, Bihar, Chhattisgarh, Gujarat, Haryana, Himachal Pradesh, Jharkhand, Karnataka, Kerala, Madhya Pradesh, Maharashtra,

Orissa, Punjab, Rajasthan, Tamil Nadu, Uttar Pradesh, Uttarakhand, and West Bengal). The 311 districts were delineated by district borders in 1965. According to the district borders in 2007, the 311 districts correspond to 498 districts. Map 2.1 shows the 311 districts. The DLS database includes the areas and production of major crops, fertilizer offtake, agricultural markets, roads, rainfall, and so on.

Long-Term Changes in Indian Agriculture

As demonstrated by Kurosaki (2015), twentieth-century Indian agriculture can be characterized by sustained growth through improving land productivity and shifts to higher value-added crops. Five figures that illustrate the long-term changes are presented below.

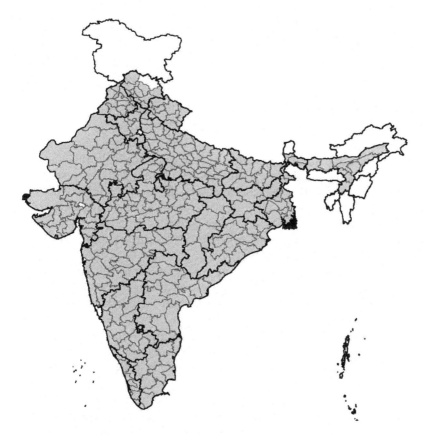

Map 2.1 Spatial distribution of the 311 districts analyzed.

Source: Kurosaki and Wada (2015).

Note: Shaded area within the thin lines corresponds to a district (boundaries in 1965) included in this study. Bold lines show state boundaries in 2013.

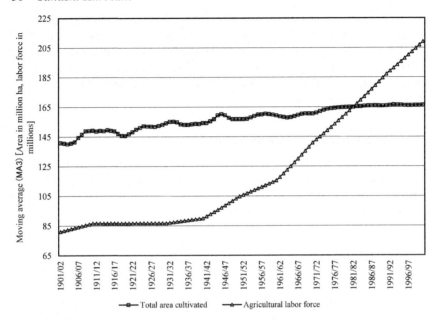

Figure 2.3 Area and labor force in Indian agriculture, 1901–02 to 2000–01.

Source: Drawn by the author using data from Kurosaki (2011).

First, both the total area cultivated (A_t) and agricultural labor force (L_t) increased during the twentieth century (Figure 2.3). Because the area increase was slower than the labor increase, the ratio of land to labor (A_t/L_t) declined from 1.7 ha in the early twentieth century to 0.8 ha at the end of the century. However, the rate of decline of land per capita was not monotonic: the area increased more in the first half of the century, whereas the labor increased more in the second half.

Second, the total agricultural output (Y_t), labor productivity (Y_t/L_t), and land productivity (Y_t/A_t) also show stagnation during the colonial period but have experienced sustained growth since, with the break period at around the early 1950s (Figure 2.4). At the end of the twentieth century, the total output and land productivity are about three times the level of that in the early twentieth century. The overlap of the two graphs of Y_t and Y_t/A_t suggests that the main engine of sustained growth has been improved land productivity.

Third, the two main foodgrain crops, rice and wheat, exhibit stagnation during the colonial period and only experience sustained growth during the second half of the twentieth century (Figure 2.5). The break did not occur in the early 1950s, as was the case of the total agricultural land productivity, but in the late 1960s. The late 1960s was the period when Green Revolution started in Indian agriculture. Figure 2.5 shows that the introduction of Green Revolution technologies brought a shift in the land productivity of these

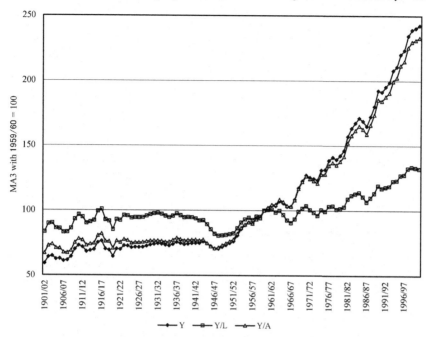

Figure 2.4 Total output, labor, and land productivity in Indian agriculture, 1901–02
to 2000–01.

Source: Drawn by the author using data from Kurosaki (2011).

two crops. Nevertheless, it is noteworthy that the overall turnaround
occurred in the early 1950s, before the Green Revolution. In Figure 2.5,
the time series of Y_t/A_t is re-produced from Figure 2.4 to emphasize the
timing gap in the breaks. As Kurosaki (2015) and references therein have
suggested, crop shifts, irrigation, and infrastructure development were
responsible for the overall breakthrough occurring before the Green
Revolution in India.

Fourth, three measures of land use among crops are presented in
Figure 2.6: Index of land use intensity (*intensity* = gross cropped area/
the total area cultivated), the share of rice and wheat in areas under
foodgrain crops (*srw*), and the share of non-foodgrain crops in the gross
cropped area (*snfg*). All of them, especially the first two, experienced a
sustained increase throughout the twentieth century. For instance, the
land use intensity was at around 100% (the current fallow area is almost
equal to areas that are cropped more than once) at the start of the twentieth century, although it reached the level of 135% at the end of the century. In other words, areas cropped more than once in a year accounted
for more than 35% of the net area sown.

Which crops experienced a relative increase in the crop mix? As the time
series for *srw* in Figure 2.6 shows, rice and wheat, two Green Revolution

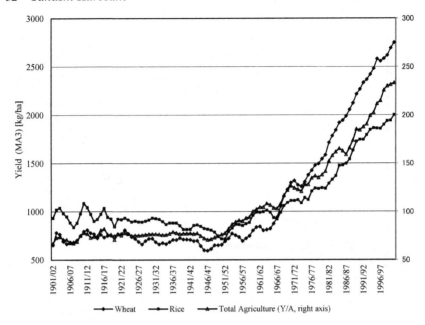

Figure 2.5 Land productivity of rice, wheat, and total agriculture in India, 1901–02 to 2000–01.

Source: Drawn by the author using data from Kurosaki (2011).

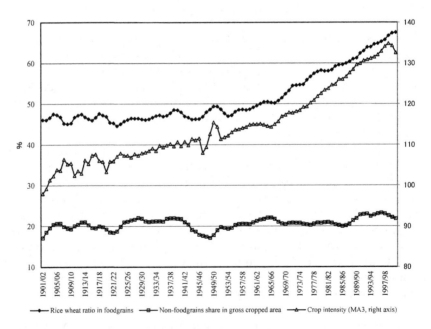

Figure 2.6 Land use patterns in Indian agriculture, 1901–02 to 2000–01.

Source: Drawn by the author using data from Kurosaki (2011).

crops, increased their shares at the cost of coarse grains. The time series for *snfg* also increased, but not as rapidly as the case of *intensity* or *srw*. Nevertheless, the average level of *snfg* after the Partition is significantly higher than that before the Partition. This implies that the importance of pure cash crops increased in India after independence.

If not accompanied by technological innovations to maintain land fertility, intensive use of agricultural land and areal expansion to marginal land might engender a decrease in the average land productivity. As Figure 2.5 demonstrates, this did not happen in post-independence India despite the increasing intensity of land use. Technological innovations such as fertilizer, modern varieties of crops, and irrigation were responsible for maintaining land fertility. As indirect evidence for such technological innovations, Figure 2.7 presents the value-added ratio. The value added ratio is defined as the gross value added from agriculture divided by the gross value of total production in agriculture. Therefore, it is close to 100% when only slight amounts of intermediate inputs are used; it becomes smaller as intermediate inputs are used more. As the figure shows, the value-added ratio was at around 95% at the start of the twentieth century. It began to decline rapidly in the late 1950s, that decline being accelerated during the Green Revolution period. It has stabilized since the 1990s.

Figure 2.7 The value added ratio in Indian agriculture, 1901–02 to 2000–01.

Source: Drawn by the author using data from Kurosaki (2011).

Heterogeneity Across Indian Districts

Have the changes described in the previous section occurred homogeneously in all districts in India? To answer this question, we compiled histograms for the district-level trends of *gca*, *intensity*,[5] *snfg*, and *srw*. The data source for this exercise is the ICRISAT-DLS dataset. The results are presented in Figure 2.8.

Figure 2.8 clearly presents substantial inter-district heterogeneity. Although the four indices were associated with positive trends at an all-India level, the trend was negative for a non-negligible number of districts. The heterogeneity is more substantial for *snfg* and *srw* than for *gca* and *intensity*. The trends for *gca* are the most homogeneous among the four indicators, which suggests that throughout India, the gross cropped area increased, mostly through the rising intensity of land use, whereas the list of crops that occupied the increased area under cultivation differed from district to district.

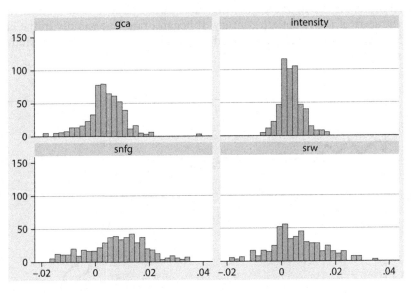

Figure 2.8 Distribution of average annual growth rates at the district level from 1965–66 to 2006–07.

Source: Kurosaki and Wada (2015).

Notes: A time series model is estimated for each of the 311 districts using the natural logarithm of gca, intensity, snfg, or srw as the dependent variable and the annual trend as the explanatory variable (gca = gross cropped area; intensity = gca/net area sown; snfg = the share of non-foodgrain crops in gca; srw = the share of rice and wheat in the areas under foodgrain crops). We then plot the distribution of the 311 parameter estimates in a histogram. To make histograms easy to compare, we trim the range between −0.02 (annual average decline at 2%) and 0.04 (annual average increases at 4%). The number of outliers outside the range is 2 for gca, 0 for intensity, 22 for snfg, and 10 for srw.

As other evidence of heterogeneity, correlation coefficients of the estimated trends shown in Figure 2.8 were calculated across districts. Trends in *intensity* and *gca* were correlated closely with the correlation coefficient of 0.591. All other correlation coefficients were positive but less than 0.24.[6] As shown in such a low correlation, district-level heterogeneity is substantial.

Furthermore, the heterogeneity of trends in *snfg* and *srw* has been increasing in recent years. When Figure 2.8 was redrawn using the subsample of the period up to 1995, the redrawn figure shows a more compact distribution for *snfg* and *srw*. As the overall shapes are highly similar to those in Figure 2.8, the redrawn figure is not reported here (but available on request from the author).

Kurosaki and Wada (2015) described the spatial shifts underlying this heterogeneity. They found that a visual perusal of GIS maps identified a shift of rice production into the interior districts of north India, a shift of wheat production to the east in north India, the new appearance of maize production centers in the interior districts of the Deccan, and a southward shift of chickpea production, among others. Although they did not provide rigorous evidence, they speculated that the spatial shift appeared consistent with the comparative advantages of the respective districts. As discussed in the Introduction of this chapter, if the spatial shifts were in the direction of comparative advantages, then we would expect the level of similarity in crop choices across districts to decline (Figure 2.2). This expectation is investigated further in the next section.

Spatial Concentration Indices Across Indian Districts

Measures of Spatial Concentration

This section follows the descriptive methodology adopted by Kurosaki (2003), who used two measures of diversification derived from the Hirschman–Herfindahl index. Because our emphasis is on specialization (concentration) rather than diversification, we use the index as it is. In the context of agricultural production, if the total area A is subdivided into its components indexed by k, i.e., $A = \Sigma_k A_k$, then the Hirschman–Herfindahl index (H) is defined as

$$H = \Sigma_k (A_k/A)^2. \tag{2.1}$$

By construction, H is bounded between 0 and 1. When the share of the largest component out of all k becomes closer to 1, H also becomes closer to 1 (a highly concentrated situation, i.e., a situation with high specialization). When the shares of all k components are the same (the least concentrated situation), H equals $1/N$, where N is the number of components (when N is extremely large, H becomes close to zero).

From the DLS dataset, data on areas for individual crops are compiled as A_{ijt}, where the subscript i denotes the crop (including the residual category of "other crops" so that the sum of all crop categories equals the gross cropped area in the district), j specifies the district, and t represents the agricultural year. We can calculate H from this data in two ways.

First, when H is calculated for a crop (A in Equation (2.1) is the total area under the particular crop in India and A_k is the area under the crop in district k), H has a meaning that two randomly selected points from the area under the crop in India are in the same district. Therefore, large H implies that cultivation of the crop of concern is concentrated in very few districts. If H thus calculated presents an increasing trend for a particular crop, then the crop experiences spatial concentration into a few districts from the earlier situation of widely spread production across India. Mathematically, this index is calculated as

$$H_{it} = \Sigma_j (A_{ijt}/A_{it})^2,\tag{2.2}$$

where A_{it} is the sum of A_{ijt} over j (which is the total area under crop i in India in period t).

Second, when H is calculated for a district (A in Equation (2.1) is the gross cropped area in the district and A_k is the area under crop k in the district), H has a meaning that two randomly selected points from the cultivated area in the district are under the same crop. Therefore, large H implies that crop cultivation in the district of concern is specialized in a few crops. Mathematically, this index is calculated as

$$H_{jt} = \Sigma_i (A_{ijt}/A_{jt})^2,\tag{2.3}$$

where A_{jt} is the sum of A_{ijt} over i (which is the gross cropped area in district j in period t).

Crop-Level Spatial Concentration

Using Equation (2.2), the crop-level concentration index H_{it} is calculated for six cereal crops (rice, wheat, maize, sorghum, pearl millet, and finger millet) and four other crops (chickpea, pigeon pea, cotton, and sugarcane). To remove the temporal variation attributable to weather and other shocks, we employ data after taking a moving average over three years. The results are shown in Figures 2.9 and 2.10. The figures are comparable to those of Figure 2 of Kurosaki (2003) for West Punjab, with the vertical axis reversed.

Figure 2.9 depicts the index for the six cereal crops. To make the graph compact, the time series for finger millet is shown on the right axis because it has an exceptionally high concentration ratio (i.e., its production is concentrated in a few specialized districts: see Kurosaki and Wada, 2015). Among

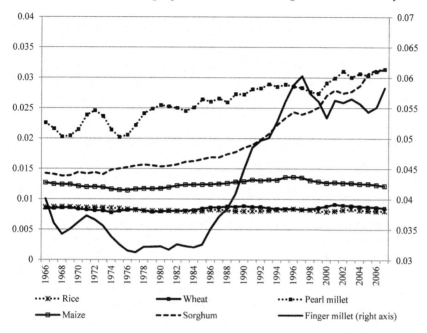

Figure 2.9 Concentration of production of the six important grains in India, 1965–66 to 2006–07.

Source: Drawn by the author using data presented in the text.

Notes: The Hirschman–Herfindahl index, calculated as Equation (2.2), is plotted on the vertical axis.

the six crops shown in Figure 2.9, rice and wheat are the most widely grown grains in India. In spite of recent shifts to these two crops out of other food-grains (as shown in Figure 2.8) and some spatial shifts that are discernible in GIS maps (Kurosaki and Wada 2015), the list of main producing districts for these two crops has not changed much. Figure 2.9 shows very low and stable levels of the concentration index for rice and wheat.

The rising trend in the concentration index for pearl millet is associated with a rapid decline in the production of this crop in India. As an inferior food in Indian consumer demand, the production and consumption of pearl millet were on the decline in most districts, but some districts known to cultivate this crop traditionally continue to grow it (Kurosaki and Wada 2015). Consequently, the concentration index has been rising. Dynamics of the index for sorghum and finger millet are similar to that for pearl millet. It is likely that interpretations similar to that for pearl millet also apply to sorghum and finger millet.

Further explanation is necessary for the dynamics of maize. The concentration level was somewhat between the lows of rice and wheat and the highs of coarse grains. From the mid-1970s to the late 1990s, the Herfindahl index was increasing (rising concentration). During this period, maize production for direct consumption by humans was on the decline, leading to a rising share of districts known as traditional regions of maize cultivation. These circumstances resemble those observed for pearl millet. Since the late 1990s, the Herfindahl index has been declining (decreasing concentration). During this period, hybrid maize production for livestock feeding was spreading in India. The total production of maize has been growing rapidly since the late 1990s as a result. As the hybrid maize production spreads into districts where maize was not a major crop in the traditional cropping patterns in India, the concentration index decreases because of the emergence of new maize production centers (Kurosaki and Wada 2015). This might be a transitory phenomenon. Once hybrid maize districts become dominant, the concentration index might rise again.

Among the four non-grain crops for which the concentration indexes are presented in Figure 2.10, cotton and sugarcane are associated with a high level of concentration and a positive trend during this study. Because cotton and sugarcane are pure cash crops, their rising concentration with the progress of agricultural transformation and urbanization is consistent with the theoretical discussion presented in the Introduction. In both crops, the rising trend was considerably strong until the early 1990s. Since then, the

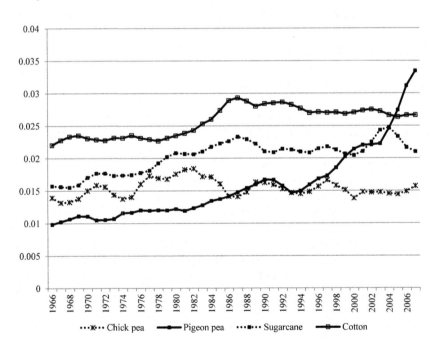

Figure 2.10 Concentration of production of the four important non-grains in India, 1965–66 to 2006–07.

Notes and source: See Figure 2.9.

Table 2.1 Summary statistics of crop-level spatial concentration

Crop	Level of concentration		Trend in concentration	
	Mean	*Std. dev.*	*OLS coeff.*	*Std. error*
Rice	0.0083	0.0002	−0.000012	0.000002
Wheat	0.0084	0.0003	0.000015	0.000003
Pearl millet	0.0261	0.0033	0.000255	0.000014
Maize	0.0125	0.0006	0.000025	0.000006
Sugarcane	0.0203	0.0024	0.000162	0.000018
Cotton	0.0257	0.0023	0.000142	0.000019
Sorghum	0.0196	0.0056	0.000432	0.000025
Finger millet	0.0431	0.0105	0.000726	0.000072
Chickpea	0.0154	0.0013	0.000001	0.000017
Pigeon pea	0.0158	0.0057	0.000411	0.000033

Source: Calculated by the author using data presented in the text.

Note: This table shows summary statistics of the Hirschman–Herfindahl index plotted in Figures 2.9 and 2.10. The number of observations is 42. The null hypothesis of zero trend is rejected at the 1% level, except for chickpea, for which the coefficient is not significant even at the 20% level.

concentration has remained stable. The monotonically rising concentration of cotton production from the mid-1960s to the early 1990s with subsequent stability is similar to the pattern observed in Pakistan Punjab (Kurosaki 2003). It is interesting to observe similar trends in India and Pakistan despite the highly different roles played by the government and cooperatives in sugarcane production.

The two most important pulses in India, i.e., chickpea and pigeon pea, show contrasting patterns. Although no trend is apparent for chickpea, the concentration index has risen rapidly since the mid-1990s. National chickpea production is stagnating, while that of pigeon pea has been increasing rapidly since the 1990s. These facts suggest that chickpea production is stagnating with little progress in spatial specialization, while the production of pigeon pea has been accelerated by spatial specialization.

In Table 2.1, the graphic information contained in Figures 2.9 and 2.10 is summarized with the mean and trend rate estimated by OLS.[7] The mean shows which crop is more specialized (level) while the trend reveals crops for which specialization is proceeding (change). The concentration level is the highest for finger millet, followed by pearl millet and cotton. It is the lowest for rice and wheat. The time trend is the highest for finger millet, followed by sorghum and pigeon peas. It is the lowest for rice, wheat, and chickpea.

District-Level Crop Concentration

Using Equation (2.3), the district-level crop concentration index H_{jt} is calculated for each of the 311 districts. Because of discontinuity in crop classification in the DLS dataset, we cannot calculate the measure using detailed crop disaggregation. For instance, in more recent years, area data are available with a finer classification for oilseed crops such as rape/mustard, groundnut, sunflower, linseed, soybean, and sesame. However, in the early years, data follow a more coarse classification, such as "oilseeds, total." Because we are interested in trends in the district-level crop concentration index, we necessarily adopted a somewhat coarse classification to maintain consistency with the crop classification list. Consequently, the final crop list of this exercise includes 15 crop groups: rice, wheat, maize, pearl millet, sorghum, finger millet, barley, chickpeas, pigeon peas, other pulses, oilseed crops, cotton, sugarcane, fresh vegetables and fruits (including potato and onion), and "other crops" (including fodder crops).

Because plotting 311 time series in a single figure does not make sense, Figure 2.11 shows the median, top 25%, and bottom 25% of the Herfindahl index out of the total 311 districts. For comparison, the same index was also calculated for the macro level by calculating the index after all district-level data were aggregated to an all-India level. In Figure 2.11, this plot is captioned as "India total," although it is the aggregated figure for the area summing up the 311 districts analyzed in this chapter. Figure 2.11

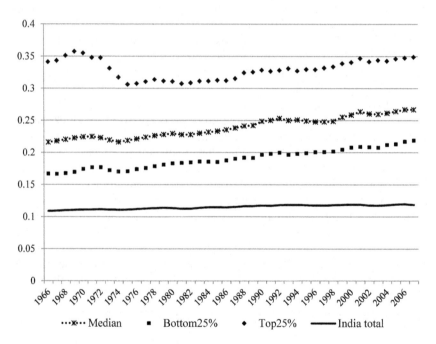

Figure 2.11 District-level crop concentration in India, 1965–66 to 2006–07.

Source: Drawn by the author using data presented in the text.

Notes: The Hirschman–Herfindahl index is plotted on the vertical axis. For each district, 15 crop groups are used to calculate the index based on Equation (2.3). "India total" shows the index calculated from the sum of the 311 districts analyzed in this article.

is therefore comparable to Figure 3 of Kurosaki (2003) for West Punjab, with the vertical axis reversed.

First, as the figure shows, the crop mix is more diversified at the macro (national) level than at the semi-macro (district) level. Second, both indices increased over the 40-year period (more concentration is occurring). Third, the speed of rising concentration is much faster at the district level than at the national level. Consequently, the difference between macro and semi-macro levels has been widening over time. Fourth, as shown by the top and bottom 25% plots, the dynamics of district-level concentration indices are heterogeneous. These patterns closely resemble those observed after the Partition in West Punjab (Kurosaki 2003).

The exact districts that account for the median, top 25%, and bottom 25% are not the same. For that reason, the time series plot of "Median" in Figure 2.11 does not show the time series of a district that has median characteristics. Therefore, for illustrative purposes, Figure 2.12 portrays changes in H_{jt} for the 11 districts in Punjab.[8]

Figure 2.12 confirms that most individual districts in Punjab experienced an increase in the concentration index. A comparison of Figures 2.11 and 2.12 readily suggests that Punjab districts are more specialized than the

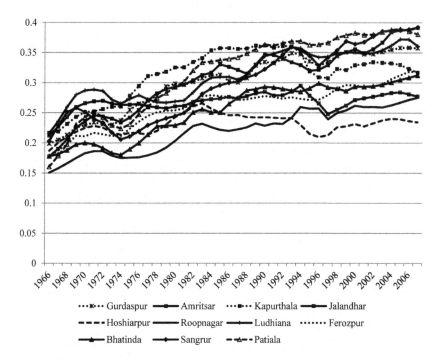

Figure 2.12 District-level crop concentration in Punjab, 1965–66 to 2006–07.

Notes and source: See Figure 2.11.

Table 2.2 Summary statistics of district-level crop concentration

District	Level of concentration		Trend in concentration	
	Mean	*Std. dev.*	*OLS coeff.*	*Std. error*
Distribution among 311 districts (1965 boundaries) in India				
Median	0.239	0.016	0.00129	0.00005
Bottom25	0.190	0.015	0.00122	0.00003
Top25	0.330	0.016	0.00024	0.00020
Herfindahl for the aggregated level ("India total" in Figure 2.11)				
	0.115	0.003	0.00027	0.00001
Punjab districts				
Gurdaspur	0.301	0.049	0.00384	0.00019
Amritsar	0.305	0.056	0.00433	0.00022
Kapurthala	0.314	0.042	0.00233	0.00040
Jalandhar	0.268	0.015	0.00076	0.00016
Hoshiarpur	0.231	0.016	0.00049	0.00020
Roopnagar	0.221	0.036	0.00284	0.00012
Ludhiana	0.312	0.041	0.00313	0.00019
Ferozpur	0.261	0.036	0.00280	0.00016
Bhatinda	0.254	0.045	0.00351	0.00018
Sangrur	0.299	0.062	0.00479	0.00024
Patiala	0.317	0.067	0.00513	0.00028

Source: Calculated by the author using data presented in the text.

Note: This table shows summary statistics of the Hirschman–Herfindahl index plotted in Figures 2.11 and 2.12. The null hypothesis of zero trend is rejected at the 1% level, except for Hoshiarpur, whose coefficient is significant at the 5% level.

median district in India (shown in Figure 2.11). Furthermore, the positive trend in the specialization is steeper than that of the average districts in India. Table 2.2 presents the level and trend of specialization in a compact form similar to that of Table 2.1. The concentration is highest for Patiala, Ludhiana, and Kapurthala; it is lowest for Roopanagar and Hoshiarpur. The time trend is the highest for Patiala, followed by Sangrur and Amritsar. It is the lowest for Hoshiarpur and Jalandhar. The pattern appears consistent with the level and speed of agricultural commercialization.

To elucidate regional characteristics of the Herfindahl indices, Table 2.3 presents the level of concentration (means obtained for each district during 42 years) and the trend of concentration (OLS coefficients from a time-series regression using 42 annual observations for each district) for each state. In terms of the level of concentration, Assam and West Bengal are ranked at the top (with the highest level of crop concentration), mostly because of the dominance of rice in their crop mix; Haryana, Karnataka, and Madhya Pradesh are at the bottom (with the highest level of crop diversification). In terms of the trend in concentration, Punjab is ranked at the top (with the most rapid increase in crop concentration), followed by Madhya Pradesh and Haryana; Orissa, followed by Assam and West Bengal, were associated

Table 2.3 Summary statistics of district-level crop concentration by state

Name of the state (1965 borders)	Number of districts in the sample (1965 borders)	Level of concentration (mean over the 42 years)		Trend in concentration (OLS coeff. from a time-series regression using 42 observations)	
		Mean	Std. dev.	Mean	Std. dev.
Andhra Pradesh	20	0.250	0.088	0.00050	0.00382
Assam	10	0.496	0.063	−0.00324	0.00306
Bihar	17	0.370	0.161	0.00271	0.00238
Gujarat	18	0.249	0.090	0.00043	0.00196
Haryana	7	0.225	0.039	0.00213	0.00230
Himachal Pradesh	10	0.339	0.062	−0.00141	0.00151
Karnataka	19	0.237	0.111	−0.00037	0.00217
Kerala	10	0.327	0.047	−0.00052	0.00190
Madhya Pradesh	43	0.239	0.100	0.00219	0.00209
Maharashtra	26	0.262	0.118	0.00009	0.00338
Orissa	13	0.381	0.104	−0.00513	0.00249
Punjab	11	0.280	0.035	0.00309	0.00149
Rajasthan	26	0.245	0.093	0.00020	0.00338
Tamil Nadu	12	0.282	0.156	0.00024	0.00355
Uttar Pradesh	54	0.240	0.067	0.00068	0.00609
West Bengal	15	0.498	0.148	−0.00171	0.00198
All	311	0.285	0.124	0.00033	0.00389

Source: Calculated by the author using data presented in the text.

Note: This table shows the means and standard deviations (both unweighted) of the time-series means and the OLS trend coefficient of the Hirschman–Herfindahl index for each of 311 districts. For example, 0.280 in Punjab (level of concentration) is the simple average of 11 means reported in Table 2.2 and 0.00309 in Punjab (trend in concentration) is the simple average of 11 trends reported in Table 2.2.

with highly negative trends, indicating that crop diversification (away from rice) is proceeding in these states. The regional contrast in concentration trends thereby reflects the difference in the initial crop mix. A more systematic analysis of the relation between the mean and trend (Tables 2.2 and 2.3) and the district-level development indicators is left as a subject for future analysis.

Conclusion

This chapter, using district-level data for 1965–2007, presented our examination of whether Indian agriculture is experiencing spatial specialization of crop production. As urbanization proceeds with more integrated agricultural markets, one would expect some local regions to specialize in agricultural production, with food consumption patterns becoming more homogeneous across regions. The empirical results presented in this chapter showed that high heterogeneity exists across districts regarding measures of trends in increasing land use intensity and shifting to Green Revolution crops or non-foodgrain crops. The rising concentration of the production of several crops in specific districts was observed for several crops, especially cotton, finger millet, and pearl millet. In addition, the rising concentration of crop mix was observed for districts in the state of Punjab. These are consistent with the expected consequences of urbanization and within-India market integration.

Several implications for development policies can be derived from the findings in this chapter. First, agricultural development through efficient resource allocation is facilitated by technology that allows flexible crop choices. In the Indian context, investment in irrigation and tractors appears to be one key factor. Another key that allows flexible crop choices is modern varieties of crops. Public sector investment in research and development could be vital in these areas. Second, district-level analysis in this chapter suggests the importance of infrastructure in realizing the benefit of regional specialization. Infrastructure for integrating markets, especially roads and marketplaces, is expected to contribute to agriculture-led economic development.

Although conceptually consistent with the comparative advantage principle, the analyses in this chapter are limited in the sense that we were unable to quantify the effects of increasing spatial specialization on aggregate productivity in Indian agriculture. This result is mostly attributable to the lack of data related to agricultural inputs for individual crops at the district level. The cost of production data from the Indian Ministry of Agriculture includes information at the state level only. Some methodological innovations or new datasets related to profitability at the district level are required to estimate the effect. Furthermore, more fundamental determinants of cropping patterns must be analyzed at various aggregation levels: plots, farms, districts, and states. These are left for further study.

Notes

1 Throughout this chapter, crop specialization is regarded as a factor that can contribute to the income growth of farmers because improved productivity in farming is likely to benefit them. In the economic history literature for Southeast Asia, however, crop specialization is often regarded as a sign of pauperization of peasants (Bassino and Baten 2016, Isham et al. 2005). That contrast is attributable to the difference in the nature of agricultural commercialization across two areas: Crop specialization was initiated by plantation agriculture in Southeast Asia, whereas plantation agriculture was not important in India as far as the period and areas analyzed in this chapter are concerned.

2 Crop shifts contributed to aggregate productivity improvement in two ways, even with little improvement in the per-acre yield of individual crops. Land productivity can increase through the reallocation of crops from low value-added to high value-added crops and from regions where productivity is low to regions where productivity is high. The contribution of crop shifts is a source of agricultural growth unnoticed in the traditional literature. On the other hand, in the traditional literature on long-term growth in agricultural

production in India, the contribution of Green Revolution since the late 1960s has been emphasized. Various authors have examined how land productivity increased with the introduction of new technology, characterized by high yielding seeds, chemical fertilizer, and irrigation (e.g., Bhalla and Tyagi 1989, Bhalla and Singh 2001, Bhalla and Singh 2009, Bhalla and Singh 2012).

3 "Annual" corresponds to an agricultural year of India, a period extending from July 1 to June 30.

4 Foodgrains are defined as crop groups containing cereals (e.g., rice, wheat, and coarse grains) and pulses (e.g., chickpea and pigeon pea). The term is widely used in India to discuss the national food balance because cereals and pulses comprise the most important parts of local diets.

5 In this section, *intensity* is defined as *gca* divided by the net area sown because of data availability. In the previous section, it was defined as *gca* divided by the total area cultivated. The total area cultivated is the sum of the net area sown and the current fallow area. The two measures of *intensity* are highly correlated.

6 The correlation coefficients in trends were as follows: *snfg* and *gca* 0.176, *snfg* and *intensity* 0.199, *srw* and *gca* 0.192, *srw* and *intensity* 0.134, and *srw* and *snfg* 0.240.

7 The estimated trend resembles that of the average annual change calculated from the data. We adopt a regression approach because it allows us to test the statistical significance of the trend.

8 Figures for other states are available on request. Punjab was chosen for illustrative purposes because the number of districts in the DLS dataset is moderate and the frequency of missing data is almost zero.

References

Bassino, J.P. and Baten, J. (2016) "A Curse of 'Pint Source' Resources? Cash Crops and Numeracy on the Philippines 19th–20th Century," *Paper presented at the HIAS Seminar*, Hitotsubashi University, March 14, 2016.

Bhalla, G.S. and Singh, G. (2001) *Indian Agriculture: Four Decades of Development*, New Delhi: Sage Publications.

Bhalla, G.S. and Singh, G. (2009) "Economic Liberalisation and Indian Agriculture: A Statewise Analysis," *Economic and Political Weekly* 46(52): 34–44.

Bhalla, G.S. and Singh, G. (2012) *Economic Liberalisation and Indian Agriculture: A District-Level Study*, New Delhi: Sage Publications.

Bhalla, G.S. and Tyagi, D.S. (1989) *Patterns in Indian Agricultural Development: A District Level Study*, New Delhi: Institute for Studies in Industrial Development.

ICRISAT [International Crops Research Institute for the Semi-Arid Tropics] (1998) *District Level Database Documentation – 13 States of India, Volume I: Documentation of Files: 1966–94 Database (1966 District Boundaries)*, Pattancheru, AP, India: ICRISAT.

Isham, J., Woolcock, M., Pritchett, L. and Busby, G. (2005) "The Varieties of Resource Experience: Natural Resource Export Structures and the Political Economy of Economic Growth," *World Bank Economic Review* 19(2): 141–174.

Kurosaki, T. (2002) "Agriculture in India and Pakistan, 1900–95: A Further Note," *Economic and Political Weekly* 37(30) July 27: 3149–3152.

Kurosaki, T. (2003) "Specialization and Diversification in Agricultural Transformation: The Case of West Punjab, 1903–1992," *American Journal of Agricultural Economics* 85(2): 373–387.

Kurosaki, T. (2011) "Compilation of Agricultural Production Data in Areas Currently in India, Pakistan, and Bangladesh from 1901/02 to 2001/02," G-COE discussion paper, No. 169/PRIMCED discussion paper, No. 6, Hitotsubashi University, February 2011.

Kurosaki, T. (2015) "Long-Term Agricultural Growth in India, Pakistan, and Bangladesh from 1901/2 to 2001/2," *International Journal of South Asian Studies* 7: 61–86.

Kurosaki, T. and Wada, K. (2015) "Spatial Characteristics of Long-Term Changes in Indian Agricultural Production: District-Level Analysis, 1965–2007," *Review of Agrarian Studies* 5(1): 1–38.

Timmer, C.P. (1988) "The Agricultural Transformation," in H. Chenery and T. N. Srinivasan (eds.), *Handbook of Development Economics, Vol I*, Amsterdam: Elsevier Science, pp. 275–331.

Timmer, C.P. (1997) "Farmers and Markets: The Political Economy of New Paradigms," *American Journal of Agricultural Economics* 79(2): 621–627.

3 Thirty Years of Change
Tamil Villages Re-Surveyed

Haruka Yanagisawa

The Indian economy has shown remarkable growth since around 1980 (Balakrishnan 2010). The expansion of agricultural production and changes in rural society has supported this growth by providing non-agrarian sectors with expanding markets for non-agrarian products and services as well as a labour force. During the three decades of economic growth, the socioeconomic structure of rural society has also changed considerably. Some important observations have been presented through repeated surveys of Tamil villages, such as Iruvelpattu and Gangaikondan, by Harriss et al. (2010; 2012) and of six villages in Tiruchirappalli examined by Djurfeldt et al. (2008). Remarkable among the changes they observed is an increasing labour shortage, a rise in the agricultural wage level, and progress in the 'social revolution'. These, together with other factors such as an increase in business opportunities in non-agrarian sectors, seem to have encouraged dominant-class villagers to either reduce the size of their farms or quit agricultural pursuits completely and also seem to have tempted farmers to reduce their dependence on hired non-family labourers.

The author surveyed a village ('M Village') in Lalgudi Taluk, Tiruchirappalli District, Tamil Nadu, in 1979–81 and surveyed it again in 2007–08. This preliminary report describes a survey mainly addressing villagers' occupations and education. The first section presents a brief summary of the 1979–81 survey findings. The second section presents an examination of changes in villagers' occupations. The third and fourth sections associate the occupational changes with changes in education level. The fifth section presents some important aspects of changes in the socioeconomic life of villagers that pertain to villagers' occupations and education. The sixth section presents a discussion of the findings from a wider perspective.

The Village in 1979–1981[1]

The village is located in a suburban area of Tiruchirappalli city, to which villagers commute by bus. In 1980, residents lived there in 470 households, among which the largest group was the Muthurajas (an OBC), who formed

DOI: 10.4324/9781003311898-4

42 per cent of all households. The second largest groups were SCs, such as the Pallans and Paraiyans, accounting for 24 per cent of the total. Pillais and Chettiyars, who belonged to the 'Forward Classes', jointly made up 12 per cent of the total. Muslim households were situated on the roadside. Nearly 40 per cent of the agricultural land in the village belonged to absentee Brahmin landlords, most of whom were living in Thiruvanaikoil town.

Brahmin Households

Our 1979–81 village survey revealed several trends for the major communities described above. As with other irrigated paddy cultivating regions in Tamil Nadu, in the nineteenth century, the Brahmins owned the major portion of village agricultural land, which they either managed, hiring labourers including Dalit farm servants, or let out to tenant cultivators. However, from the end of the nineteenth century, Brahmins in Tamil Nadu were increasingly engaged in urban white-collar jobs such as government service, as advocates or teachers, prompting a greater number of Brahmin families to leave the village society to engage in these urban jobs and make higher education available to their family members. This process was accompanied by a reduction in their ownership of village land (Yanagisawa 1996: Chapter 7).

In addition to income from their land, which was either managed themselves or let out to tenants, most of the Brahmin landlords who owned land in this village were also temple priests in Thiruvanaikoil. Here too, many of them had gradually shifted their main occupation to urban white-collar jobs as Table 3.1 shows. Their involvement in agriculture ceased. They gave their sons a higher education to degree level and allowed them to take work in government offices or to take up executive and engineering posts in public enterprises. Brahmin ownership of village land decreased from 52 per cent in 1952 to 38 per cent in 1980. Table 3.2 shows that the largest group of Brahmin earners (43 per cent) comprised employees in urban jobs, of whom

Table 3.1 Distribution of households by non-farm occupations, 1980 (%)

| | | Urban employment | | | | |
| | *Small businesses in villages* | *Total* | Per month income | | | *Total non-farm households* |
			Less than Rs. 300	*Rs. 300–499*	*Rs. 500 and more*	
Brahmin	37%	37%	7%	0%	93%	74%
Pillai	41%	22%	43%	14%	43%	63%
Chettiyar	54%	8%	0%	50%	50%	62%
Muthuraja	19%	7%	7%	50%	43%	26%
SCs	14%	5%	20%	40%	40%	19%

Source: Yanagisawa (1983).

Table 3.2 Distribution of workers by non-farm occupation, 1980 (%)

	Small businesses in villages	Urban employment				Total non-farm households
		Total	Per month income			
			Less than Rs. 300	Rs. 300–499	Rs. 500 and more	
Brahmin	39%	43%	22%	9%	70%	81%
Pillai	36%	32%	45%	14%	41%	68%
Chettiyar	52%	17%	36%	18%	45%	70%
Muthuraja	18%	12%	30%	33%	37%	30%
SCs	10%	8%	40%	35%	25%	19%

Source: Yanagisawa (1983).

70 per cent earned a monthly salary of more than Rs. 500 in 1980, indicating that they were in the elite group of urban workers.

Pillai and Chettiyar Households

The Pillais and Chettiyars, although forming only about 12 per cent of the village population, have long held high socioeconomic status among the village population. Most had been small farmers managing their own land. By 1980, while still doing so, they had started expanding into non-agrarian activities. As Table 3.2 shows, about 70 per cent of the earners from these two communities were engaged in non-farm jobs. A group among them ran small businesses such as rice mills, a cinema, and various small shops in and around the village. Another group obtained jobs in urban areas. Some were employed in Bharat Heavy Electricals Limited (BHEL), Tiruchirappalli, and the Ordnance Factory as skilled workers. Some worked as sales workers in Tiruchirappalli city. The households of the two communities often sent their sons to private schools so that they would be sufficiently qualified to be employed as skilled workers and supervisors in big companies. Although working in the non-agrarian sector to a large extent, they still had not abandoned agricultural management by 1980, partly because the village was located in a suburban area within commuting distance of the city. Most hired agricultural labourers to manage their land and took leave from their factories at busy times on the farm, such as harvest times.

Muthuraja Households

The Muthurajas, who formed more than 40 per cent of the village population, had been tenants cultivating land that was owned by absentee landlords. In the three decades of the land reforms and the Green Revolution, the Muthurajas grew to become the core group of farmers in the village. By 1980, a group of them had purchased land from other communities, expanded their rented lands, and therefore came to be larger-scale farmers, digging wells and progressively introducing new technologies. At the same time, some of the Muthuraja villagers had lost their tenancy rights and had become hired labourers. As shown in Tables 3.1 and 3.2, in 1980, 74 per cent of the households and 70 per cent of the earners from this community were engaged in the agricultural sector. Generally speaking, villagers registered their names at the employment exchange office to obtain urban employment when they passed the Secondary School Leaving Certificate (SSLC) examination. The sons of Muthuraja large farmers, however, often did not dare to register at the office even though they had passed the examination. Therefore, in 1980, the core groups of Muthuraja villagers must have chosen to be progressive farmers with less concern for non-agrarian occupations.

Scheduled Castes

SC households, as described above, accounted for one-fourth of the village total. As in other Tamil regions, the SC villagers' ancestors were mostly agricultural labourers, of whom a considerable number were formerly either attached permanent labourers or servants to influential farmers. However, their situation changed markedly in the 1950s, when an anti-caste movement among the Pallan villagers led to the formation of an agricultural labour trade union. The union organized a strike demanding tenancy rights over Brahmans' land and successfully acquired about 50 acres, which were distributed among the Pallan households. In this way, each SC family, formerly purely landless agricultural labourers, became tenants-cum-labourers with 0.5 acres of tenancy land. Thereby, they were able to strengthen their bargaining position with influential landowners. By 1980, village society reflected this remarkable empowerment of the SC and other lower classes of villagers and a weakening of elite control over subaltern villagers. Although the SCs thus raised their status in village agrarian society, their activities were confined mainly to the agrarian sector, 81 per cent of SC households being mainly engaged in agriculture. The main non-agricultural activity among them was trading in paddy straw.

Changes in Occupations

Expansion of Non-Farm Activities and Agriculture

The occupational structure of the villagers changed remarkably during the three decades after 1980, with some important variations among communities. Table 3.3 shows the present situation for the occupations of villager groups. Although data for 'Pillai and Chettiyar' pertain to all households living in this village, 'No. 1 Ward' data was collected from all households living in this street, most of whom were Muthurajas. Almost all households in 'No. 5 Ward' were SCs.

Table 3.3 Distribution of households by occupation, 2007

	Pillai, Chettiyar		No. 1 ward (Muthuraja, etc.)		No. 5 ward (Mostly SCs)	
	N	%	N	%	N	%
AG	1	2%	8	7%	2	2%
AL	2	3%	10	9%	29	25%
AG + AL	2	3%	22	20%	6	5%
(Agricultural occupations: total)	5	9%	40	37%	37	32%
AG + Non-AG	0	0%	6	6%	2	2%
AL + Non-AG	2	3%	8	7%	8	7%
AL + AG + Non-AG	0	0%	2	2%	2	2%
(Mainly agricultural occupations + Non-AG: total)	2	3%	16	15%	12	10%
Non-AG + AG	8	14%	11	10%	10	9%
Non-AG + AL	2	3%	9	8%	23	20%
Non-AG + AL + AG	0	0%	8	8%	1	1%
(Mainly Non-AG + agricultural occupations: total)	10	17%	28	26%	34	29%
Business (local)	2	3%	4	4%	8	7%
Professional	2	3%	1	1%	2	2%
Other non-AG	32	55%	19	18%	23	20%
Gem polishing	5	9%	0	0%	0	0%
No income	0	0%	0	0%	0	0%
(Non-AG only: total)	41	71%	24	22%	33	28%
Total	58	100%	108	100%	116	100%

Source: Data collected during my fieldwork in 2007.

As expected, the agrarian sector reduced its weight in the village economy, the Pillais and Chettiyars are conspicuous in that most of their households have ceased agricultural management. Of the households in these two communities, 71 per cent are not engaged in agriculture at all. In 1980, more than 30 per cent of Pillai and Chettiyar households depended on agriculture as the main source of income, the corresponding figure had dropped as low as 12 per cent by 2007. Therefore, most Pillais and Chettiyars, who had already by 1980 extended their activities beyond the non-agrarian sectors, had stopped agrarian activity. Reduction in the weight of agriculture as the source of income is more conspicuous. Table 3.4 shows the total income that these two communities earn, where 'agricultural management, milk production and agricultural labourer' account for only 12 per cent. That said, one exceptional case should be presented: a Pillai villager manages more than 10 acres of farmland but commutes by car to a state-run enterprise where he works as an executive.

Among the OBC and SC population, the three decades brought a remarkable increase in the number of those engaged in non-agrarian activities. As Table 3.3 shows, in No. 1 Ward, where most residents are Muthurajas,

Table 3.4 Average income per worker and distribution of income by job group

Job group	Job	Pillais and Chettiyars		Muthurajas, etc.		SCs	
		Average income per male worker (Rs.)	Distribution of sources of total household income (%)	Average income per male worker (Rs.)	Distribution of sources of total household income (%)	Average income per male worker (Rs.)	Distribution of sources of total household income (%)
A	Agricultural management	2,167	2	3,939	17	5,900	5
	Milk production	6,283	4	2,400	1		0
	Agricultural labourer	2,741	6	3,059	23	2,399	31
	Agricultural labourer + Agricultural management	-	0	4,467	2	3,854	1
	Trade in and around the village	3,375	4	5,037	3	4,000	1
	Other business in and around the village	2,992	6	4,250	2	9,250	12
	Village artisan, service person	2,759	3	2,530	3	2,937	4
	Artificial diamond polishing	2,679	5	4,875	4		0
	Total	2,912	29	3,537	56	3,512	54
B	Total	3,013	6	2,766	9	2,902	6
C	Total	3,610	8	3,992	7	3,817	8
D	Total	3,720	10	3,714	10	3,469	10
E	Total	6,015	23	6,383	8	7,125	10
F	Total	9,083	24	7,817	10	10,125	11
	Grand total (average)	4,308	100	3,853	100	4,035	100

Source: Data collected during the author's fieldwork in 2007.

48 per cent of the households work in non-agrarian jobs as their main occupation, marking an increase since 1980 when the corresponding figure was only 26 per cent. Households earning any income from non-agrarian activities account for 63 per cent. Furthermore, Table 3.4 shows that the income earned by the inhabitants of No. 1 Ward from agrarian activities constitutes only 43 per cent of the total income earned. Consequently, in terms of income, the agrarian sector is less important than the other sectors. The decline in SCs' dependence on agriculture is more noteworthy than the Muthurajas'. The proportion of households engaged in non-agrarian activities as their main occupation increased from 19 per cent in 1980 to 57 per cent in 2007. Those with any non-agrarian income were 68 per cent. Agrarian income accounts for only 37 per cent of the total income of the SCs. The Muthurajas and SCs account for more than two-thirds of the village population. Therefore, one can say that village life is supported mainly by non-agrarian activities even though they reside in a village.

However, in stark contrast to the case of the Pillais and Chettiyars, that of the Muthurajas and SCs demonstrates that their larger involvement in off-farm activities does not automatically lead them to cease their agrarian activities. As shown in Table 3.3, 52 per cent of Muthuraja households are reportedly engaged in agriculture as their main occupation; adding the 26 per cent who work in this sector as their secondary occupation, 78 per cent are more or less engaged in agrarian activities. This is also the case for SC households, with 42 per cent of household members working in the agrarian sector as their main occupation and 72 per cent participating in some kind of agrarian activity (mostly as hired labourers). The important finding here is that the increasing participation of the Muthuraja (OBC) and SC communities in non-agrarian activities does not mean a total departure from agrarian occupations. Rather it implies that they combine agrarian and non-agrarian activities within their households.

Occupation and Income

To clarify differences among communities with respect to the connection between agrarian and non-agrarian economic activities, the structure of their occupations shall be examined further. First, as shown in Table 3.5, fewer differences in the rate of workers in the adult population (older than 16 years, excluding students) exist for men in communities, between 92 per cent and 96 per cent. For women, the differences are large: for the SCs 52 per cent, for the Muthurajas 26 per cent, and for the Pillais and Chettiyars 19 per cent. Female workers mostly work in and around the village: 72 per cent and 53 per cent of the SC and Muthuraja female workers, respectively, are agricultural labourers. The other female earners work mostly in and around the village engaged, for example, in traditional village services, handicrafts, and artificial diamond polishing.

Table 3.5 Distribution of workers by occupation, 2007 (%)

Job group	Job	Pillais and Chettiyars		Muthurajas, etc.		SCs	
		Male	*Female*	*Male*	*Female*	*Male*	*Female*
A	Agricultural management	4	0	18	4	4	2
	Milk production	1	6	1	0	0	0
	Agricultural labourer	10	13	26	53	40	72
	Agricultural labourer + agricultural management	0	0	2	2	1	0
	Trade in and around the village	5	6	2	2	1	2
	Other business in and around the village	10	0	5	13	6	0
	Village artisan, service person	5	13	3	11	6	2
	Artificial diamond polishing	8	19			0	1
	Total	42	56	59	84	58	79
B	Construction worker	0	0	4	2	1	1
	Urban manual worker, watchman, auto rickshaw driver, etc.	10	13	9	4	8	2
	Total	10	13	13	5	9	3
C	Trade in urban areas	0	0	0	0	4	5
	Salesperson, computer operator, etc.	10	13	6	5	3	5
	Urban business (including auto rickshaw owner)	0	0	1	0	1	0
	Total	10	13	7	5	8	10
D	Nurse (less than Rs. 5,000)	0	0	0	2	0	2
	Teacher (less than Rs. 5,000)	0	0	0	2	1	3
	Electrician (less than Rs. 5,000)	1	0	5	0	2	0
	Lorry driver, etc. (less than Rs. 5,000)	0	0	3	0	1	0
	Bus driver (less than Rs. 5,000)	6	0	2	0	5	0
	Conductor (less than Rs. 5,000)	6	0	1	0	4	0
	Total	13	0	11	4	13	5

(Continued)

Table 3.5 Distribution of workers by occupation, 2007 (%) (Continued)

Job group	Job	Pillais and Chettiyars		Muthurajas, etc.		SCs	
		Male	*Female*	*Male*	*Female*	*Male*	*Female*
E	Driver (Rs. 5,000 and more)	1	0	1	0	3	0
	Conductor (Rs. 5,000 and more)	2	0	1	0	3	0
	Electrician (Rs. 5,000 and more)	1	0	0	0	0	0
	Others (Rs. 5,000 and more)	6	0	0	0	0	0
	Sales supervisor, etc.	2	0	1	0	1	0
	Nurse (Rs. 5,000 and more)	0	13	0	0	0	0
	Teacher (Rs. 5,000 and more)	0	6	1	0	0	1
	Clerk, other white-collar job	0	0	1	0	0	1
	Total	13	19	5	0	6	1
F	Skilled worker in the formal sector, government employee	2	0	2	0	3	0
	Management staff in the formal sector	2	0	0	2	0	0
	Professional	4	0	1	0	1	1
	Retired (pensioner)	4	0	1	0	1	0
	Employed abroad	1	0	1	0	0	0
	Total	13	0	5	2	5	1
	Grand total	100	100	100	100	100	100
	Percentage of workers in the total adult (excluding students) population (%)	93	19	92	26	96	52

Source: Data collected during the author's fieldwork in 2007.

In Tables 3.4 and 3.5, the occupations of the villagers are shown in six groups.

> Group A: Occupations in and around the village, such as agriculture, village services, and handicrafts
> Group B: Construction work and other manual work with a low income
> Group C: Salesmen/women and other low-wage white-collar jobs
> Group D: Drivers, electricians, etc. with a monthly income of less than Rs. 5,000
> Group E: Drivers, electricians, etc. with a monthly income of Rs. 5,000 or more (or those presumed to be hired in the formal sector)
> Group F: Skilled workers, etc. in big companies, government employees, professionals, etc.

Table 3.4 presents the average amount of income per worker for each occupation. It reveals the following points with respect to the workers. First, roughly speaking, there is no severe difference in income levels between the occupations in Groups A and B. Both those working in and around the village, as represented by agricultural wage labour and manual labourers such as construction workers, are more or less in the same income group category. Second, the income level of low-wage urban white-collar workers such as sales workers is higher than that in Groups A and B. Third, the income level further increases in the order of C–F. Fourth, within each group, there is less difference by community. Fifth, in Group A there is a conspicuous job that has a very high income level per worker, a business related to the trade of river sand and other construction materials, in which some SCs are engaged. As demonstrated below, the last decades have brought numerous new construction projects of *pucca* (well-built) houses in many of the villages, including the SCs' street. This construction boom has provided villagers with good business opportunities.

As expected, the distribution of these occupations differs by community. Agriculture-related occupations (management, labourer, milk production) account for only 15 per cent of the Pillai and Chettiyar male workers, in contrast to those of the Muthuraja and SC male workers, of whom 45 per cent and 44 per cent, respectively, are engaged in the agrarian sector. By contrast, the occupations of Group E (drivers, etc. with income exceeding Rs. 5,000) and Group F (skilled workers in the formal sector, etc.) account for 26 per cent of the Pillai and Chettiyar male workers, whereas the corresponding figures for the Muthurajas and SCs are as low as 10 per cent and 11 per cent. Consequently, more than two-thirds of the OBC and SC male workers are engaged in occupations in Groups A and B, with incomes more or less equal to those of agricultural labourers. It might be concluded that since only a small portion of the Muthuraja and SC male workers successfully got jobs in Groups E and F, which offer a reasonable level of income as well as job security, most of the families in these communities must manage their family budgets by combining agrarian and non-agrarian incomes while continuing to work in the agrarian sector.

At the same time, the table shows that it is not easy for the Pillai and Chettiyar households to depend entirely on the non-agrarian sectors to maintain their livelihoods. Only 26 per cent of the male workers in these communities work in jobs in Groups E and F. Therefore, they can expect a somewhat stable life with a reasonable level of income and job security. Although the higher rate of men working in better paid occupations with job security among Pillai and Chettiyar households does partly account for their cessation of farm management, another reason is necessary to elucidate the situation. As described above, some re-surveys of Tamil villages have shown a rising trend in wage levels of agricultural labourers and an increasing difficulty in securing farm workers and controlling non-elite villagers by the dominant groups. As shown there, M village had already undergone the empowerment of the lower classes of villagers by 1980. The remarkable increase in their participation in non-farm jobs might have further strengthened their position with regard to the richer section of the villagers. This continuing 'social revolution' (Harriss et al. 2010; 2012) might have also partly influenced the decisions made by the Forward Class people in this village regarding their jobs. This point will be discussed further below.

Education

As expected, the educational levels of the villagers have risen considerably during the last three decades. Table 3.6 shows the rate of workers having the SSLC or the Indian Technical Institute (ITI) certificates in 1980. Although 30 per cent of the Pillai workers had such certificates, the figures were below 20 per cent for other communities.

In Table 3.7, based on 2007 data, villagers older than 17 are classified into two groups by age: the younger group, 18–40, and the older group, older than 40. Even for the older group, 63 per cent of the Pillai and Chettiyar

Table 3.6 Proportion of SSLC and ITI certificate holders, 1980

	Rate of SSLC • ITI certificate holders among the total number of workers (%)	Rate of households with SSLC • ITI holder(s) among total households (%)
Pillai	30.4	43.8
Chettiyar	19	30.8
Muthuraja	19.4	26.1
SCs	8.3	15.3
Villagers' total	16.2	23.4
Brahmin	109.3	76.3

Source: Yanagisawa (1983, Table 21-A, pp. 133–136).

Table 3.7 Distribution of villagers in two age groups by years of education, 2007

Age groups	Male			Female		
	18–40 years old	41 and older	Total	18–40 years old	41 and older	Total
Pillais and Chettiyars						
No education (%)	0	4	2	0	24	10
1–5 years (%)	9	11	10	14	27	19
6–9 years (%)	14	21	18	27	30	28
10 years (%)	27	40	34	14	11	13
11–12 years (%)	14	19	16	29	3	18
13–17 years (%)	36	4	20	16	5	11
Total (%)	100	100	100	100	100	100
Average years	11.09	9	10.01	9.98	5.54	8.11
Rate of increase ('41 and more' group = 100)	123	100		180	100	
Muthurajas, etc.						
No education (%)	1	8	4	14	46	26
1–5 years (%)	12	37	23	19	30	23
6–9 years (%)	28	24	26	32	19	27
10 years (%)	26	20	24	19	4	13
11–12 years (%)	21	8	16	12	2	8
13–17 years (%)	12	3	8	5	0	3
Total (%)	100	100	100	100	100	100
Average years	9.57	6.59	8.31	7.26	3.12	5.69
Rate of increase ('41 and more' group = 100)	145	100		232	100	
SCs						
No education (%)	8	11	9	8	50	25
1–5 years (%)	7	26	15	14	18	16
6–9 years (%)	26	30	28	22	24	23
10 years (%)	24	23	23	22	8	16
11–12 years (%)	22	9	16	16	1	10
13–17 years (%)	14	1	8	18	0	11
Total (%)	100	100	100	100	100	100
Average years	9.38	7.1	8.37	9.25	3.5	6.94
Rate of increase ('41 and more' group = 100)	132	100		264	100	

Source: Data collected during the author's fieldwork in 2007.

male population have more than ten years of education (corresponding to SSLC or higher levels). The corresponding figures for the Muthurajas are 31 per cent and for the SCs 33 per cent. Those results underscore the progress that has been made in educational attainment by villagers since 1980. A comparison between the younger and older groups also highlights the remarkable rise in educational level. Particularly impressive is that of women: SC and Muthuraja women increased the number of years spent in education by 164 per cent and 132 per cent, respectively, between the two age groups. It is especially interesting that only a slight difference remains in the average years of education between male and female SC villagers.

Having identified overall trends in the education level of the villagers, we shall examine differences among communities in relation to male education. The proportion of male Pillais and Chettiyars educated up to 13–17 years, i.e., up to college and beyond, has significantly increased in the last 20 years, accounting for 36 per cent of the younger group. Including those with an 11–12-year education, those with an education of 11 years or more form more than half the group. In sharp contrast to these communities, the proportion of male SC members with fewer than five years of education has been reduced considerably, whereas the 11–12-year group has expanded, showing a trend to concentrate on the range of 6–12 years. A similar trend is apparent among Muthuraja men. Consequently, the Pillai and Chettiyar male group and the Muthuraja and SC male group differ in the proportions of those with 13 or more years of education. This difference presents important implications in connection with the availability of jobs in the formal sector, as described below.

It is notable that there has been a radical reduction in the number of SC female villagers without education, while the proportion of those with 13 or more years of education is larger for women than for men. Muthuraja female members 'without education' have also decreased remarkably, but female villagers with 13 or more years of education are far outnumbered by men with 13 or more years of education.

Occupations and Years of Education

Table 3.8 presents the years of education of male workers for each occupational category. First, the average number of years of education expands in order from Group A to Group F. As demonstrated earlier, the average income increases in the same order. Consequently, as expected, the number of years of education is closely related to a villager's wish to obtain work with a better income. The table indicates that it would be very difficult for a person to get any job outside Groups A and B without an education of more than nine years.

The connection between years of education and occupation differs considerably between the younger (18–39 years old) and older (more than 40) groups. Except for Group C jobs, the years of education for each

Table 3.8 Average years of education of male workers for each job group

	Age group	
Job group	18–40 years old	41 and more
A	8.1	6.6
B	8.4	7.6
C	10.4	10.4
D	10.6	9.9
E	12.4	10.2
F	13	10.5
Total (average)	10	7.6

Source: Date collected during the author's fieldwork in 2007.

occupational group are longer in the younger groups than in the older. The rise is particularly noticeable for occupations in the higher income groups: E (10.2–12.4 years) and F (10.5–13.0 years). A person from the older-aged group with an SSLC qualification could get a job in Group E (e.g., a bus conductor) or could be employed in a big company or as a government employee. A person in the younger group would need on average more than 11 or 12 years of education to get such a job.

This difference in urban-job availability between the generations is confirmed by Table 3.9, which shows the distribution of villagers engaged in jobs other than those in Group A (those available in and around the village) for each of the younger and older groups of villagers. It shows that 75 per cent of urban-employed workers with a 13–17-year education from the older

Table 3.9 Percentage of workers engaged in urban jobs by years of education

	No education	1–5 years	6–9 years	10 years	11–15 years	13–17 years	Total
	Age group: Below 41						
B Group	67	56	50	22	19	3	26
C Group	33	22	14	35	29	15	25
D Group	0	11	31	29	24	21	25
E Group	0	11	3	10	26	42	18
F Group	0	0	3	4	2	18	6
Total	100	100	100	100	100	100	100
	Age group: 41 and more						
B Group	0	80	45	15	6	0	22
C Group	0	20	0	7	19	25	11
D Group	0	0	27	19	13	0	16
E Group	0	0	9	30	19	0	19
F Group	100	0	18	30	44	75	33
Total	100	100	100	100	100	100	100

Source: Date collected during the author's fieldwork in 2007.

group are employed in Group F jobs, whereas the corresponding figure for the younger group is only 18 per cent. Even after adding Group E workers, those with such good urban occupations together form only 60 per cent for the younger group. For the lower education group with an 11–12-year education, 44 per cent and 19 per cent of the older workers are in Groups F and E, respectively, while for the younger group, the corresponding figures are as low as 2 per cent and 26 per cent. This indicates that, with such a level of education, it is difficult for younger people to get jobs that provide a reasonable income. For urban-employed workers with a 10-year education (SSLC), about 60 per cent of the older group obtained jobs in Groups F and E, but only 14 per cent of the younger workers below 41 were able to do so. SSLC enabled villagers over 40 to be employed in decent urban jobs, although younger villagers have to be educated more than 13 years to obtain such jobs. To get a job in Group F, a BA degree does not guarantee a post. An MA might be needed.

This data indicates a considerable rise over the last two decades in the number of years of education needed by villagers to get non-agrarian jobs. This trend is even more apparent regarding permanent employment in government and companies in the formal sector (Groups F and E). In other words, the hurdle in terms of education which villagers must clear to enter urban jobs has become higher over time. The longer the time spent in education by villagers is, as described above, a result of their efforts to clarify the rising barrier. At the same time, a difference became apparent among communities in this regard, that is, half of the men younger than 40 from the Pillai and Chettiyar communities have been educated for 11 years and more. In so doing, they have generally been successful in getting Groups E and F jobs. In fact, those with 11 and more years of education, respectively, account for only 33 per cent and 36 per cent of the Muthuraja and SC men younger than 40. Therefore, a lower percentage of workers are engaged in Groups E and F for these villager groups. Because of the raised barrier in terms of education, the villagers are divided with regard to benefiting from urban job opportunities.

Changes in the Villagers' Life

As expected, the last three decades have produced some important changes in villagers' living conditions, consumption, and lifestyle. Improvements have been made in infrastructure. Each household now has tap water. Most roads inside the village are now paved, making it easier to drive cars and two-wheelers in the village. Consumer durables have penetrated villagers' lives to a considerable extent. Of these changes, only those that directly relate to occupational changes and education are discussed here.

First, an important change that is noticeable in the re-survey of the village was a remarkable improvement in housing on SC streets. Whereas in 1980, only two or three houses in SC streets were built of brick and had tiled roofs, and most houses were thatched with leaves, now, 27 years later, more than 80 per cent of SC houses are *pucca* houses with tiled or concrete roofs. The government provides a subsidy to poor families for the construction of houses. This scheme has contributed considerably to the construction of *pucca* houses by SCs, but the increase of their family income might be another factor. It is noteworthy that the mushrooming construction of houses in the villages and of apartment buildings in a semi-urban town located between Tiruchirappalli city and the village provides villagers with new job opportunities related to construction work such as brick manufacturing, building work, and transporting river sand (as described above).

Second, with education of more than 12 years now necessary to obtain good urban jobs, villagers' demands for education have developed remarkably. At the time of 1980 survey, except for the Pillai and Chettiyar villagers for whom a considerable number of children were either educated at boarding schools or commuted to study in urban schools by bus and train, most villagers sent their children to primary schools in the village and the secondary school in the neighbouring village. The situation had changed by 2007. Among the Pillai and Chettiyar children attending primary and secondary schools, those attending schools located in and around the village comprised only 36 per cent of the boys and 44 per cent of the girls. Even among Muthuraja and SC children, about 30 per cent attend schools located in Lalgudi town and other remote areas. The villagers are now demanding higher-quality education even at primary and secondary levels, to provide their sons and daughters with higher education, including college and MA level courses.

Conclusion

One can examine the implications of the findings from a wider perspective. First, not only Forward Class communities such as the Pillais and Chettiyars but also OBCs such as the Muthurajas and SCs have increased their non-farm economic activities, the income from which now forms the major part of a villager's income. This finding is in accord with information from other parts of India. As Lanjouw and Murgai (2009) have described, in a considerable number of states in India, non-farm sectors account for nearly half of rural household income.

Increased participation in non-farm activities has not only increased the total income villagers earn. It has also strengthened the bargaining position of agricultural labourers and other subaltern groups with village elite landowners. As reported in some village surveys conducted around 1980 in Tamil Nadu, villages have been involved in the expansion of non-farm job opportunities, which tightened the rural labour market and empowered the agricultural labourer classes (Bardhan 1989; Yanagisawa 1996). The trend was further confirmed by village surveys conducted in other states in the 1990s (Byres et al. 1999). Agricultural wage levels in India had started to rise in real terms by 1980 (Vaidyanathan, 1994; Bhalla et al. 2006; Jose 2013).

Helped by a tightening of the labour market, as was the case in M village, Dalits and other subaltern villagers strengthened their movements to achieve emancipation from dominant village elites. Recent re-survey reports on Tamil villages confirm the further consolidation of this trend. Harriss et al. (2010) report a general tightening of the labour market with the increased availability of non-farm employment and state that since 1981 'in real terms, agricultural wage rates have roughly doubled, moving well beyond the long-run historic mean. They recount that the complaints of the Reddiyars and others in the case village about the costs of labour and 'labour problems' are understandable'. Low caste villagers who have been thus empowered prefer working outside their villages to being employed by village landowners. The previously dominant village elites have lost their power to control subaltern groups of villagers. As Harriss et al. (2012) reports, Tamil villages are now involved in a 'social revolution'.

Second, as shown by the village data, this increasing involvement in non-farm activities by villagers has not led rural households to stop working in agriculture or, other than certain dominant elite villagers, to leave the village entirely. Our village re-survey reveals that while the progress in the villagers' educational attainment in the last three decades is remarkable, only a small fraction of the OBC and SC households are able to get their sons educated to more than 11 years. The survey reveals a rise in the years of education needed for the villagers to get well-paid jobs in the formal sector, indicating that without an education of more than 11 years it is difficult for a villager to be employed in such posts. Therefore, most non-farm occupations available to OBC and SC households are those such as construction work and other poorly paid unstable jobs that provide people a low-level income more or less equal to agricultural wages. In view of such meagre and insecure sources of non-farm income, they cannot stop working in the agrarian sector, needing income from agriculture to support their family budget.

A rise in the number of years of education necessary for a male worker to get a job is apparently common throughout India. An examination of the sectoral distribution of wage workers by Eswaran et al. (2009) reveals that in 1983 for male workers with a middle school education 'public administration and service' accounted for 49 per cent of their working days. The corresponding figures dropped to only 16 per cent in 2004–05, indicating that middle school education only slightly qualifies a male worker for a government job, as it did in 1983. Consequently, although lower caste and other subaltern people in India have improved their socioeconomic conditions and have been empowered, most are unable to get secure and well-paid jobs in the formal sector. They must continue to work at a range of precarious small-scale and insecure informal sector activities spread across the agricultural and non-agricultural sectors (Harriss et al. 2010). Therefore, most rural households neither stop working in agriculture nor completely leave the villages for urban areas.[2] This fact probably partly explains the slow progress of urbanization in India.

Third, the re-survey reveals an important difference in the proportion of those having left agriculture by community. Forward Classes villagers such as the Pillais and Chettiyars have ensured that their sons receive a higher education. A larger proportion of their households have succeeded in getting well-paid jobs in the formal sector and government.[3] This partly explains why most households from these two communities have completely left agriculture. However, considering that fewer than one-third of their male workers are in Groups F and E jobs, there must be other factors that have induced families in these communities to leave agriculture. The progress of the 'social revolution', as indicated above, might be another related element. As described above, M village had already experienced a social movement by the SCs by 1980, which led to a severe decline in the controlling power of dominant villager groups over subaltern villagers. It is likely that, as occurred in other villages in Tamil Nadu, the increasing difficulty in hiring labour induced them to leave agriculture.

Fourth, the radical change in the proportion of *pucca* houses in the SC streets in M village also likely reflects a rise in the socioeconomic status of the lower classes of villagers. This finding also accords closely with all-India base data. Extraordinary progress in the construction of *pucca* houses in rural India has already been reported in the National Sample Survey data. The percentage of *katcha* houses in rural areas decreased from 51 per cent in 1983 to 17 per cent in 2008–09, whereas the figure for *pucca* houses rose from 17 per cent to 55 per cent in the same period.[4] The houses are constructed in greater numbers in rural areas than in urban areas. A 2002 NSS on housing conditions in India revealed that, in terms of the number of houses constructed (including additions, alterations, and major repairs) during the last five years, rural areas accounted for 82 per cent, and in terms of costs incurred, rural areas accounted for 60 per cent. Even if one includes the cost for the purchase of new residential units such as flats, which is much more common in urban areas, the total cost incurred in constructing, repairing, and purchasing residential units in rural areas accounted for 54 per cent.[5] As shown by Denis et al. (2012), where the employment share was examined by sector, the share of rural areas for construction workers increased from 56.7 per cent in 1993–94 to 70.3 per cent in 2009–10. Thomas (2012) reveals that the new employment opportunities created in India during the second half of the 2000s were predominantly in rural construction. Therefore, further clarification of the house construction boom in rural areas, as evidenced in M village, might contribute meaningfully to an understanding of the nature of contemporary economic growth in India.

Notes

1 For the survey of M village in 1979–81, see Yanagisawa (1983) and Yanagisawa (1996: Chapter 7).

2 A resurvey of six villages in Tiruchirappalli District by Djurfeldt et al. (2008) suggests that only about 15 per cent of the households completely left their villages between 1979–80 and 2005–06.

3 Our observation of a difference in attainment in higher level education between communities is in accord with the findings by Knatkovska et al. (2012), which reveal that between 1983 and 2004–05, although gaps between the SC/ST and the other communities in regard to education, occupation, wages, and income rapidly narrowed, the gap slightly widened with respect to higher education. It also widened for attaining white-collar jobs, in contrast to blue-collar jobs, for which the gap narrowed.

4 National Sample Survey Organisation, Government of India, *Dwellings in India: NSS 50th Round (July 1993–June 1994), Fifth Quinquennial Survey on Consumer Expenditure*, March 1997, 18; National Sample Survey Organisation, Government of India, *Housing Condition in India, Housing Stock and Constructions, NSS 58th Round (July 2002–December 2002); Housing Conditions and Amenities in India, 2008–09*, NSS 65th Round (July 2008–June 2009), National Sample Survey Office, Government of India, 2010.

5 National Sample Survey Organisation, Government of India, *Housing Condition in India, Housing Stock and Constructions*: NSS 58th Round (July 2002–December 2002), Report No. 488, Statements 28, 29, Tables 75, 104.

References

Balakrishnan, P. (2010) *Economic Growth in India: History and Prospect*, Delhi: Oxford University Press.

Bardhan, P., ed. (1989) *Conversations between Economists and Anthropologists: Methodological Issues in Measuring Economic Change in Rural India*, Delhi: Oxford University Press.

Bhalla, S., Karan, A. K. and Shobha T. (2006) 'Rural Casual Labourers, Wages and Poverty: 1983 to 1999–2000', in Aasha Kapur Mehta and Andrew Shepherd, eds., *Chronic Poverty and Development Policy in India*, New Delhi: Sage.

Byres, T. J., Kapadia, K. and Lerche, J. eds. (1999) *Rural Labour Relations in India*, London: Frank Cass.

Denis, E., Mukhopadhyay, P. and Zérah, M. (2012) 'Subaltern Urbanisation in India', *Economic and Political Weekly*, July 28, 47(30): 52–62.

Djurfeldt, G., Athreya, V., Jayakumar, N., Lindberg, S., Rajagopal, A. and Vidyasagar, R. (2008) 'Agrarian Change and Social Mobility in Tamil Nadu', *Economic and Political Weekly*, November 8, 43(45): 50–61.

Eswaran, M., Kotwal, A., Ramasawami, B. and Wadhwa, W. (2009) 'Sectoral Labour Flows and Agricultural Wages in India, 1983–2004: Has Growth Trickled Down?', *Economic and Political Weekly*, January 10, 44(2): 46–55.

Harriss, J., Jeyaranjan, J. and Nagaraj, K. (2010) 'Land, Labour and Caste Politics in Rural Tamilnadu in the 20th Century: Iruvelpattu (1916–2008)', *Economic and Political Weekly*, July 31, 45(31): 47–61.

Harriss, J., Jeyaranjan, J. and Nagaraj, K. (2012) 'Rural Urbanism in Tamil Nadu, Notes on a 'Slater Village': Gangaikondan, 1916–2012', *Review of Agrarian Studies*, 2(2): 29–59.

Jose, A.V. (2013) 'Changes in Wages and Earnings of Rural Labourers', *Economic and Political Weekly*, 48(26 & 27): 107–114.

Knatkovska, V., Lahiri, A. and Paul S. (2012) 'Castes and Labor Mobility', *American Economic Journal: Applied Economics*, 4(2): 274–307.

Lanjouw, P. and Murgai, R. (2009) 'Poverty Decline, Agricultural Wages, and Nonfarm Employment in Rural India: 1983–2004', *Agricultural Economics*, 40: 243–263.

Thomas, J. Jose. (2012) 'India's Labour Market during the 2000s: Surveying the Changes', *Economic and Political Weekly*, December 22, 47(51): 39–51.

Vaidyanathan, A. (1994) 'Employment Situation: Some Emerging Perspectives', *Economic and Political Weekly*, December 10, 29(50): 3147–3156.

Yanagisawa, H. A. (1983) *Socio-Economic Changes in a Village in the Paddy Cultivating Areas in South India*, Tokyo: Institute for the Study of Languages and Cultures in Asia and Africa, Tokyo University of Foreign Studies.

Yanagisawa, H. (1996) *A Century of Change: Caste and Irrigated Lands in Tamilnadu, 1860s–1970s*, Delhi: Manohar.

4 Recent Changes in Employment Structure in India

Yoshifumi Usami and Vikas Rawal

The Indian economy has transformed greatly since 1991 when the process of liberalization of the economy began. Although the average rate of GDP growth has been high, growth has been extremely uneven across different sub-periods, regions, and sectors. In most years since 1991, the growth of agriculture and manufacturing sectors has been sluggish. Growth, even in periods during which it increased, was driven primarily by the service sector. It occurred in urban, particularly metropolitan, areas. Trade and foreign investment have played only a marginal role as drivers of economic expansion. These dynamics have been associated with sweeping changes in the structure of employment. Apart from changes in the sectoral composition of growth and those in employment elasticity of growth in different sectors, the expansion of education has affected the structure of employment. Since the mid-2000s, the provision of employment under the Mahatma Gandhi National Rural Employment Guarantee Act Programme (MGNREGA) has also had an impact.

Recent NSS Employment Unemployment Surveys show a considerable contraction of employment, especially in agriculture, during the second half of the 2000s. There is substantial literature that has discussed this decline. Mehrotra et al. (2014) provided a broad overview of changes in employment since 1993–94. They examined employment trends in the Indian economy as a whole and showed that employment in agriculture decreased while that in non-agriculture increased. They have argued that the decline in work participation rates of women was primarily a result of their increased participation in schooling. Rangarajan et al. (2011) also explained the decline in work participation rates of women after 2004–05 on the basis of the rise in school enrolment. Mehrotra et al. (2014) claimed that the withdrawal of adult women from the labour force was also a result of higher school attendance rates among girls and increased outmigration of adult men, which made housework more time-demanding for adult women. Abraham (2013) has maintained that, while agrarian distress forced more women into work between 1999–2000 and 2004–05, better economic conditions in a patriarchal society created social pressures that withdrew them from the labour force and confined them to doing housework. Rawal and Saha (2015) have argued that the long-term decline in women's workforce participation rate was a result

DOI: 10.4324/9781003311898-5

of contraction of employment in agriculture and the lack of corresponding rise in employment opportunities in rural non-farm sector. They contend that more concentrated land coupled with labour-displacing machines led to the drop in labour absorption in agriculture. On the other hand, lack of access to basic amenities and serious problems of safety for women impede their physical mobility, limiting migration of rural women to the urban labour markets.

This chapter presents an analysis of overall trends in the structure of employment, differentiating these trends between men and women, between rural and urban workers, and across different sectors. The emphasis of this chapter is on using age cohort analysis to elucidate the dynamics of change in the employment structure. Such analyses are limited by the fact that data related to age in NSS surveys and censuses, particularly for older people, are not accurate. Particularly, this makes it difficult to use age cohort analysis to examine the long-term dynamics of changes in employment structure. Consequently, age cohort analyses in this chapter are limited to the 61st and 68th round NSS Employment Unemployment Surveys (hereinafter, EUS), which are combined with age cohort population data from the 2001 and 2011 Censuses. In addition, because of these limitations, the analyses primarily examine changes in the youth employment structure and especially throw light on the role of education.

The first section of this chapter presents an overview of changes in the overall size of the labour force and in work participation rates between 1993–94 and 2011–12. An explanation of the changes in employment structure across different industries is presented next, followed by two sections discussing the results of age cohort analyses and the impact of improvement in educational attainment on employment conditions of young workers. This chapter concludes with a summary of the main findings.

Change in Workforce

Since the early 1990s, when full-scale economic reform was undertaken, the Indian economy has experienced sweeping changes including those in the overall composition of employment, with a strong shift from agriculture to non-agriculture. It is important, however, to assess the employment structure not only throughout the Indian economy as a whole but in rural and urban areas separately and in terms of both men and women. A decline in agricultural employment has taken place in rural areas, but the corresponding level of non-agricultural employment in rural and urban areas shows different patterns. Another reason for investigating the employment structure in rural and urban areas separately is a peculiar feature of Indian urbanization: the mushrooming of census towns. Although the delay of notification of a village as a statutory town by the State government is a major reason for the upsurge, this phenomenon reflects the fact that the employment structure in rural areas has been morphing very rapidly from agricultural to non-agricultural. It is also important to elucidate the employment structures used by men and women separately. A great difference exists between men and women in terms of work participation, not only in intensity but also in the types of employment. Therefore, it is expected that both have different patterns when agricultural employment declines and new employment opportunities emerge, particularly in the construction and other services sectors.

Table 4.1 presents population and workers, along with worker–population ratios of people aged 15 years and above in India, for rural and urban men and women. Rural men of this age group swelled from 186.3 million in 1993–94 to 234.5 million in 2004–05 and further to 267.4 million in 2011–12. The female population of the same age group in rural areas increased from 181 million to 233.2 million and to 263.5 million during the same period. A decline in population growth is apparent. The average annual growth rate for rural men decreased from 2.3 per cent during the first period (1993–94 to 2004–05) to 1.3 per cent during the second period (2004–05 to 2011–12). The population of women rose at the rate of 2.5 per cent in the first period and 1.2 per cent per year in the second period. Urbanization (a result of rural–urban migration as well as transformation of some villages into towns) is reflected in higher population growth in urban areas. The population of urban men of age 15 years and above grew at 3.1 per cent during the first

Table 4.1 Population and labour force in India (age 15 and over) (Million persons)

	Year	Population	Workers (PS + SS)	Unemployed	Students	Other non-workers	Worker population ratio
Rural male	1993	186.3	160.9	2.4	13.5	9.5	86.4%
	2004	234.5	198.4	3.2	19.2	13.8	84.6%
	2011	267.4	213.8	3.7	33.9	16.0	80.0%
Rural female	1993	181.5	88.3	0.7	5.4	87.0	48.7%
	2004	233.2	113.1	2.1	11.5	106.5	48.5%
	2011	263.5	92.8	1.5	22.4	146.7	35.2%
Urban male	1993	67.7	52.0	2.2	8.6	4.8	76.8%
	2004	91.9	70.1	2.7	11.5	7.6	76.3%
	2011	119.6	88.7	2.7	17.9	10.4	74.1%
Urban female	1993	61.5	13.7	0.9	5.9	41.0	22.3%
	2004	84.6	19.2	1.4	8.5	55.4	22.7%
	2011	112.7	21.9	1.2	13.7	75.8	19.5%

Source: Author's estimation using NSS's 50th, 61st, and 68th Employment and Unemployment Surveys unit data.

Note: This table is based on the NSS EUS estimates. It is difficult to estimate rural/urban population in 1993/94 because the 1991 census was not undertaken in Jammu and Kashmir. NSS Employment and Unemployment Surveys under-estimate the absolute size of the population.

period and at 2.7 per cent during the second period; it reached 119.8 million in 2011–12. For urban women, population growth was 3.2 per cent and 2.9 per cent per annum, respectively, for the same periods.

The increase in the number of workers, including principal and subsidiary status workers, slowed from the first period to the second; it was negative for rural women. As Table 4.1 shows, the expansion of schooling is an important reason for the slower proliferation of male workers in both rural and urban areas. A rise in the likelihood of population attending educational institutions took place also for women workers, but in their case, a greater increase took place in the population of other non-workers. It is noteworthy that the number of other non-workers, which mainly include persons engaged in housework, increased considerably, from 87.0 million to 146.7 million for rural women and from 40.0 million to 75.8 million for urban women. In the NSSO data, such people are classified as being outside the labour force.

As a result of these changes, the worker–population ratio (WPR) fell. For men, the decline of the WPR was rather slight, from 86.4 per cent in 1993–94 to 80.0 per cent in 2011–12 for rural men and from 76.8 per cent to 74.1 per cent for urban men. The major decline occurred in the 15–24 years age group and can be explained mainly by an increase in the number of people attending secondary and higher educational institutions. In contrast, the female WPR declined markedly in both rural and urban areas. In rural areas, it was 48.7 per cent in 1993–94. It remained at an almost identical level until 2004–05 but dropped to 35.2 per cent in 2011–12.[1] Similarly, the female WPR in urban areas fell from 22.3 per cent in 1993–94 to 19.5 per cent in 2011–12. It is unlikely that educational improvement alone explains this because it occurred across all age groups, as we will see later.

Industrial Distribution of Workers

Table 4.2 presents changes in the industrial distribution of workers during the last two decades. According to the NSS usual and subsidiary activity status definition, workers are as (a) self-employed, which includes family helpers and employers, (b) regular wage/salaried employees (hereinafter, regular wage workers), and (c) casual labour. The activity status and industry are combined to show the different employment statuses of workers in Table 4.2.

It is noteworthy that self-employment and casual labour in agriculture were the major occupations for rural male workers. In 1993–94, 44.8 per cent of rural male workers were self-employed; 27.7 per cent of rural male workers worked as casual labourers in agriculture. The shares of both occupations waned substantially over the following two decades. The share of self-employed among rural male workers fell to 42.2 per cent in 2004–05 and further to 38.9 per cent in 2011–12. The share of casual labourers dropped to 23.2 per cent in 2004–05 and further to 20.0 per cent in 2011–12. On the whole, the share of total employment in agriculture (including regular wage workers in agriculture) fell sharply, from 73.7 per cent in 1993–94 to 59.4 per cent in 2011–12.

Table 4.2 Percentage distribution of workers by employment status and industry

Employment status	Industry	Rural male			Rural female			Urban male			Urban female		
		1993/94	2004/05	2011/12	1993/94	2004/05	2011/12	1993/94	2004/05	2011/12	1993/94	2004/05	2011/12
Self-employed	Agriculture	44.8%	42.2%	38.9%	50.3%	53.8%	48.1%	5.4%	4.3%	3.9%	14.4%	11.5%	6.4%
	Mining	0.1%	0.1%	0.0%	0.0%	0.0%	0.0%	0.1%	0.1%	0.0%	0.1%	0.0%	0.0%
	Manufacturing	3.5%	4.1%	3.6%	4.6%	6.3%	7.4%	7.3%	7.7%	7.5%	13.3%	18.7%	19.8%
	Electricity	0.1%	0.0%	0.0%	0.0%	0.1%	0.0%	0.1%	0.0%	0.1%	0.1%	0.1%	0.2%
	Construction	0.5%	1.2%	1.3%	0.0%	0.0%	0.0%	1.7%	2.4%	2.1%	0.1%	0.1%	0.1%
	Trade	4.9%	6.6%	6.4%	2.0%	2.4%	2.5%	16.3%	19.7%	17.7%	8.7%	10.0%	9.9%
	Transport	0.8%	1.7%	1.8%	0.0%	0.1%	0.0%	3.2%	5.0%	4.4%	0.2%	0.5%	0.1%
	Other services	2.7%	2.1%	2.4%	1.3%	1.0%	1.0%	7.5%	5.6%	6.1%	7.8%	6.3%	6.1%
Regular wage workers	Agriculture	1.2%	0.9%	0.5%	0.5%	0.4%	0.4%	0.4%	0.3%	0.3%	0.3%	0.3%	0.3%
	Mining	0.2%	0.1%	0.1%	0.0%	0.0%	0.0%	1.0%	0.7%	0.6%	0.2%	0.1%	0.1%
	Manufacturing	1.6%	1.8%	2.5%	0.6%	0.7%	0.9%	12.5%	11.6%	12.0%	4.0%	5.1%	5.4%
	Electricity	0.2%	0.2%	0.2%	0.0%	0.0%	0.0%	1.4%	0.9%	1.2%	0.8%	0.3%	0.7%
	Construction	0.1%	0.2%	0.3%	0.0%	0.0%	0.0%	0.8%	0.6%	1.4%	0.1%	0.2%	0.5%
	Trade	0.5%	1.1%	1.1%	0.0%	0.1%	0.3%	4.4%	6.7%	6.8%	0.8%	1.6%	2.3%
	Transport	1.0%	1.4%	1.7%	0.0%	0.1%	0.1%	5.2%	5.4%	6.5%	0.9%	1.1%	2.5%
	Other services	3.8%	3.3%	3.6%	1.5%	2.4%	3.9%	16.8%	14.5%	14.7%	22.1%	27.2%	31.1%
Casual labourers	Agriculture	27.7%	23.2%	20.0%	35.6%	29.2%	26.4%	3.2%	1.5%	1.5%	10.3%	6.4%	4.2%
	Mining	0.5%	0.5%	0.4%	0.3%	0.2%	0.2%	0.2%	0.1%	0.2%	0.3%	0.1%	0.2%
	Manufacturing	1.8%	1.9%	2.0%	1.7%	1.2%	1.4%	3.4%	3.2%	2.7%	6.1%	3.3%	3.3%
	Electricity	0.0%	0.0%	0.0%	0.0%	0.0%	0.0%	0.1%	0.1%	0.0%	0.2%	0.0%	0.1%
	Construction	2.6%	5.5%	11.4%	0.8%	1.4%	6.6%	4.5%	6.2%	7.2%	4.0%	3.5%	3.4%
	Trade	0.2%	0.6%	0.5%	0.0%	0.0%	0.1%	1.2%	1.6%	1.5%	0.6%	0.8%	0.6%
	Transport	0.5%	0.8%	0.8%	0.0%	0.0%	0.1%	1.9%	1.2%	1.0%	0.3%	0.1%	0.1%
	Other services	0.7%	0.4%	0.4%	0.5%	0.4%	0.4%	1.6%	0.6%	0.7%	4.3%	2.5%	2.5%
Total		100.0%	100.0%	100.0%	100.0%	100.0%	100.0%	100.0%	100.0%	100.0%	100.0%	100.0%	100.0%

Source: Same as Table 4.1.
Note: Workers in this table include both usual principal and subsidiary activity status workers.

It is also apparent that the proportion of self-employed and regular wage workers in manufacturing, trade, and transport rose between 1993–94 and 2004–05, but stagnated or fell thereafter. Employment in other service sectors, either as self-employed, regular wage worker, or casual labour, remained at the level of 1993–94 or flagged slightly. Although the share of every other sector either stagnated or declined, it was casual labour in construction that rose substantially during the period under study. The share of construction labourers rose from 2.6 per cent in 1993–94 to 5.5 per cent in 2004–05 and then sharply to 11.4 per cent in 2011–12. In 2011–12, construction became the second largest industry aside from agriculture to employ rural male labourers. Between 1993–94 and 2004–05, numerous rural male workers lost employment in agriculture but found it in services (trade and transport). Between 2004–05 and 2011–12, they were pushed out of agriculture and found jobs in construction.

Some points are particularly noteworthy. First, the rural–urban demarcation in the NSS EUS is based on the usual place of residence of a household. Second, a short-term migrant who might be away from their usual place of residence for up to six months is included as a household member. According to the NSS 64th E&U and Migration Survey, short-term migrants from rural areas were estimated to be around 12 million, of whom about 40 per cent were employed as construction labourers. In other words, a substantial proportion of rural male workers are presumably working as construction labourers away from home.

Major occupations of rural female workers were self-employed and casual labour in agriculture, which together accounted for 85.9 per cent in 1993–94. The percentage of workers engaged in these occupations fell to 83 per cent in 2004–05 and fell further to 74.5 per cent in 2011–12. As it happened for male workers, in non-agricultural employment, the share of female casual labour in construction rose substantially from 1.4 per cent in 2004–05 to 6.6 per cent in 2011–12. The shares of self-employed in manufacturing and regular wage workers in the other services sector rose gradually. It is possible that this rise in the share of construction labourers was related to the MGNREGA. The MGNREGA was implemented from 2005–06 in selected districts and from 2007–08 in all districts. According to NSS 68th EUS results, it is estimated that 34.3 million men and 23.6 million women were engaged in MGNREGA works, although the number of days worked in MGNREGA work is limited. Female workers in public works (status 41) accounted for 45.1 per cent of all casual labourers (categories 41 and 51) in non-agriculture. About 57 per cent of those who reported construction labour as their principal or subsidiary activity had done construction labour under public works programmes. MGNREGA was the single most important public works programme. Therefore, it would be reasonable to conclude that MGNREGA accounted for the bulk of women's employment in construction.

Most urban male workers were engaged in manufacturing, trade, and the other services sector in 1993–94. Employment in manufacturing as either self-employed, regular wage worker, or casual labour remained almost constant or slightly declined during the period. Among the various service sectors, the portion of self-employed people in trade went up from 16.3 per cent in 1999–2000 to 19.7 per cent in 2004–05. The share of those in transport rose from 3.2 per cent in 1999–2000 to 5.0 per cent in 2004–05. Between 2004–05 and 2011–12, however, these shares remained either unchanged or fell slightly. Self-employed or regular wage workers in other services sectors decreased their respective shares from 16.9 per cent to 14.7 per cent. For urban men, the share of casual labour in construction rose, whereas the share of the manufacturing and other services sector declined. Major employment opportunities are available to urban male workers in the service sector. The slow growth of employment in manufacturing is an important concern because job seekers with secondary and higher level education are increasing, as we examine later.

In contrast with rural women who mostly worked in agriculture, most urban women workers found employment in manufacturing, trade, and other services sectors. It is noteworthy that, within these sectors, a shift occurred from employment as casual workers and as self-employed to a higher proportion of workers being employed as regular workers. Particularly, the share of regular workers in the other services sector rose substantially from 22.1 per cent in 1993–94 to 31.1 per cent in 2011–12, although self-employed and casual labour in this sector declined. In addition, the share of self-employed workers in manufacturing rose from 13.3 per cent in 1993–94, to 18.7 per cent in 2004–05, and to 19.8 per cent in 2011–12, whereas the share of casual labour in the sector fell. Similarly, workers in trade rose from 10.1 per cent, to 15.9 per cent, and to 16.2 per cent, and other services sectors, from 34.3 per cent, to 36.1 per cent, and to 38.7 per cent.

Change in Distribution of Workers by Age Cohort, Employment Status, and Industry During 2004–05 and 2011–12

The percentage distribution of workers sometimes conceals changes in the actual magnitude of each category because of fluctuation in the total number of workers. Estimation of the numbers of workers in different age cohorts allows for an examination of the shift of the workforce across different sectors. Let us first explain the method of age cohort analysis and its limitations.

Generally speaking, a change in employment structure takes place through the following:

a Entry of young workers into different sectors
b Changes in occupations of existing workers
c Exit or retirement of workers from the labour force

Dividing the workers into age cohorts and making comparisons across two rounds of NSS EUS provides some clues that elucidate the impact of these three processes on changes in the employment structure. Considering the

7-year gap separating the 61st and 68th EUSs of NSS, we divide the sample into 7-year age groups starting from 15 years of age (that is, 15–21 years, 22–28 years, and so on). Then, the employment structure of an age group (say, 15–21 years) in 2004–05 is compared with the employment structure of the next age group (22–28 years) from the 2011–12 survey. Since people who were in the 15–21 years age group at the time of 2004–05 would have been in the 22–28 years age group at the time of 2011–12 survey, a comparison of the employment structure of these two age groups enables us to examine how employment conditions of this age group changed during this period.

In principle, one should be able to compare the employment structure of each age cohort in 2004–05 with the employment structure of the next age cohort in 2011–12. However, NSS data pose two limitations in doing so. First, NSS surveys underestimate the population. Results show that these data must be adjusted using population data from population censuses. Doing so requires age cohort population estimates from the population censuses. Second, because many respondents do not know their exact age, information related to age is an approximation. This approximation leads to a problem of age heaping, with a disproportionately high number of people reporting their age in numbers with terminal digits '5' or '0', and among other numbers, a smaller preference for numbers ending with '1' and '9'. For comparing data of the two NSS EUS rounds, 7-year age cohorts are necessary to address the seven-year gaps separating the two survey rounds. For that reason, the age heaps (at 5s, 0s, and other minor heaps) are not evenly distributed across these cohorts. Given improvements in the recording of age in recent times, the extent of heaping is not so severe for the youngest age groups (15–21 years and 22–28 years). Therefore, it least affects comparisons of data for these groups.

Given that the problem of age-heaping is not severe in the youngest two age cohorts, one can start by comparing data for the 15–21 years age cohort in 2004–05 with data for the 22–28 years age cohort in 2011–12. Of those who had been working in 2004–05, some would have continued working in the same industry, and some would have moved into a different industry, although some would have exited, retired, or migrated (from rural to urban or vice versa) by the time the 2011–12 survey took place. In 2004–05, persons in the 15–21 years age group who were non-workers included students, unemployed persons, and other non-workers. Some students would have completed education and entered the labour market (as workers or unemployed persons) by the time the 2011–12 survey took place (and they were in the 22–28 years age group), although others would have gone on to further studies. Some persons who were unemployed or were a part of the category of other non-workers in 2004–05 might have found work by 2011–12. Those who gained employment constitute fresh entrants into the labour market. Combined with educational attainment, employment patterns of young fresh entrants are apparent.

The employment structure changed during the seven years. Table 4.3(A) shows the number of rural male workers by age cohort, employment status,

Table 4.3(A) Age group-wise number of workers by employment status and
industry (rural male) (1,000 persons)

2004/05	Age at 2004/05		15–21	22–28	29–35	36–49	50+	Total
	SE Ag		12,308	16,051	14,423	21,849	25,624	90,254
	Ag labourers		8,885	10,570	10,875	13,623	8,556	52,509
	Manufacturing		3,006	3,977	3,697	4,198	2,446	17,323
	Construction		2,690	3,678	3,324	3,507	1,535	14,735
	Service sector		4,908	8,284	8,681	10,297	6,005	38,175
	Total		31,797	42,559	41,001	53,474	44,166	2,12,997
2011/12	Age at 20011/12	15–21	22–28	29–35	36–42	43–56	57+	Total
	SE Ag	8,468	14,827	14,795	13,162	21,348	16,100	88,701
	Ag labourers	5,437	9,159	9,367	7,842	10,828	4,957	47,589
	Manufacturing	2,487	4,788	3,859	2,979	3,506	1,585	19,204
	Construction	4,567	7,140	6,197	4,914	5,298	1,677	29,793
	Service sector	3,361	9,019	9,198	7,800	9,686	3,407	42,471
	Total	24,319	44,933	43,416	36,697	50,666	27,727	2,27,759
Change	SE Ag	8,468	2,519	–1,256	–1,261	–500	–9,524	–1,554
	Ag labourers	5,437	274	–1,203	–3,033	–2,795	–3,599	–4,920
	Manufacturing	2,487	1,782	–118	–718	–691	–860	1,881
	Construction	4,567	4,450	2,520	1,590	1,790	142	15,058
	Service sector	3,361	4,111	914	–881	–611	–2,598	4,296
	Total	24,319	13,136	856	–4,303	–2,808	–16,439	14,762

Source: Author's estimation using age tables of population census of 2001 and 2011 and NSS
61st and 68th EUS unit data.

Note: Workers in this table include both usual principal and subsidiary activity status
workers.

and industry. The total number of rural male workers increased by
14.8 million during the seven years: from 213.0 million in 2004–05 to 227.8 million in 2011–12. The number of self-employed people in agriculture (that is,
cultivators) decreased by 1.6 million, although the number of agricultural
labourers decreased by 4.9 million. Construction was the largest employer
of the increased labour force, accounting for 15.1 million persons, followed
by the service sector (4.3 million persons). The rise in the number of workers
in manufacturing was less than 2.0 million.

Cohort data show that there were 31.8 million workers in the 15–21 years
age group in 2004–05. Persons in this age cohort moved to the 22–28 years
age group by 2011–12; the number of workers increased to 44.9 million. The
increase by 13.1 million in the number of workers among this group consists
mainly of ex-students who completed education and who entered the labour
market during the seven years. There were also some unemployed and other
non-workers who found jobs as they moved to the 22–28 years age group.
Sector data show that the number of workers in manufacturing increased by
2.5 million, the number of workers in construction increased by 1.8 million,
the number of workers in services increased by 4.5 million, and the number

of self-employed persons in agriculture increased by 4.1 million. We examine the employment patterns of fresh entrants more closely with consideration of their educational attainment in the next section.

For the next age cohort, persons of the 22–28 years age group in 2004–05, it is apparent that only a small increase (0.8 million) in the number of workers occurred among them as they moved into the 29–35 year age group in 2011–12. Two factors are likely to have been responsible for the fact that the increase in work participation rates for rural men in this age group was small: first, the increase in the number of students in higher education was limited (estimated as 1.1 million students in 2004–05); second, migration of workers from this age cohort to urban areas increased. In this age cohort, the number of workers engaged in self-employment in agriculture and agricultural labour diminished by 1.3 million and 1.2 million, respectively, during the period. Workers in the construction and services sectors, respectively, increased by 2.5 million and 0.9 million. Judging from the amount of change in the number of workers, it is most likely that workers shifted from agriculture to construction.

As for the age cohorts of 29–49 in 2004–05, it is not possible to compare them strictly because of severe heaping in age tables. It is striking that the pattern of change is the same across all cohorts: decreases in employment in agriculture, manufacturing, and service sector and an increase in construction labour suggest shifts of occupation to construction labour from other sectors. A drop of 16.4 million workers occurred in the age cohort of 50 and over in 2004–05, which is attributable to retirement from the labour force.

Table 4.3(B) shows the distribution of rural female workers by age cohort, employment status, and industry. A marked falling-off occurred in the number of rural women workers: from 116.2 million in 2004–05 to 95.1 million in 2011–12. The decrease (21.1 million), which accounts for 18.1 per cent of all female workers in 2004–05, took place across all age cohorts. Moreover, the fall in self-employed workers in agriculture (16.7 million) was much greater than that of rural male workers who left cultivation (1.6 million). This fact suggests that the decline in women's work participation rate was not driven merely by a higher participation in education. Many women had to give up cultivation and agricultural labour, and were left only household work to do.[2]

Female construction workers increased by 4.6 million. As described earlier, it is probable that some MGNREGA workers were classified as construction workers. Therefore, MGNREGA might have contributed to the larger number of rural women employed in construction. It is noteworthy that, among service sector workers, an increase was found for young women, although workers of age 29 and above exhibited a decline over time. In such cases, young educated women started working in the other services sector, as discussed later.

The number of urban male workers increased by 19.2 million during the period, as shown in Table 4.3(C). A clear upsurge was apparent

Table 4.3(B) Age group-wise number of workers by employment status and industry (rural female) (1,000 persons)

2004/05	Age at 2004/05		15–21	22–28	29–35	36–49	50+	Total
	SE Ag		8,191	11,114	11,995	18,285	12,987	62,572
	Ag labourers		5,049	6,609	7,648	9,905	5,450	34,661
	Manufacturing		2,305	2,132	1,884	2,299	1,025	9,645
	Construction		346	370	382	433	176	1,706
	Service sector		673	1,532	1,627	2,312	1,450	7,593
	Total		16,563	21,757	23,536	33,235	21,088	1,16,178
2011/12	Age at 20011/12	15–21	22–28	29–35	36–42	43–56	57+	Total
	SE Ag	4,584	7,403	8,553	8,622	11,476	5,192	45,830
	Ag labourers	2,617	3,924	5,249	4,853	6,557	2,506	25,706
	Manufacturing	2,010	2,055	1,832	1,357	1,425	660	9,337
	Construction	477	981	1,364	1,395	1,404	658	6,278
	Service sector	622	1,435	1,621	1,615	1,856	813	7,963
	Total	10,309	15,798	18,619	17,842	22,718	9,829	95,114
Change	SE Ag	4,584	−787	−2,561	−3,373	−6,809	−7,795	−16,742
	Ag labourers	2,617	−1,124	−1,360	−2,796	−3,348	−2,944	−8,955
	Manufacturing	2,010	−251	−301	−527	−874	−365	−308
	Construction	477	635	994	1,014	970	482	4,571
	Service sector	622	762	90	−12	−456	−637	370
	Total	10,309	−765	−3,138	−5,694	−10,517	−11,259	−21,064

Source: Same as Table 4.3(A)

Note: Same as Table 4.3(A).

among young workers. Chiefly, workers of the 15–21 years age cohort doubled from 10.1 million in 2004–05 to 21.7 million in 2011–12. This increase was partly attributable to fresh entrants to the labour market and partly to rural–urban migration. Employment in the service sector (10.2 million), manufacturing (4.5 million), and construction (3.3 million) grew. It is noteworthy that most of the added workers in these sectors are young workers: more than two-thirds of the increase in industry and service sector workers was attributable to workers in the 15–21 years age cohort in 2004–05. Workers belonging to the 22–28 years age cohort in 2004–05 rose by 4.3 million, most of whom were employed in the service sector.

Table 4.3(D) shows that urban female workers increased from 24.1 million in 2004–05 to 26.6 million in 2011–12. The additional workers were mostly employed as regular workers in the services sector (2.4 million). Change in employment structure by age cohort shows that there was a rise in young workers of age 28 and younger in 2004–05 (2.2 million in the 15–21 years age cohort and 1.3 million in the 22–28 years age cohort) during the seven years, which suggests that, like urban men, the fresh entrants from this age group outnumbered those that exited from labour market. However, the number of female workers of age cohorts 29 years and above shrank, indicating mostly exit from employment in agriculture. As in the case of rural women,

Table 4.3(C) Age group-wise number of workers by employment status and industry (urban male) (1,000 persons)

2004/05	Age at 2004/05	15–21	22–28	29–35	36–49	50+	Total
	Agriculture	591	905	967	1,863	1,983	6,309
	SE manufacturing	952	1,312	1,367	2,023	1,294	6,948
	RW manufacturing	1,527	2,997	2,416	2,852	1,311	11,103
	Construction	1,296	2,011	1,877	2,125	954	8,263
	SE service	2,329	5,295	6,379	8,371	4,678	27,052
	RW service	2,093	4,651	5,009	7,842	4,073	23,669
	CL manuf. + service	1,309	1,534	1,253	1,262	503	5,861
	Total	10,097	18,704	19,269	26,339	14,795	89,205
2011/12	Age at 20011/12	15–21	22–28	29–35	36–42	43–56	57+	Total
	Agriculture	484	956	1,170	1,123	2,107	1,270	7,110
	SE manufacturing	788	1,381	1,464	1,545	2,210	891	8,279
	RW manufacturing	1,360	3,720	3,157	2,344	3,099	557	14,237
	Construction	1,269	2,597	2,624	2,027	2,417	604	11,538
	SE service	1,520	4,766	6,701	6,190	8,283	3,102	30,562
	RW service	1,726	6,792	6,547	5,609	8,098	1,605	30,376
	CL manuf. + service	1,005	1,485	1,375	901	1,126	389	6,281
	Total	8,152	21,696	23,039	19,738	27,340	8,419	1,08,383
Change	Agriculture	484	365	265	156	244	–712	802
	SE manufacturing	788	428	152	178	186	–402	1,330
	RW manufacturing	1,360	2,193	161	–72	246	–754	3,134
	Construction	1,269	1,300	613	150	293	–351	3,274
	SE service	1,520	2,437	1,406	–189	–88	–1,576	3,510
	RW service	1,726	4,698	1,896	599	256	–2,468	6,707
	CL manuf. + service	1,005	176	–159	–352	–137	–114	419
	Total	8,152	11,598	4,334	469	1,001	–6,377	19,178

Source: Same as Table 4.3(A).

Note: Same as Table 4.3(A).

more young educated women in urban areas were engaged as regular wage workers in the services sector.

Employment Structure of Fresh Entrants by Educational Attainment

The observations presented above confirm that differences in the nature of employment of those who enter the labour market and those who leave the labour market are important drivers of changes in the employment structure. In this section, we examine the changes in employment conditions of young people who freshly enter the labour market. There has been an improvement in the levels of educational attainment in this age group.

Table 4.3(D) Age group-wise number of workers by employment status and industry (urban female) (1,000 persons)

2004/05	Age at 2004/05	15–21	22–28	29–35	36–49	50+	Total
	Agriculture	523	653	914	1,389	927	4,406
	SE manufacturing	949	859	1,108	1,170	490	4,576
	RW manufacturing	236	325	323	322	119	1,325
	Construction	3	22	24	17	11	77
	SE service	414	767	878	1,267	708	4,034
	RW service	747	1,494	1,537	2,341	1,039	7,157
	CL manuf. + service	337	403	645	761	343	2,489
	Total	3,208	4,523	5,429	7,266	3,637	24,064
2011/12	Age at 20011/12	15–21	22–28	29–35	36–42	43–56	57+	Total
	Agriculture	186	353	525	672	883	359	2,978
	SE manufacturing	748	1,058	1,176	1,052	966	335	5,334
	RW manufacturing	266	360	352	362	263	36	1,639
	Construction	9	26	73	28	19	0	155
	SE service	196	725	944	962	1,065	379	4,271
	RW service	690	2,435	2,144	1,617	2,269	383	9,538
	CL manuf. + service	215	401	590	580	634	218	2,638
	Total	2,312	5,358	5,803	5,273	6,098	1,708	26,553
Change	Agriculture	186	–169	–128	–243	–506	–568	–1,428
	SE manufacturing	748	109	317	–56	–204	–155	759
	RW manufacturing	266	124	27	39	–59	–83	314
	Construction	9	23	50	4	2	–11	78
	SE service	196	311	178	84	–202	–329	238
	RW service	690	1,688	649	80	–72	–656	2,380
	CL manuf. + service	215	64	187	–65	–127	–125	149
	Total	2,312	2,150	1,280	–156	–1,168	–1,928	2,489

Source: Same as Table 4.3(A).

Note: Same as Table 4.3(A).

An important question to ask here is whether a rise in educational attainment had any bearing on the nature of young workers' occupation. For this purpose, two types of comparison are needed: first, a comparison between the employment situation of 'less-educated' fresh entrants into labour market in 2004–05 and that of 2011–12, and second, a comparison of employment situations between 'less-educated' and 'educated' fresh entrants.

Table 4.4 shows the distribution of rural and urban populations of the 15–21 years age group according to educational attainment and activity status in 2004–05 and 2011–12 separately for men and women. It is readily apparent that the educational attainment of this age group improved substantially

Table 4.4 Distribution of the population of age group 15–21 years by educational attainment and usual activity status, 2004–05 and 2011–12 (1,000 persons)

Age group	Sector and sex	Usual activity status	Educational attainment							
			Below Primary	Primary	Middle	Secondary	Higher Secondary	Diploma	College +	Total
Age group 15–21 years in 2004/05	Rural male	Workers	11,186	6,915	8,616	3,358	1,321	175	224	31,797
		Unemployed	365	293	435	432	236	60	90	1,911
		Student	640	2,372	7,765	5,956	2,927	143	263	20,071
		Other non-workers	916	342	358	77	61	0	8	1,763
		Total	13,108	9,923	17,174	9,823	4,545	379	586	55,542
	Rural female	Workers	8,741	2,763	3,238	1,169	486	86	75	16,563
		Unemployed	74	72	168	182	171	35	61	762
		Student	416	1,496	4,364	3,363	1,895	70	170	11,782
		Other non-workers	9,945	3,415	3,978	1,818	686	23	120	19,986
		Total	19,175	7,747	11,748	6,532	3,238	214	426	49,093
	Urban male	Workers	2,438	2,357	3,146	1,253	578	156	168	10,097
		Unemployed	161	195	446	235	129	79	117	1,364
		Student	212	651	3,326	4,091	3,597	204	367	12,451
		Other non-workers	293	110	192	56	30	1	28	710
		Total	3,104	3,313	7,110	5,635	4,334	440	679	24,622
	Urban female	Workers	1,080	613	710	331	242	83	148	3,208
		Unemployed	17	68	94	89	120	33	114	536
		Student	106	495	2,506	3,396	3,018	170	417	10,108
		Other non-workers	2,405	1,445	2,068	1,084	552	19	145	7,719
		Total	3,609	2,621	5,378	4,900	3,931	304	825	21,572

(Continued)

Table 4.4 Distribution of the population of age group 15–21 years by educational attainment and usual activity status, 2004–05 and 2011–12 (1,000 persons) (Continued)

Age group	Sector and sex	Usual activity status	Educational attainment							Total
			Below Primary	Primary	Middle	Secondary	Higher Secondary	Diploma	College +	
Age group 15–21 years in 2011/12	Rural male	Workers	6,494	4,831	6,817	3,886	1,846	260	186	24,319
		Unemployed	385	378	591	313	205	70	82	2,024
		Student	368	2,411	10,761	12,486	7,388	408	577	34,400
		Other non-workers	747	317	363	207	93	8	18	1,754
		Total	7,993	7,937	18,532	16,893	9,533	746	863	62,498
	Rural female	Workers	3,774	2,137	2,246	1,298	669	53	131	10,309
		Unemployed	74	17	159	150	100	54	67	620
		Student	366	1,867	7,841	8,360	4,916	184	409	23,943
		Other non-workers	7,327	3,605	5,169	3,109	1,538	45	227	21,021
		Total	11,541	7,627	15,415	12,916	7,223	336	834	55,893
	Urban male	Workers	1,948	1,658	2,087	1,370	752	158	177	8,152
		Unemployed	156	131	211	180	256	67	110	1,110
		Student	108	665	3,841	6,614	5,712	636	640	18,215
		Other non-workers	255	120	91	49	61	13	22	611
		Total	2,467	2,574	6,230	8,213	6,781	875	948	28,088
	Urban female	Workers	628	369	474	298	284	81	177	2,312
		Unemployed	26	22	56	91	65	25	82	368
		Student	62	380	3,167	4,851	5,519	445	787	15,211
		Other non-workers	1,818	1,154	1,850	1,361	880	33	299	7,396
		Total	2,535	1,926	5,547	6,601	6,748	584	1,345	25,286

Source: Same as Table 4.3(A).

Note: Workers in this table include both usual principal and subsidiary activity status workers.

during the seven years. Nevertheless, a considerable number of workers were aged 15–21 years with primary school education and below. Because of various social, economic, and other reasons, they were unable to continue attending a school and started working at a young age. They are designated as 'less-educated' workers. With improvement in educational attainment in general, the number of less-educated male workers in rural areas dropped from 18.1 million in 2004–05 to 11.3 million in 2011–12. Similarly, less-educated female workers in rural areas decreased from 11.5 million to 5.9 million during the same period. However, it is notable that the less-educated workers account for more than 40 per cent of young people aged 15–21 years.

A comparison of the employment situation of less-educated fresh entrants in 2004–05 and those in 2011–12 is presented in Table 4.5. Marked differences were found in the nature of employment of young persons who had freshly entered the labour market by the time of 2004–05 survey and those who had freshly entered the labour market by the time when the 2011–12 survey was administered. Historically, agriculture has been the sector that employed a large share of rural workers who had low levels of education. It is apparent that 34.1 per cent of them had joined the labour force to work on their household landholding and 35.1 per cent to work as agricultural labourers if one looks at rural male workers who were in the 15–21 years age group in 2004–05 (Table 4.5(A)). The table also shows that the shares declined to 30.4 per cent and 28.0 per cent, respectively, by 2011–12. A similar fall was apparent for rural women of this age group: 47.9 per cent and 34.8 per cent in 2004–05 to 43.4 per cent and 29.2 per cent in 2011–12, for self-employed people in agriculture and agricultural labour, respectively.

Although a smaller share of less-educated fresh entrants into the rural workforce was employed in agriculture, construction emerged as a sector that employed a much larger share of young rural male workers. In 2011–12, about 21 per cent of rural male workers of the 15–21 years age group were employed in construction; the corresponding share in 2004–05 had been only 9.9 per cent. For rural women, the decline in absorption of young workers in agriculture caused a large share of them to be unable to enter the labour force at all, although some found employment in manufacturing, services, and construction. Unlike rural workers, changes in the nature of employment of less-educated fresh labour market entrants in urban areas were not very striking (see Table 4.5(B)). A slight shift occurred in the shares in favour of construction and manufacturing, whereas the proportion of workers freshly entering the labour market through self-employment in the service sector shrank.

Next, we present a comparison of employment situations between 'less-educated' and 'educated' fresh entrants. We explored this question by examining the employment structure of people in the age cohort who were in the 15–21 years age group in 2004–05 and in 22–28 years age group in 2011–12. Table 4.6 presents the distribution of population of this age cohort by educational attainment and usual activity status (PS+SS). From this table, we can estimate the number of 'educated' workers, higher secondary

Table 4.5 Percentage distribution of less-educated workers by employment status and industry

(A) Rural

Employment status and industry	Educational attainment (male)				Educational attainment (female)			
	2004/05		2011/12		2004/05		2011/12	
	Primary & below	Middle	Primary & below	Middle	Primary & below	Middle	Primary & below	Middle
SE agriculture	34.1%	42.9%	30.4%	35.8%	47.9%	53.2%	43.4%	42.7%
Ag labourers	35.1%	22.2%	28.0%	20.8%	34.8%	24.7%	29.2%	26.3%
Manufacturing	9.0%	9.9%	9.5%	10.6%	12.5%	16.1%	19.1%	21.4%
Construction	9.9%	7.4%	21.1%	19.3%	2.6%	1.2%	5.8%	2.6%
Services sector	12.0%	17.6%	11.0%	13.5%	2.2%	4.7%	2.5%	7.0%
Total	100.0%	100.0%	100.0%	100.0%	100.0%	100.0%	100.0%	100.0%
Total workers (1,000 persons)	18,102	8,616	11,325	6,816	11,504	3,238	5,911	2,246

(B) Urban

Employment status and industry	Educational attainment (male)				Educational attainment (female)			
	2004/05		2011/12		2004/05		2011/12	
	Primary & below	Middle	Primary & below	Middle	Primary & below	Middle	Primary & below	Middle
Agriculture	6.6%	4.7%	5.9%	6.8%	21.9%	13.3%	9.9%	9.9%
SE manufacturing	10.9%	8.4%	11.6%	10.0%	33.4%	34.3%	42.2%	32.5%
RW manufacturing	13.9%	16.7%	18.2%	16.3%	5.6%	10.5%	6.7%	16.6%
Construction	15.5%	14.0%	19.2%	15.8%	3.2%	1.3%	4.4%	3.4%
SE services sector	20.8%	21.2%	13.6%	18.3%	7.0%	12.3%	5.1%	7.0%
RW services sector	16.8%	21.1%	15.3%	20.4%	20.1%	13.6%	22.6%	25.4%
CL manuf. + services	15.6%	13.9%	16.2%	12.5%	8.7%	14.6%	9.1%	5.3%
Total	100.0%	100.0%	100.0%	100.0%	100.0%	100.0%	100.0%	100.0%
Total workers (1,000 persons)	4,795	3,146	3,607	2,087	1,693	710	997	474

Source: Same as Table 4.3(A).

Note: Workers in this table include both usual principal and subsidiary activity status workers.

Table 4.6 Distribution of the population of age cohort aged 15–21 years in 2004/05 by educational attainment and usual activity status (1,000 persons)

Sector	Age group	Usual (PS+SS) Activity status	Below Primary	Primary	Middle	Secondary	Higher Secondary	Diploma	College +	Total
Rural male	Age group 15–21 years in 2004/05	Workers	11,186	6,915	8,616	3,358	1,321	175	224	31,797
		Unemployed	365	293	435	432	236	60	90	1,911
		Student	640	2,372	7,765	5,956	2,927	143	263	20,071
		Others	916	342	358	77	61	0	8	1,763
		Non-workers	1,921	3,008	8,558	6,465	3,224	203	361	23,745
		Total	13,108	9,923	17,174	9,823	4,545	379	586	55,542
	Age group 22–28 years in 2011/12	Workers	11,481	6,655	10,583	7,622	4,652	930	3,008	44,933
		Unemployed	46	83	179	258	255	159	710	1,690
		Student	8	8	65	227	1,221	100	1,297	2,924
		Others	326	78	147	188	36	1	51	828
		Non-workers	380	169	391	673	1,512	260	2,057	5,442
		Total	11,861	6,824	10,974	8,295	6,164	1,190	5,065	50,375
Rural female	Age group 15–21 years in 2004/05	Workers	8,741	2,763	3,238	1,169	486	86	75	16,563
		Unemployed	74	72	168	182	171	35	61	762
		Student	416	1,496	4,364	3,363	1,895	70	170	11,782
		Others	9,945	3,415	3,978	1,818	686	23	120	19,986
		Non-workers	10,434	4,984	8,510	5,363	2,752	129	351	32,531
		Total	19,175	7,747	11,748	6,532	3,238	214	426	49,093
	Age group 22–28 years in 2011/12	Workers	7,521	2,494	2,546	1,499	795	164	779	15,798
		Unemployed	21	4	72	123	135	40	329	725
		Student	8	1	17	126	435	21	638	1,246
		Others	12,435	4,495	5,783	3,676	2,514	186	1,537	30,627
		Non-workers	12,464	4,500	5,872	3,926	3,084	247	2,504	32,598
		Total	19,985	6,994	8,419	5,425	3,879	412	3,282	48,396

Educational attainment (general)

(Continued)

Table 4.6 Distribution of the population of age cohort aged 15–21 years in 2004/05 by educational attainment and usual activity status (1,000 persons) (*Continued*)

Sector	Age group	Usual (PS+SS) Activity status	Educational attainment (general)							
			Below Primary	Primary	Middle	Secondary	Higher Secondary	Diploma	College +	Total
Urban male	Age group 15–21 years in 2004/05	Workers	2,438	2,357	3,146	1,253	578	156	168	10,097
		Unemployed	161	195	446	235	129	79	117	1,364
		Student	212	651	3,326	4,091	3,597	204	367	12,451
		Others	293	110	192	56	30	1	28	710
		Non-workers	666	956	3,964	4,382	3,757	284	512	14,525
		Total	3,104	3,313	7,110	5,635	4,334	440	679	24,622
	Age group 22–28 years in 2011/12	Workers	3,058	2,450	4,441	3,652	2,498	803	4,794	21,696
		Unemployed	76	49	149	121	220	82	939	1,635
		Student	7	0	25	133	909	269	1,677	3,020
		Others	112	23	45	42	75	4	88	392
		Non-workers	195	73	218	296	1,204	356	2,703	5,047
		Total	3,253	2,522	4,659	3,948	3,701	1,159	7,498	26,743
Urban female	Age group 15–21 years in 2004/05	Workers	1,080	613	710	331	242	83	148	3,208
		Unemployed	17	68	94	89	120	33	114	536
		Student	106	495	2,506	3,396	3,018	170	417	10,108
		Others	2,405	1,445	2,068	1,084	552	19	145	7,719
		Non-workers	2,529	2,008	4,668	4,569	3,689	221	677	18,363
		Total	3,609	2,621	5,378	4,900	3,931	304	825	21,572
	Age group 22–28 years in 2011/12	Workers	1,053	478	723	462	483	190	1,969	5,358
		Unemployed	17	20	27	54	73	36	600	828
		Student	0	0	32	65	539	68	1,301	2,006
		Others	3,331	1,741	3,172	3,110	2,632	263	3,251	17,500
		Non-workers	3,348	1,762	3,231	3,229	3,244	368	5,152	20,334
		Total	4,401	2,240	3,954	3,691	3,727	558	7,121	25,692

Source: Same as Table 4.3(A).

Note: Workers in this table include both usual principal and subsidiary activity status workers.

and above, who freshly entered the labour market during the seven years between 2004–05 and 2011–12. According to Table 4.6, in rural areas, there were 17.1 million male students of secondary level and above in 2004–05. During the seven years between 2004–05 and 2011–12, some of these students in 2004–05 completed their education and started working. Thereby, they constituted educated fresh entrants to the labour market. The remaining students proceeded to higher education and remained as students. It is estimated that there were 1.2 million higher secondary students and 1.3 million students with college-plus students when the 2011–12 survey was undertaken. The difference in the number of workers with higher secondary, diploma or college-plus in 2004–05 (aged 15–21 years) and 2011–12 (aged 22–28 years) are presumably freshly entered 'educated' workers during the period. Consequently, it is estimated that among rural men 4.3 million with educational attainment of secondary school, 3.3 million of higher secondary school, 0.7 million with diploma, and 2.8 million of college graduates are freshly entered educated workers during the period under study.

Similarly, the number of fresh entrants with the educational attainment of secondary school and above were 1.4 million for rural women, 9.6 million for urban men, and 2.3 million for urban women.

Table 4.7 presents a distribution of workers of this age cohort by educational attainment and employment status and industry. Table 4.7(A), for rural men, presents some interesting patterns. Rural male workers of this age cohort went up from 31.8 million in 2004–05 to 44.9 million in 2011–12. Consequently, the fresh entrants to the labour market were 13.1 million, most of whom had educational attainment of secondary school and above (11.1 million). Consequently, the number of workers of this age cohort with educational attainment of higher-secondary, diploma, and college graduates increased, respectively, by 3.3 million, 0.7 million, and 2.8 million. They are fresh entrants during the seven years. It is also noteworthy that the difference in the numbers of 'less-educated' workers between two points of time was negligible. This fact suggests that there were very few additions in this category of young workers during the period. Most of the workers of this category are those already employed at the time of the 2004–05 survey.

It is particularly interesting that not only between 'less-educated' and highly educated workers but also even among rural men with more than ten years of education, clear differences are apparent in the kind of employment gained by persons with different kinds of education. Persons with higher secondary education came to be employed primarily in agriculture, working on their household landholdings and as agricultural labourers, which suggests a lack of non-agricultural employment opportunities suitable to their educational attainment. In contrast, a markedly higher share of persons who obtained technical diplomas found employment in manufacturing (40.1 per cent) and service sectors (30.1 per cent). In addition, persons with college education became employed in household landholdings (38.4 per cent), and in various service sectors (44.3 per cent).

Table 4.7(A) Number of workers by employment status, industry, and level of educational attainment (Age cohorts 15–21 years in 2004/05 and 22–28 years in 2011/12) (rural male) (1,000 persons)

Sector, sex and age	Employment status and industry	Educational attainment (general)							
		Below primary	Primary	Middle	Secondary	Higher secondary	Diploma	College+	Total
Age 15–21 in 2004/05	SE Ag	3,710	2,456	3,694	1,592	699	53	103	12,308
	Ag labourers	4,299	2,048	1,912	489	117	5	15	8,885
	Manufacturing	814	810	855	381	98	38	10	3,006
	Construction	1,124	674	639	173	68	10	2	2,690
	Service sector	1,239	927	1,516	723	339	69	94	4,908
	Total	11,187	6,915	8,616	3,358	1,321	175	224	31,797
Age 22–28 in 2011/12	SE Ag	3,115	1,786	3,604	2,953	2,050	162	1,155	14,827
	Ag labourers	3,672	1,660	1,949	1,177	546	50	105	9,159
	Manufacturing	905	687	1,203	803	550	343	297	4,788
	Construction	2,493	1,429	1,824	855	349	72	118	7,140
	Service sector	1,297	1,095	2,002	1,834	1,157	303	1,332	9,019
	Total	11,481	6,655	10,583	7,622	4,652	930	3,008	44,933
Change	SE Ag	-595	-671	-90	1,361	1,350	109	1,053	2,519
	Ag labourers	-628	-388	37	688	429	45	90	274
	Manufacturing	91	-123	347	422	452	305	288	1,782
	Construction	1,369	755	1,186	682	281	62	116	4,450
	Service sector	58	167	486	1,110	818	234	1,237	4,111
	Total	294	-260	1,966	4,264	3,331	755	2,784	13,136

Source: Same as Table 4.3(A).

Note: Workers in this table include both usual principal and subsidiary activity status workers.

However, it is noteworthy that those less-educated workers, who had already been employed in 2004–05, changed the pattern of employment. The number of cultivators and agricultural labours decreased, respectively, by 1.3 million and 1.0 million. Construction labourers increased by 2.1 million. Therefore, with an increased number of men with higher secondary and college education joining the workforce, workers who joined the workforce early and with low levels of educational attainment were not only excluded from jobs in the manufacturing and services sectors but were also edged out of employment in agriculture to work mainly in construction. During the period of our study, construction emerged as the sector that used increasing numbers of workers with low levels of education, whereas educated workers cornered a disproportionate share of the limited new jobs in manufacturing and services sectors.

Why were so many educated fresh entrants engaged in self-employment in agriculture? Two interpretations might be made. A sort of mismatch in the labour market might be occurring because educated fresh entrants, particularly college graduates in arts, were unable to find employment of their choice. For them, few options are available aside from employment in family farming. If this is true, then it reflects the problem of invisible unemployment among the educated youth. Another interpretation is that the recent economic environment related to agriculture has been changing towards more market orientation, which requires more management skills of farmers. Consequently, highly educated fresh entrants would have found future prospects on family farms. Further exploration of the reasons behind the increased participation of educated workers in agriculture remains a subject for future study.

Table 4.7(B) presents similar data for rural women who were in the 15–21 years age cohort in 2004–05 and who moved to the 22–28 years age group in 2011–12. Unlike rural men, the most important feature of rural female workers of this age cohort is that numerous such women who had joined the workforce early (in 2004–05) with limited educational attainment dropped out of the labour force altogether. The number of less-educated workers decreased from 11.5 million in 2004–05 to 10.0 million in 2011–12.

The relation between educational status and employment among rural women of this age cohort was similar to that for rural men in terms of increased employment of persons with higher levels of education and the edging out of persons with low levels of education. Many female workers were employed in the service sector, some of the most important occupations being school teachers, *anganwadi*[3] workers, and workers for cooking mid-day meals in schools. Like rural men, the most commonly available employment opportunities for less-educated female workers were self-employment in agriculture and agricultural labourers. With a decline in employment in agriculture, 1.8 million workers who were engaged in agriculture in 2004–05 left. Some of them were engaged in construction, most likely in MGNREGA works, but most were engaged in domestic duties.

Table 4.7(B) Number of workers by employment status, industry, and level of educational attainment (age cohorts 15–21 years in 2004/05 and 22–28 years in 2011/12) (rural female) (1,000 persons)

Sector, sex and age	Employment status and industry	Below primary	Primary	Middle	Secondary	Higher secondary	Diploma	College+	Total
Age 15–21 in 2004/05	SE Ag	4,117	1,395	1,723	625	281	16	27	8,191
	Ag labourers	3,263	739	800	198	39	9	1	5,049
	Manufacturing	928	513	523	221	83	26	11	2,305
	Construction	261	36	40	9	0	0	0	346
	Service sector	171	80	151	116	83	35	36	673
	Total	8,741	2,763	3,238	1,169	486	86	75	16,563
Age 22–28 in 2011/12	SE Ag	3,623	1,047	1,321	731	469	14	198	7,403
	Ag labourers	2,264	768	557	286	40	2	9	3,924
	Manufacturing	793	483	380	210	124	11	54	2,055
	Construction	644	132	132	59	5	2	6	981
	Service sector	196	64	157	214	157	136	511	1,435
	Total	7,521	2,494	2,546	1,499	795	164	779	15,798
Change	SE Ag	−494	−348	−402	106	188	−2	171	−787
	Ag labourers	−999	29	−244	88	1	−7	8	−1,124
	Manufacturing	−135	−31	−143	−11	40	−15	44	−251
	Construction	383	96	91	50	5	2	6	635
	Service sector	25	−16	6	97	74	101	475	762
	Total	−1,220	−270	−692	330	309	79	704	−765

Source: Same as Table 4.3(A).

Note: Workers in this table include both usual principal and subsidiary activity status workers.

With few employment opportunities for rural women of this age cohort, the main trend in the case of young rural women is that many of them drop out of the labour force in their early twenties to mid-20s.

The number of urban male workers of this cohort doubled from 10.1 million in 2004–05 to 21.7 million in 2011–12 (Table 4.7(C)). This large increase by 11.6 million during the period is partly attributable to fresh young entrants with higher education and partly to rural–urban migration. Improvement of workers' educational attainment is clear. A marked expansion (4.6 million) of college graduates and more educated people is apparent during the period. The new entrants of this age group were employed as regular workers in manufacturing (2.2 million), the service sector (7.1 million), and construction (1.3 million). However, no large change has occurred in the employment structure of less-educated workers, except for a slight rise in manufacturing and construction workers.

Urban female workers of this cohort increased by 2.2 million during the seven years, as shown in Table 4.7(D). It is noteworthy that the number of workers with the least educational attainment fell. Those workers with middle and higher education increased. Like urban men, many young female college graduates entered the labour market. Most of these fresh entrants were employed as regular wage workers in the service sector.

Concluding Remarks

An extensive and severe contraction of employment took place in India between 2004–05 and 2011–12. NSS surveys show a fall in work participation rates in rural and urban areas and for men and women. Sectoral data show a considerable decline in employment in agriculture. After 2004–05, employment in manufacturing and services sectors stagnated or declined. Between 1993–94 and 2004–05, numerous rural male workers lost employment in agriculture but found employment in services (mainly trade and transport), between 2004–05 and 2011–12, they left agriculture to find employment in construction. In 2011–12, construction became the second largest industry next to agriculture to employ a rural labour force: it accounted for employment of 11 per cent of rural male workers, 6.6 per cent of rural women workers, 7.2 per cent of urban male workers, and 3.7 per cent of urban women workers. Although data also show an expansion of employment in construction for rural women, much of this was attributable to employment under public works programmes, mainly reflecting the impact of MGNREGA.

The chief contribution of this chapter is its detailed age cohort analysis of employment. Age cohort analysis can yield clues to how changes in employment conditions of fresh entrants, changes in employment conditions of existing workers, and changes in employment conditions of workers who leave the labour force affect the overall employment structure. Given the seven-year gap separating the NSS two EUS surveys, this study uses seven-year age cohorts.

Table 4.7(C) Number of workers by employment status, industry, and level of educational attainment (age Cohorts 15–21 years in 2004/05 and 22–28 years in 2011/12) (urban male) (1,000 persons)

Sector, sex and age	Employment status and industry	Educational attainment (general)							Total
		Below primary	Primary	Middle	Secondary	Higher secondary	Diploma	College+	
Age 15–21 in 2004/05	Agriculture	172	146	147	93	24	3	6	591
	SE manufacturing	221	300	265	119	39	4	4	952
	RW manufacturing	340	325	527	190	73	35	36	1,527
	Construction	409	332	439	90	11	12	3	1,296
	SE service	536	461	667	351	222	52	41	2,329
	RW service	366	438	665	321	183	44	74	2,093
	CL manuf. + service	394	355	436	88	25	6	4	1,309
	Total	2,438	2,357	3,146	1,253	578	156	168	10,097
Age 22–28 in 2011/12	Agriculture	166	138	240	172	106	6	129	956
	SE manufacturing	263	190	386	205	135	11	191	1,381
	RW manufacturing	486	514	835	546	361	322	655	3,720
	Construction	704	407	624	458	176	80	147	2,597
	SE service	563	469	872	1,056	647	110	1,049	4,766
	RW service	481	425	1,068	983	1,008	242	2,584	6,792
	CL manuf. + service	394	307	416	232	64	33	38	1,485
	Total	3,058	2,450	4,441	3,652	2,498	803	4,795	21,696
Change	Agriculture	-6	-8	93	79	82	3	123	365
	SE manufacturing	42	-110	120	85	96	7	187	428
	RW manufacturing	146	189	309	356	288	287	619	2,193
	Construction	295	74	185	368	165	68	145	1,301
	SE service	27	8	206	705	425	58	1,008	2,437
	RW service	116	-13	403	662	825	198	2,510	4,699
	CL manuf. + service	0	-48	-20	144	40	27	34	176
	Total	620	92	1,296	2,399	1,920	647	4,627	11,599

Source: Same as Table 4.3(A).

Note: Workers in this table include both usual principal and subsidiary activity status workers.

Table 4.7(D) Number of workers by employment status, industry, and level of educational attainment (age cohorts 15–21 years in 2004/05 and 22–28 years in 2011/12) (urban female) (1,000 persons)

Sector, sex and age	Employment status and industry	Educational attainment (general)							
		Below primary	Primary	Middle	Secondary	Higher secondary	Diploma	College+	Total
Age 15–21 in 2004/05	Agriculture	265	106	95	41	11	5	1	522
	SE manufacturing	353	213	244	77	31	26	5	949
	RW manufacturing	29	66	75	35	9	14	8	236
	Construction	36	18	9	2	4	1	0	71
	SE service	79	40	88	75	88	8	36	414
	RW service	236	105	96	100	87	25	98	747
	CL manuf. + service	83	65	104	2	12	3	0	269
	Total	1,080	613	710	331	242	83	148	3,208
Age 22–28 in 2011/12	Agriculture	202	29	40	51	22	0	9	353
	SE manufacturing	340	154	274	122	86	13	69	1,058
	RW manufacturing	42	78	42	68	27	23	80	360
	Construction	87	27	2	0	2	5	24	147
	SE service	86	81	123	80	89	16	250	725
	RW service	216	66	173	96	238	124	1,521	2,435
	CL manuf. + service	79	43	69	44	19	10	16	280
	Total	1,053	478	723	462	483	190	1,969	5,358
Change	Agriculture	-62	-77	-55	10	12	-5	8	-169
	SE manufacturing	-13	-59	30	45	55	-13	64	109
	RW manufacturing	13	12	-33	33	18	9	72	124
	Construction	50	9	-7	-2	-2	3	24	76
	SE service	7	41	35	6	0	8	213	311
	RW service	-19	-39	77	-3	151	99	1,423	1,688
	CL manuf. + service	-4	-22	-35	43	7	7	16	11
	Total	-27	-135	13	131	241	107	1,820	2,150

Source: Same as Table 4.3(A).

Note: Workers in this table include both usual principal and subsidiary activity status workers.

There are two limitations of the age cohort analysis using NSS data. First, the age cohort data from NSS surveys must be combined with age cohort population data from the population censuses to correct underestimation of population in the NSS surveys. Second, because of inaccuracies in age reporting and because of the consequent age heaping at certain numbers, information cannot be extracted reliably for all age cohorts. In general, information related to age is more accurate for younger cohorts. For this reason, the age cohort analysis specifically examines younger age cohorts.

The most interesting results from age cohort analysis are those obtained for rural men. The rural male workforce increased by 14.7 million between 2004–05 and 2011–12. This larger workforce was employed mainly by the construction sector. The greatest increase in the size of the workforce, 13.7 million workers, took place among those who were in the 15–21 years age cohort in 2004–05. By the time they moved to the 22–28 years age group (at the time of 2011–12 survey) many more persons in this age group had finished their education and had joined the workforce. About 65 per cent of these workers came to be employed in agriculture, and only 13 per cent in construction. While the young workers entered the workforce, and while many of them sought employment in agriculture, older people had to shift from agriculture to construction. This point is readily apparent in the dynamics of change for the 22–28 years age cohort. In this age cohort, the number of workers engaged in agriculture (as cultivators or as agricultural labour) declined by about 2.5 million, whereas the number of workers in construction increased by roughly the same amount between 2004–05 and 2011–12.

Contraction of employment in agriculture affected rural women much more. Other than the youngest age group in 2011–12 (15–21 years), all age cohorts, including the 15–21 years age cohort in 2004–05, showed a stark drop in the number of workers. This decline was not merely attributable to the expansion of education, as suggested by Mehrotra et al. (2014); it was also attributable to a large contraction of agricultural employment.

Cross-tabulating the age cohort data with education shows that, although agriculture had historically employed the bulk of the workers with little or no education, between 2004–05 and 2011–12, contraction of agricultural employment caused workers with higher secondary education to leave agriculture, in addition to edging out some workers with low levels of education. Construction emerged as the sector employing workers with the lowest educational attainment. Many persons in the 15–21 years age cohort in 2004–05 obtained higher secondary, technical, and college education and joined the workforce by the time the 2011–12 survey was administered. Among such young workers, workers with education up to higher secondary level moved into agriculture as both cultivators and agricultural workers, persons with technical diplomas cornered manufacturing sector jobs, whereas workers with college degrees came to be employed in household enterprises (as cultivators) or in the service sector as regular wage workers.

Notes

1 The 1999–2000 survey showed a lower female WPR, perhaps because 1999–2000 was a drought year (Himanshu, 2011). However, it rose in 2004–05 to almost the same level as in 1993–94. It seems likely that female work participation started falling since the mid-2000s if one considers 1999–2000 data as an aberration. An alternative explanation has been that the 2004–05 data were an anomaly (Rawal and Saha, 2015). If one treats 2004–05 data rather than 1999–2000 data as an aberration, then the decline in female WPR seems to have started earlier.

2 Rangarajan et al. (2011) explained the decline in work participation rates of women after 2004–05 based on the increase in school enrolment. Mehrotra et al. (2014) argued that the withdrawal of adult women from the labour force was also a result of increased school attendance rates among girls and increased outmigration of adult men, which made housework more time-demanding for adult women. Rawal and Saha (2015) have argued that the long-term decline in the women's workforce participation rate has derived from a contraction of employment in agriculture and the lack of a corresponding rise in employment opportunities in the rural non-farm sector. Kapsos et al. (2014) showed that a general lack of employment opportunities for women, rather than income and education effects, is the major cause of the decline in female labour force participation.

3 Child care centres in rural areas.

References

Abraham, Vinoj (2013) 'Missing Labour or Consistent "De-Feminisation"?', *Economic and Political Weekly*, 48(31): 99–108.

Himanshu (2011) 'Employment Trends in India: A Re-Examination', *Economic and Political Weekly*, 46(37): 43–59.

Kapsos, S., Silberman, A. and Bourmpoula, E. (2014) *Why a Female Labour Force Participation Declining so Sharply in India?* ILO Research Paper No.10, International Labour Office, Geneva.

Mehrotra, Santosh, Parida, J. Sinha, S. and Gandhi, A. (2014) 'Explaining Employment Trends in the Indian Economy: 1993–94 to 2011–12', *Economic and Political Weekly*, 49(32): 49–57.

Rangarajan, C., Kaul, P.I. and Seema (2011) 'Where Is the Missing Labour Force?', *Economic and Political Weekly*, 46(39): 68–72.

Rawal, Vikas and Saha, Partha (2015), 'Women's Employment in India: What Do Recent NSS Surveys of Employment and Unemployment Show?', *Statistics on Indian Economy and Society*, January 28, http://archive.indianstatistics.org/misc/women_work.pdf.

5 Food Consumption Among Low-Income Households in India in the Era of Economic Growth

Daizo Sugimoto

In spite of rapid economic growth during the last 25 years in India, the growth rate of real agricultural wages has been discouragingly low, being 1.3 per cent between 1993–94 and 1999–2000 and 0.1 per cent between 2000–01 and 2005–06 (Drèze and Sen 2013; Usami 2011; Usami 2012). The sluggish growth of earnings for low-income earners seems to have severely hindered them from improving their living standards. According to National Sample Survey (NSS) results, monthly per-capita expenditure (MPCE) of the poorest 20 per cent in real terms is estimated as having grown at 1 per cent between 1993–94 and 2009–10 in rural India, and less than 1 per cent in urban India.[1]

It is important to examine the ways in which low-income people made ends meet and the social and economic conditions under which they live, including the functions of village society, the role of the family, and the economic and social policies implemented by their respective governments. These investigations are also expected to reveal the background of the extremely low level of Indian wages, which have paradoxically persisted despite the economic prosperity prevailing since the 1990s. Particularly, this study will assess how low-income households managed to maintain their diets after the inception of economic liberalization in the 1990s by studying the consumption of food items, including cereals, pulses, milk, and edible oils based on NSS results.

In the literature related to food consumption, key focal points have included the effects of consumers' income and food prices on consumption.[2] Although income and price play critically important roles in determination of the level of food consumption, they are not the exclusive factors determining it. For example, tastes influence food consumption, as Atkin (2013) demonstrated rigorously. Trade policies and measures to supply subsidized foods to poorer people also influence food consumption. This study addresses these factors while examining changes in food consumption patterns. Another issue addressed in this chapter is the classification of food regions. Most analyses in the literature related to food consumption in India are based on the average rural and urban food consumption in India. The real lives of the people, however, cannot be ascertained from Indian

DOI: 10.4324/9781003311898-6

averages because considerable inter-regional variation exists. Therefore, this study first classifies the 62 NSS regions into six food regions and secondly examines the changing food consumption.

The data source is unit-level data collected during the NSS conducted in 1993–94, 2004–05, and 2009–10. Each survey examines around 100,000 households. The primary geographical unit for analyses is the NSS region: one or more districts in each state. The original NSS regions constructed by the National Sample Survey Office (NSSO) were modified by the author to make them identical throughout the period of investigation because the number and boundaries of NSS regions have often been revised.[3] In addition to the revision of NSS regions, bifurcation implemented in Uttar Pradesh, Madhya Pradesh, and Bihar should be addressed carefully. As a result of bifurcation, the three states of Uttarakhand, Chhattisgarh, and Jharkhand were created. This study will follow the newly created names and boundaries of the states even if the analysis relates to the years before division.

This study is organized into seven sections. The first section will present the creation of the six food regions based on an examination of the food consumption patterns in the NSS regions. The second to fifth sections will investigate the respective consumption patterns related to cereals, pulses, edible oils, and milk, considering household expenditures, food prices, government interventions in food markets, the effects of trade liberalization, and self-produced food consumption. Concluding remarks will be presented in the final section of the chapter.

Classification of NSS Regions

A close examination of foods consumed in different areas reveals several regional patterns of food consumption. Table 5.1 reports quantities of various food items consumed in rural areas in NSS regions in the year 1993–94. Figures in boldface signify that the corresponding figures exceed the criteria fixed by the author for the individual food items. The criteria are shown on the second row of the table. Based on these patterns, NSS regions can be grouped into six food regions, as shown in Table 5.1 and Map 5.1.

The diversity in dietary patterns among the food regions is clearly observed in Figure 5.1. In this figure, per-capita quantities of food items consumed in rural areas in the food regions are converted into indices using the Indian average as 100 and are displayed in the form of bar charts. The figure indicates regional differences with respect to the cereals consumed primarily, the edible oils most preferred, and the quantity of dairy products consumed. The figure also shows that the food consumption pattern in each food region was almost maintained between 1993–94 and 2009–10. The consistency confirms that the classification based on the food consumption in 1993–94 is valid for 2009–10 and naturally for 2004–05.

Table 5.1 Monthly per-capita consumption of food in 1993/94 in rural India

		Rice (kg)	Wheat (kg)	Coarse grains (kg)	Pulses (kg)	Milk (litre)	Ghee (kg)	Vanaspati (kg)	Mustard oil (kg)	Groundnut oil (kg)	Coconut oil (kg)	Other edible oils (kg)	Non-veg foods (kg)	Sugar (kg)
Criteria for marking		3.0	3.0	3.0	0.7	3.0	0.1	0.1	0.1	0.1	0.1	0.1	0.3	0.8
Food region	NSS region													
North-western region	JK Mountainous	5.0	8.1	0.9	1.2	7.8	0.0	0.1	0.4	0.0	0.0	0.0	0.1	1.0
	JK Outer hills	3.7	6.5	7.2	0.9	5.6	0.0	0.0	0.3	0.0	0.0	0.0	0.2	0.7
	PB Northern	1.0	9.2	0.2	0.9	12.9	0.0	0.4	0.1	0.0	0.0	0.0	0.1	1.9
	PB Southern	0.4	10.8	0.1	0.8	16.2	0.0	0.3	0.1	0.0	0.0	0.0	0.1	2.3
	HR Eastern	0.9	11.9	0.2	0.6	12.8	0.0	0.2	0.1	0.0	0.0	0.0	0.1	1.7
	HR Western	0.4	11.9	0.5	0.6	15.3	0.2	0.2	0.1	0.0	0.0	0.0	0.0	2.1
	HP Himachal	3.6	6.3	3.5	1.1	7.5	0.0	0.2	0.3	0.0	0.0	0.0	0.1	1.0
	UTR	5.5	6.5	1.4	1.1	7.4	0.0	0.1	0.4	0.0	0.0	0.0	0.1	1.1
	UP Western	2.1	10.0	1.1	0.9	8.1	0.0	0.1	0.3	0.0	0.0	0.0	0.2	1.2
	UP Southern	0.8	14.5	1.1	0.8	4.1	0.0	0.1	0.3	0.0	0.0	0.0	0.1	0.5
	CHD	2.1	7.3	0.2	0.8	8.6	0.0	0.3	0.3	0.0	0.0	0.0	0.1	1.2
	DEL	2.8	7.7	0.0	1.1	8.7	0.2	0.2	0.6	0.0	0.0	0.1	0.4	1.5
	MP Northern	0.4	12.2	2.5	1.1	7.0	0.1	0.0	0.4	0.0	0.0	0.1	0.1	1.1
	RJ Western	0.1	8.0	6.5	0.6	12.4	0.1	0.0	0.2	0.0	0.0	0.1	0.0	1.4
	RJ North-eastern	0.1	11.3	4.3	0.6	12.2	0.1	0.0	0.3	0.0	0.0	0.1	0.1	1.2
	RJ Southern	0.6	7.6	5.5	0.7	5.5	0.0	0.0	0.1	0.1	0.0	0.0	0.0	0.8
	RJ South-eastern	0.3	9.3	4.4	0.7	5.5	0.1	0.0	0.1	0.2	0.0	0.1	0.1	0.9
	GJ Northern	2.3	5.0	3.8	0.8	5.3	0.1	0.0	0.0	0.6	0.0	0.0	0.0	1.3
	GJ Western	1.1	4.9	5.0	0.8	6.7	0.1	0.0	0.0	0.7	0.0	0.0	0.0	1.3
	MP Malwa	0.3	8.0	6.4	1.0	4.3	0.0	0.0	0.0	0.2	0.0	0.2	0.2	1.1
	MP Central	1.1	10.5	0.5	0.8	3.1	0.0	0.0	0.0	0.1	0.0	0.3	0.1	0.7

(Continued)

Table 5.1 Monthly per-capita consumption of food in 1993/94 in rural India (*Continued*)

		Rice (kg)	Wheat (kg)	Coarse grains (kg)	Pulses (kg)	Milk (litre)	Ghee (kg)	Vanaspati (kg)	Mustard oil (kg)	Groundnut oil (kg)	Coconut oil (kg)	Other edible oils (kg)	Non-veg foods (kg)	Sugar (kg)
North-central region	BH Northern	7.1	6.4	0.8	0.7	2.4	0.0	0.0	0.3	0.0	0.0	0.0	0.3	0.4
	BH Central	7.0	6.8	0.8	0.8	3.3	0.0	0.0	0.3	0.0	0.0	0.0	0.1	0.4
	UP Central	4.3	10.1	0.6	1.1	3.9	0.0	0.0	0.4	0.0	0.0	0.0	0.1	0.8
	UP Eastern	5.7	7.7	0.4	1.0	3.8	0.0	0.0	0.3	0.0	0.0	0.0	0.2	0.7
	MP Vindhya	5.7	8.6	0.7	1.4	3.1	0.0	0.0	0.2	0.0	0.0	0.0	0.1	0.7
	MP South	7.0	4.5	2.0	0.9	1.6	0.0	0.0	0.1	0.1	0.0	0.1	0.1	0.6
Eastern region	AP Coastal	12.1	0.1	0.6	0.6	2.9	0.0	0.0	0.0	0.3	0.0	0.1	0.5	0.4
	AS	12.5	0.6	0.0	0.5	1.2	0.0	0.0	0.3	0.0	0.0	0.0	0.7	0.5
	JRK	10.7	2.5	0.8	0.6	1.2	0.0	0.0	0.2	0.0	0.0	0.0	0.2	0.4
	CHT	13.8	0.6	0.3	0.8	0.8	0.0	0.0	0.1	0.1	0.0	0.1	0.2	0.5
	MAN Hills	15.5	0.0	0.4	0.6	0.1	0.0	0.0	0.1	0.0	0.0	0.0	0.8	0.4
	MEG	11.9	0.3	0.1	0.4	1.3	0.0	0.0	0.3	0.0	0.0	0.0	1.0	0.6
	MIZ	12.2	0.2	0.8	0.9	0.7	0.0	0.0	0.3	0.0	0.0	0.0	0.9	0.6
	OR Coastal	15.4	0.5	0.2	0.4	1.0	0.0	0.0	0.2	0.0	0.0	0.0	0.5	0.4
	OR Southern	13.2	0.1	1.2	0.5	0.5	0.0	0.0	0.1	0.0	0.0	0.1	0.3	0.3
	OR Northern	16.1	0.3	0.0	0.5	0.5	0.0	0.0	0.1	0.0	0.0	0.0	0.3	0.4
	WB Himalayan	12.6	2.6	0.1	0.4	1.4	0.0	0.0	0.2	0.0	0.0	0.0	0.5	0.4
	WB Eastern plains	13.5	1.5	0.1	0.4	1.7	0.0	0.0	0.3	0.0	0.0	0.0	0.8	0.4
	WB Central plains	13.4	0.9	0.0	0.5	1.6	0.0	0.0	0.4	0.0	0.0	0.0	0.9	0.5
	WB Western plains	14.9	0.6	0.1	0.4	1.4	0.0	0.0	0.3	0.0	0.0	0.0	0.7	0.4

(*Continued*)

Table 5.1 Monthly per-capita consumption of food in 1993/94 in rural India (*Continued*)

		Rice (kg)	Wheat (kg)	Coarse grains (kg)	Pulses (kg)	Milk (litre)	Ghee (kg)	Vanaspati (kg)	Mustard oil (kg)	Groundnut oil (kg)	Coconut oil (kg)	Other edible oils (kg)	Non-veg. foods (kg)	Sugar (kg)
Middle-western region	GJ Eastern	2.8	2.3	**5.1**	**1.0**	**3.1**	0.0	0.0	0.0	**0.5**	0.0	0.1	0.2	**1.1**
	KT Inland-northern	**3.3**	1.1	**8.2**	**0.8**	**3.0**	0.0	0.0	0.0	**0.3**	0.0	0.1	0.1	**0.9**
	MP South-western	0.9	**5.0**	**6.6**	**0.9**	2.7	0.0	0.0	0.0	**0.2**	0.0	**0.1**	0.1	0.7
	MH Inland-western	2.4	2.1	**6.5**	**0.8**	**3.6**	0.0	0.0	0.0	**0.4**	0.0	0.1	0.2	**1.2**
	MH Inland-northern	1.2	2.4	**6.3**	**0.9**	2.3	0.0	0.0	0.0	**0.5**	0.0	0.0	0.2	**1.0**
	MH Inland-central	0.9	2.2	**9.0**	**1.1**	2.6	0.0	0.0	0.0	0.0	0.0	**0.3**	0.1	**1.1**
	MH Inland-eastern	1.2	2.7	**7.9**	**1.1**	1.8	0.0	0.0	0.0	**0.2**	0.0	**0.2**	0.1	**1.1**
Southern region	AP Inland-northern	**11.1**	0.2	2.1	**0.8**	2.3	0.0	0.0	0.0	**0.4**	0.0	0.0	**0.4**	0.6
	AP South-western	**9.7**	0.4	**3.9**	**0.8**	2.8	0.0	0.0	0.0	**0.4**	0.0	0.0	**0.3**	0.7
	AP Inland-southern	**12.9**	0.2	1.1	0.6	2.2	0.0	0.0	0.0	**0.3**	0.0	0.0	**0.3**	0.4
	KT Inland-eastern	**9.4**	0.6	**5.1**	**0.8**	2.9	0.0	0.0	0.0	**0.2**	0.0	0.0	**0.4**	**1.1**
	KT Inland-southern	**5.7**	0.7	**7.3**	**0.8**	2.7	0.0	0.0	0.0	**0.2**	0.0	0.0	0.3	0.8
	MH Eastern	**8.9**	1.9	1.7	**1.0**	1.2	0.0	0.0	0.0	0.0	0.0	**0.4**	0.2	0.8
	TN Coastal-northern	**10.0**	0.2	1.2	0.6	1.9	0.0	0.0	0.0	**0.3**	0.0	0.0	**0.3**	0.4
	TN Coastal	**11.8**	0.3	0.6	**0.8**	2.8	0.0	0.0	0.0	**0.2**	0.0	**0.1**	**0.5**	0.5
	TN Southern	**10.4**	0.2	0.6	0.6	1.7	0.0	0.0	0.0	**0.1**	0.0	**0.1**	**0.5**	0.5
	TN Inland	**9.5**	0.6	1.7	**0.9**	2.3	0.0	0.0	0.0	**0.3**	0.0	0.0	0.3	0.6
West-coastal region	KT Coastal & Ghats	**11.2**	0.6	0.4	0.5	**3.0**	0.0	0.0	0.0	**0.1**	**0.1**	0.0	**1.4**	**0.9**
	KE Northern	**9.2**	0.5	0.0	0.4	2.1	0.0	0.0	0.0	0.0	**0.3**	0.0	**1.6**	**0.9**
	KE Southern	**9.4**	1.0	0.0	0.4	2.9	0.0	0.0	0.0	0.0	**0.2**	0.0	**1.8**	**0.9**
	MH Coastal	**8.8**	1.8	0.9	**0.8**	1.7	0.0	0.0	0.0	**0.4**	0.0	0.0	**0.9**	**1.0**

Source: Calculated by the author from NSSO (2012a).

Notes:

Non-veg. foods include egg, chicken, sheep/goat, beef/buffalo, and fish/prawn. Sugar includes sugar and gur. Pulses include pulses and chickpeas.

Figures in boldface mean that they exceed the criteria shown in the second row of the table.

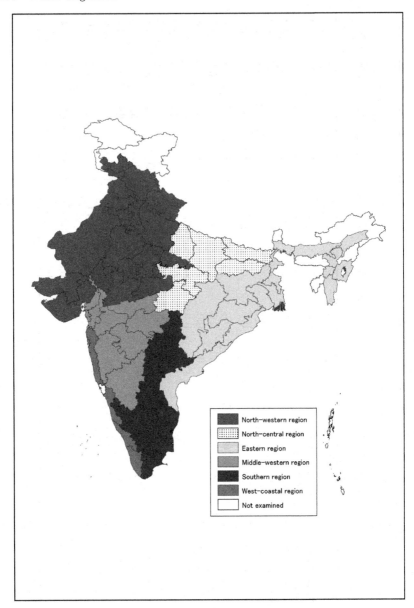

Map 5.1 Food regions.

It should also be ascertained whether the classification is useful for analyses of urban areas as the classification is based on rural food consumption. Table 5.2 presents the monthly per-capita consumption of food items in 1993–94 in rural and urban areas and the coefficients of correlation between the consumption in both areas. The strong coefficients reflect that urban

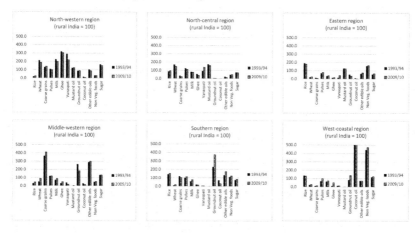

Figure 5.1 Per-capita consumption indices by food item in rural areas in the six food regions.

Source: Drawn by the author using data from NSSO (2011) and NSSO (2012a).

Table 5.2 Monthly per-capita consumption in rural and urban areas in 1993/94 (kg)

		Rice and wheat	Coarse grains	Cereals total	Pulses	Milk (litre)	Edible oils	Non-veg. foods	Sugar
Rural	North-western region	10.7	2.6	13.3	0.8	8.9	0.5	0.1	1.3
	North-central region	13.6	0.7	14.3	0.9	3.3	0.3	0.2	0.6
	Eastern region	14.2	0.3	14.5	0.5	1.4	0.3	0.5	0.4
	Middle-western region	4.3	7.2	11.5	0.9	2.8	0.5	0.2	1.1
	Southern region	10.4	2.3	12.7	0.8	2.3	0.3	0.4	0.6
	West-coastal region	10.4	0.2	10.6	0.5	2.5	0.3	1.5	0.9
	All India	11.4	2.0	13.4	0.8	3.9	0.4	0.3	0.8
Urban	North-western region	9.8	0.4	10.2	0.9	7.3	0.7	0.2	1.3
	North-central region	11.6	0.1	11.7	1.0	4.1	0.5	0.3	0.9
	Eastern region	11.9	0.0	11.9	0.7	2.9	0.5	0.8	0.7
	Middle-western region	6.9	3.1	10.0	0.9	3.9	0.7	0.3	1.1
	Southern region	10.1	0.6	10.7	0.9	4.0	0.5	0.5	0.7
	West-coastal region	8.7	0.2	8.9	0.8	5.1	0.6	1.2	1.0
	All India	10.0	0.6	10.6	0.9	4.9	0.6	0.5	1.0
Coefficient of correlation		0.958	0.966	0.944	0.939	0.927	0.772	0.966	0.976

Source: See Table 5.1.

Note: Edible oils include vegetable edible oils and ghee. Non-veg. foods include egg, chicken, sheep/goat, beef/buffalo, and fish/prawn. Sugar includes sugar and gur. Pulses include pulses and chickpeas.

areas tend to have similar patterns of food consumption with the rural areas in the same food region. It can be readily inferred that the classification is also applicable to urban areas.

Cereal Consumption

Table 5.3 reports the monthly per-capita consumption of cereals in households of the first to fifth quintiles of MPCE. First, cereal consumption in urban areas shows a departure from the conventional pattern in which the amount of consumption increases with a rise in MPCE. The table shows that the wealthiest group in urban areas consumed the smallest amount of cereals in half of the food regions in 2009–10 and that urban households of the middle class consumed the largest amount of cereals in all food regions. For rural areas, the conventional tendency has remained discernible, but the gap separating the wealthiest 20 per cent and the poorest 20 per cent has narrowed since 1993–94. The conventional pattern of cereal consumption is apparently disappearing. The smaller amounts of cereals consumed by the wealthier segments of the population apparently reflect that they are beginning to consume a wider variety of foods while reducing their cereal consumption. They are gradually diversifying their dietary patterns.

Another issue raised in Table 5.3 is that cereal consumption showed a quite consistent tendency to decrease from 1993–94 to 2009–10. That tendency was observed in all MPCE classes in all food regions in both rural and urban sectors. The fall in cereal consumption in the higher MPCE classes can be interpreted as dietary diversification. However, it is difficult to believe that the low-income Indian population of the lowest 20 per cent of MPCE class has been reducing its cereal consumption because of a diversification of diets. Drivers would be others for the poor.

To elucidate the reasons for lower cereal consumption in households with smaller incomes, this study sheds light on the fact that a household in India has at least three ways to procure cereals. The first is to purchase them in markets. However, this method only accounts for a portion of cereal consumption in India. The second is self-produced cereal consumption, which is an option confined to households engaged in agricultural production. The third is to make use of the Public Distribution System (PDS). Under the Targeted PDS introduced in 1997, all households are provided with Above Poverty Line (APL), Below Poverty Line (BPL), or Anchodaya cards, which are intended for use by 'the poorest of the poor'. The BPL card holders are given a fixed amount of wheat and rice at Fair Price Shops (FPSs) at a cost even lower than market prices. Anchodaya card holders are subsidized more than BPL card holders are. State governments are in charge of implementing the PDS. For that reason, the amount of the cereals provided to a household under the PDS, the number of households eligible for the scheme, and the prices of the subsidized cereals differ among states. States located in southern

Table 5.3 Monthly per-capita cereal consumption in different MPCE quintile classes (kg)

		Rural		Urban	
		1993/94	*2009/10*	*1993/94*	*2009/10*
North-western region	0–20%	11.7	10.0	10.1	8.8
	20–40	12.7	10.7	10.3	9.1
	40–60	13.5	10.9	**10.5**	**9.1**
	60–80	14.3	11.3	**10.2**	**8.9**
	80–100	15.1	11.6	**9.9**	**8.5**
	Average	13.3	10.8	10.2	8.9
North-central region	0–20%	11.7	10.7	10.9	10.8
	20–40	13.6	11.9	11.9	11.3
	40–60	14.6	12.4	12.0	**11.5**
	60–80	15.4	13.0	12.0	**11.0**
	80–100	16.8	14.2	12.0	**10.8**
	Average	14.3	12.3	11.7	11.1
Eastern region	0–20%	12.1	11.0	11.2	10.4
	20–40	14.0	11.9	12.2	**10.6**
	40–60	14.8	12.5	**12.6**	10.4
	60–80	15.6	12.5	**12.1**	10.3
	80–100	16.7	13.0	**11.6**	10.0
	Average	14.5	12.1	11.9	10.4
Middle-western region	0–20%	9.8	8.8	9.5	8.5
	20–40	11.2	9.6	10.1	9.0
	40–60	11.5	10.1	**10.4**	9.2
	60–80	12.1	10.6	**10.1**	**9.2**
	80–100	13.6	11.6	**10.1**	8.8
	Average	11.5	10.0	10.0	8.9
Southern region	0–20%	10.4	9.7	9.4	9.3
	20–40	12.1	10.5	10.7	**10.1**
	40–60	13.3	11.1	11.2	**9.8**
	60–80	14.0	11.6	**11.4**	9.6
	80–100	14.9	12.3	**11.1**	8.8
	Average	12.7	10.9	10.7	9.6
West-coastal region	0–20%	8.8	8.1	8.3	7.3
	20–40	10.2	8.8	9.1	**7.9**
	40–60	10.7	9.6	**9.4**	**7.9**
	60–80	11.6	9.6	**9.0**	7.5
	80–100	12.5	10.5	**8.7**	7.6
	Average	10.6	9.2	8.9	7.6
All India	0–20%	11.3	10.2	10.0	9.2
	20–40	12.8	11.1	10.8	**9.6**
	40–60	13.7	11.5	**11.1**	**9.6**
	60–80	14.4	11.9	**10.9**	9.4
	80–100	15.6	12.6	**10.6**	**9.0**
	Average	13.4	11.3	10.6	9.4

Source: Calculated by the author from NSSO (2011) and NSSO (2012a).

Note: Bold figures denote reverse or unclear relations between the amount of consumption and MPCE.

parts of India, including Andhra Pradesh and Tamil Nadu, have a larger percentage of the population covered under the PDS and even have lower fixed prices compared to those of other states. Many states have undertaken PDS reforms recently with the major purpose of attaining popularity among the people to win elections. The PDS in these states has improved considerably in terms of the coverage of population, the prices of the commodities, and the operation of FPSs (Khera 2011; Drèze and Sen 2013).

Table 5.4 presents nominal prices of cereals purchased through the PDS and a market. Prices of rice and wheat purchased through PDS remained almost unchanged between 1993–94 and 2009–10 in the four food regions: the north-western region, the north-central region, the middle-western region, and the west-coastal region. The prices of the cereals provided through the PDS relative to those purchased at markets have decreased substantially in these regions because the latter rose steeply during the period, whereas the former remained almost unchanged.

Unlike the other four regions, in the last two food regions, i.e., the eastern region and the southern region, the prices of PDS cereals shrank between 2004–05 and 2009–10 in nominal terms. Consequently, the price of PDS rice in the southern region in 2009–10 was less than 10 per cent of the market price in rural areas and 6 per cent in urban areas. It is noteworthy that the greater part of the southern region includes Andhra Pradesh and Tamil Nadu, which are known for the successful implementation of the PDS. The substantial reduction in prices of PDS cereals in the region appears to reflect the PDS policies adopted in these states. However, it is significant that the amount of PDS cereals assigned to a household is limited in accordance with stipulations by state governments. That the supply of PDS cereals has made coarse grains expensive is also striking. In 1993–94, the cheapest cereals were coarse grains in most of the food regions. However, in 2009–10 the prices of coarse grains became almost twice as high as those of wheat or rice provided through the PDS. The rise in the relative prices of coarse grains is estimated as having markedly discouraged consumption, although the tastes of these cereals also played an important role. The monthly per-capita consumption of the people belonging to the first quintile of MPCE decreased from 2.4 kg in 1993–94 to 0.9 kg in 2009–10 in rural India and from 1.0 kg to 0.5 kg in urban India. The decreasing trend was found both in rural and urban areas in all food regions.

The reduced consumption of coarse grains accounted for a substantial portion of the decline in total cereal consumption. For the lowest MPCE group, the contribution ratio of the coarse grains to the total decrease in cereal consumption during 1993–94 and 2009–10 was 139 per cent for rural India and 55 per cent for urban India. However, the declining consumption of coarse grains cannot entirely explain the reduction in total cereal consumption.

Table 5.5 presents the monthly per-capita consumption of rice and wheat by source for the poorest 20 per cent of the population. The eastern region has shown a drop in the consumption of rice and wheat in both rural and

Table 5.4 Nominal cereal prices (1993/94, 2004/05, and 2009/10) (Rs./kg)

		Rural									Urban								
		1993/94			2004/05			2009/10			1993/94			2004/05			2009/10		
		Rice	Wheat	Coarse grains	Rice	Wheat	Coarse grains	Rice	Wheat	Coarse grains	Rice	Wheat	Coarse grains	Rice	Wheat	Coarse grains	Rice	Wheat	Coarse grains
North-western region	Market price	7.9	4.7	3.1	12.6	9.0	5.7	21.8	15.9	8.9	9.2	5.0	2.9	14.9	9.4	6.1	25.5	15.5	9.5
	PDS price	5.8	3.7	–	5.7	4.2	–	6.1	4.8	–	6.3	4.0	–	6.1	4.6	–	6.1	6.1	–
North-central region	Market price	6.4	4.9	2.9	10.0	9.4	5.3	15.7	14.8	7.8	7.0	4.9	2.3	11.0	9.1	5.7	17.8	14.9	8.9
	PDS price	5.4	4.1	–	5.0	4.0	–	5.1	4.3	–	5.7	3.9	–	5.3	4.3	–	5.6	5.8	–
Eastern region	Market price	6.8	6.5	5.2	11.3	11.7	8.7	17.9	19.5	10.3	7.4	6.8	5.0	12.3	12.3	8.5	20.6	20.4	12.8
	PDS price	4.2	3.9	–	5.4	4.7	–	3.1	5.1	–	5.0	4.1	–	5.8	5.8	–	2.8	5.9	–
Middle-western region	Market price	8.0	6.3	3.2	12.8	11.7	7.0	21.1	18.2	11.4	8.1	6.3	3.8	13.7	11.3	7.9	24.2	17.9	13.1
	PDS price	5.6	3.7	–	5.0	4.1	–	5.2	4.3	–	6.1	4.1	–	5.6	4.9	–	5.5	5.6	–
Southern region	Market price	7.0	8.0	3.7	11.6	14.8	7.1	20.4	22.3	11.5	7.9	8.0	4.5	14.1	15.6	9.5	26.4	24.8	14.5
	PDS price	3.9	3.7	–	4.2	5.1	–	1.9	6.8	–	4.2	3.9	–	4.1	7.0	–	1.5	7.9	–
West-coastal region	Market price	7.6	7.6	5.1	12.4	15.2	9.5	20.3	25.0	13.9	9.0	7.7	5.1	14.8	13.9	9.4	25.7	23.2	13.0
	PDS price	5.9	4.0	–	6.7	6.1	–	5.6	7.0	–	6.2	4.4	–	7.1	7.1	–	6.9	8.4	–
All India	Market price	7.2	5.8	3.5	11.6	11.1	6.7	19.1	17.8	10.1	8.2	6.2	3.9	13.7	11.6	7.9	24.0	19.1	12.3
	PDS price	4.8	3.8	–	5.0	4.5	–	3.8	5.2	–	5.3	4.1	–	5.1	5.7	–	3.4	6.8	–

Source: Calculated by the author from NSSO (2011), NSSO (2012a), and NSSO (2012b).

Table 5.5 Monthly per-capita consumption of rice and wheat by source (for population of the poorest 20%) (kg)

		Home-grown		PDS		Market		Total		
		1993/94	2009/10	1993/94	2009/10	1993/94	2009/10	1993/94	2009/10	"'09/10 - '93/94"
Rural	North-western region	3.0	2.6	0.7	1.7	4.9	4.4	8.6	8.7	0.2
	North-central region	3.4	1.8	0.1	1.9	6.9	6.7	10.5	10.4	-0.1
	Eastern region	3.3	1.6	0.6	3.6	7.4	5.6	11.3	10.8	-0.5
	Middle-western region	0.4	0.5	0.5	2.5	1.1	2.0	2.0	5.1	3.1
	Southern region	0.6	0.2	1.9	4.6	4.6	3.9	7.1	8.7	1.6
	West-coastal region	1.0	0.8	3.8	3.3	3.4	3.7	8.2	7.8	-0.5
	All India	2.5	1.6	0.8	2.7	5.4	4.9	8.7	9.2	0.5
Urban	North-western region	0.7	0.4	0.7	1.4	8.0	6.7	9.4	8.5	-0.9
	North-central region	1.2	0.5	0.2	1.6	9.1	8.6	10.5	10.6	0.0
	Eastern region	0.5	0.4	1.2	2.2	9.3	7.8	11.0	10.4	-0.6
	Middle-western region	0.1	0.0	0.6	1.8	3.6	4.4	4.3	6.2	1.9
	Southern region	0.2	0.0	2.0	4.2	6.2	4.6	8.3	8.8	0.5
	West-coastal region	0.0	0.1	3.9	1.8	4.1	5.2	8.0	7.1	-1.0
	All India	0.5	0.3	1.3	2.2	7.1	6.2	8.9	8.7	-0.2

Source: See Table 5.3.

urban areas, and it remained almost unchanged in both rural and urban areas in the north-central region. In rural areas in the two regions, the people in the poorest group reduced their consumption of cereals grown at home as well as those purchased at markets and markedly increased their consumption of PDS cereals. In urban areas, people decreased their consumption of market-bought cereals and increased consumption of cereals obtained through the PDS. The growth in cereals purchased through the PDS and the decrease in cereals purchased at markets suggest that the demand for cereals was possibly not satisfied and that the consumption might have been higher if the state governments had provided larger amounts of cereals through the PDS than the amount stipulated by them. The lower cereal consumption suggests neither saturation of the demand for cereals nor diversification of dietary patterns, as far as the poorer households are concerned.

In contrast, the middle-western region and the southern region showed increased cereal consumption of the poorest people among the population in both rural and urban areas. The table reveals that consumption of PDS cereals expanded markedly in rural and urban areas in both regions and contributed to the overall rise in rice and wheat consumption. Around 50 per cent of the rice and wheat consumed in the regions in 2009–10 was accounted for by cereals purchased through PDS in rural and urban areas in the southern region and in rural areas in the middle-western region. The PDS transformed the cereal consumption in the era of economic growth after the 1990s. It plays a crucial role in supporting poorer people in India.

The importance of cereals purchased through the PDS is well understood when cereal consumption in labour households is investigated. Table 5.6 presents the percentage share of consumption of rice and wheat by source in labour households in rural and urban areas. The table shows data of household types assigned by NSSO to all surveyed households.[4] First, rural households earning income mainly from labour work in agricultural or non-agricultural sectors increased their dependence on the PDS for the consumption of rice and wheat in all food regions. The share of rice and wheat bought this way rose from approximately 10 per cent to 30 per cent, incorporating households engaged in agricultural labour and other labour in rural India. The middle-western region and the southern region reported high shares of about 20 per cent in 1993–94. They increased sharply to as high as 40 per cent in 2009–10.[5] Another development in the sources of cereals in rural labour households is the declining share of home-grown cereals. Households engaged in agricultural labour in rural India reported a decrease in the share of home-grown cereals from 13 per cent in 1993–94 to 8 per cent in 2009–10. This trend was observed in all food regions except the north-western region. The self-produced cereals accounted for a certain portion of the total cereal consumption in labour households and presumably functioned as a safety net to some degree in 1993–94. However, they almost disappeared in 2009–10. They have been replaced by rice and wheat supplied through the PDS.

Table 5.6 Percentage share of rice and wheat consumed in labour households
by source

Food region	Sector	Household type	1993				2009			
			HG	PDS	MRK	Total	HG	PDS	MRK	Total
North-western region	Rural	Ag. labour	15	5	81	100	18	20	62	100
		Other labour	11	12	77	100	8	21	71	100
	Urban	Casual labour	5	7	89	100	2	15	83	100
North-central region	Rural	Ag. labour	15	1	84	100	10	16	74	100
		Other labour	17	2	81	100	9	19	72	100
	Urban	Casual labour	6	2	92	100	3	18	79	100
Eastern region	Rural	Ag. labour	14	6	80	100	7	27	66	100
		Other labour	11	6	83	100	5	23	71	100
	Urban	Casual labour	3	11	86	100	1	21	78	100
Middle-western region	Rural	Ag. labour	9	27	64	100	3	49	48	100
		Other labour	9	18	73	100	3	34	63	100
	Urban	Casual labour	1	13	86	100	0	28	72	100
Southern region	Rural	Ag. labour	7	23	69	100	2	48	50	100
		Other labour	6	21	74	100	1	45	54	100
	Urban	Casual labour	0	21	78	100	0	44	55	100
West-coastal region	Rural	Ag. labour	7	41	52	100	4	43	53	100
		Other labour	4	43	53	100	2	34	63	100
	Urban	Casual labour	1	46	53	100	0	30	70	100
All India	Rural	Ag. labour	13	10	78	100	8	30	62	100
		Other labour	10	13	77	100	6	26	68	100
	Urban	Casual labour	3	15	82	100	1	28	71	100

Source: See Table 5.3.

Note: Home-grown rice and wheat = HG, Rice and wheat purchased through PDS = PDS, and
Rice and wheat purchased at market = MRK.

Thirdly, the supply of PDS rice and wheat became vital for urban households engaged in casual labour work. The Indian average share of the
PDS cereals in the urban labour households increased from 15 per cent to
28 per cent. The same trends were observed in all food regions except for the
west-coastal region. The shares of rice and wheat provided through PDS in

2009–10 reached as high as 44 per cent in the southern region and 28 per cent in the middle-western region. Cereals supplied through PDS play an indispensable role in maintaining the diet in the urban households engaged in labour work. The enlarged share of PDS in both rural and urban areas and the diminished share of home-grown cereals in rural areas showed similarity between the sources of cereals consumed by labour households in rural and urban areas.

Pulse Consumption

Pulses constitute a fundamental part of the Indian diet, being a major source of protein along with milk. Nevertheless, pulse consumption has declined in most regions, as has that of cereals. The monthly per-capita consumption of pulses fell from 0.76 kg in 1993–94 to 0.66 kg in 2009–10 in rural India and from 0.86 kg to 0.80 kg in urban India. An important difference between pulse and cereal consumption lies in the fact that the disparity in pulse consumption among the MPCE classes was not reduced. The wealthiest 20 per cent in the MPCE class ate twice as much in pulses as the poorest 20 per cent. That disparity persisted for 16 years. A similar difference was found in cereal consumption, but it narrowed during the same period.[6]

The decrease in pulse consumption can be attributed to price hikes. The real price of pulses evaluated based on the prices in 1986 went from Rs. 8.2 to Rs. 11.1 in rural areas and Rs. 9.4 to Rs 12.3 in urban areas, with respective growth rates of 36.1 per cent and 31.5 per cent. Contrary to pulses, the average prices of cereals in real terms including those purchased in markets and those purchased through PDS were maintained at the same level during the same period. The supply of cheap cereals enabled by the expansion of the PDS seems to have kept the price stable in real terms in spite of the considerable increase in market prices. In contrast, the PDS does not cover pulses in most states, although some states recently started to deal with them in that context (Khera 2011). Therefore, the price hike of pulses directly constrained the consumption and further aggravated the low consumption of pulses in poorer households.

Edible Oil Consumption

The investigation of cereal consumption revealed that low-income people were able to maintain a minimum level of cereal consumption by virtue of cheap PDS cereals, but they failed to do so in the case of pulses, presumably because pulses were not covered by the PDS. Edible oil consumption presents another story. The most impressive change in edible oil consumption has been the steep rise in consumption. The per-capita monthly consumption of total edible oils increased from 0.38 kg in 1993–94 to 0.57 kg in 2009–10 in rural India and from 0.61 kg to 0.77 kg in urban India, representing respective growth rates of 50.0 per cent and 26.2 per cent. All food regions underwent a sharp rise in per-capita edible oil consumption in both rural and urban areas. The second development was a substantial reduction of the disparities among the MPCE classes. The ratio of the amount consumed by the wealthiest 20 per cent to the poorest 20 per cent shrank from 2.8 to 2.0 in rural India and from 2.9 to 2.0 in urban India. The lessening of the difference in edible oil consumption took place in all food regions without exception. Low-income households have been catching up with the wealthier households with respect to edible oil consumption, although the gap remains large.

The third development related to edible oil consumption since the 1990s has been the increased consumption of 'other edible oils' and the corresponding decline in the consumption of groundnut oil. Table 5.7 shows that the poorest 20 per cent in the north-western region bought mainly mustard oil and groundnut oil in 1993–94 in both rural and urban areas, but the major edible oils used in the region in 2009–10 changed to mustard oil and 'other edible oils' as the substantial growth of the latter marginalized groundnut oil. Similarly, the middle-western region and the southern region, where groundnut oil accounted for a major part of total edible oil consumption in 1993–94, showed a marked increase in 'other edible oils', which almost completely replaced groundnut oil in 2009–10. A drastic shift in edible oil use caused by the ascendancy of 'other edible oils' is found in all regions except for the north-central region. The increased consumption of 'other edible oils' is witnessed not only in the poorest 20 per cent but also in the other MPCE classes. But it is particularly important for the poor because it can easily raise their caloric intake.

A plausible reason for the expanded consumption of 'other edible oils' is their low price relative to other conventional oils. Table 5.7 reports that, in rural areas of the middle-western region and the southern region, both of which underwent a major shift in the consumption of primary edible oils, 'other edible oils' have been the cheapest throughout the period. Moreover, the difference between the prices of them and groundnut oil, which was ranked second in 2009–10, widened further. In the other food regions, 'other edible oils' were the cheapest in 2009–10, along with vanaspati. The increased consumption of cheaper edible oils reduced the real price of edible oils consumed in India overall. The average price of edible oils in real terms based on 1986 decreased from Rs. 19.4 to Rs. 12.8 in rural India and Rs. 21.6 to Rs. 13.9 in urban India with a growth rate of −33.9 per cent and −35.8 per cent, respectively. The markedly lower real price allowed not only the wealthy households but also the poor to consume a larger amount of edible oils.

'Other edible oils' chiefly comprised palm oil imported from Indonesia and Malaysia. The large-scale import of palm oil began in the mid-1990s after the government liberalized its import in response to a price hike at that time on the one hand and in accordance with the agreement on agriculture in World Trade Organization (WTO) on the other, and reduced the tariff on them (World Bank 1999; Chand 2004). Palm oil imports to India increased

Table 5.7 Monthly per-capita consumption of edible oils, percentage share of different edible oils consumed, and the prices (for population of the poorest 20%)

Food region	Year	Rural								Urban							
		Total consumption of edible oils (kg)	Total	Ghee	Vanaspati	Mustard oil	Groundnut oil	Coconut oil	Other edible oils	Total consumption of edible oils (kg)	Total	Ghee	Vanaspati	Mustard oil	Groundnut oil	Coconut oil	Other edible oils
North-western region	1993/94	0.29	100% (35.1)	3% (92.7)	10% (37.9)	52% (29.4)	19% (38.7)	0% (38.5)	16% (32.3)	0.42	100% (39.7)	5% (89.9)	16% (38.0)	37% (29.7)	30% (38.0)	0% (44.0)	11% (35.4)
	2009/10	0.46	100% (65.9)	2% (255.7)	7% (56.7)	58% (61.1)	2% (73.5)	0% (106.6)	31% (58.9)	0.56	100% (76.5)	4% (250.9)	8% (55.9)	47% (62.5)	3% (72.7)	0% (89.6)	37% (61.3)
North-central region	1993/94	0.21	100% (31.7)	0% (88.5)	3% (38.7)	91% (30.7)	2% (35.4)	0% (40.0)	4% (30.1)	0.28	100% (34.4)	0% (91.4)	6% (39.1)	82% (30.9)	7% (35.9)	0% (44.8)	4% (32.3)
	2009/10	0.33	100% (66.3)	0% (264.1)	5% (54.9)	86% (66.5)	1% (65.9)	0% (122.2)	8% (57.8)	0.40	100% (69.3)	0% (268.9)	7% (56.0)	80% (66.7)	1% (80.6)	0% (107.4)	12% (62.4)
Eastern region	1993/94	0.19	100% (33.3)	0% (101.8)	0% (41.2)	61% (32.9)	20% (35.5)	0% (38.2)	18% (26.9)	0.29	100% (35.0)	0% (102.8)	2% (41.8)	62% (33.0)	29% (36.2)	0% (38.8)	7% (37.3)
	2009/10	0.34	100% (64.4)	0% (231.5)	2% (57.6)	59% (68.7)	1% (66.1)	0% (100.5)	38% (54.5)	0.46	100% (66.6)	0% (253.6)	1% (60.7)	64% (68.7)	2% (68.5)	0% (92.4)	32% (61.4)
Middle-western region	1993/94	0.25	100% (35.6)	0% (91.1)	1% (40.5)	0% (33.4)	51% (37.2)	1% (37.4)	48% (30.0)	0.35	100% (36.9)	0% (91.4)	2% (40.7)	0% (37.0)	65% (37.1)	0% (40.6)	33% (29.4)
	2009/10	0.53	100% (56.8)	0% (249.1)	0% (57.0)	0% (64.9)	8% (66.8)	1% (77.6)	91% (54.4)	0.64	100% (64.4)	1% (240.9)	0% (62.3)	0% (71.0)	9% (71.2)	0% (93.0)	90% (55.4)
Southern region	1993/94	0.21	100% (35.0)	0% (76.5)	0% (40.3)	1% (34.6)	78% (35.0)	3% (40.0)	18% (30.9)	0.26	100% (36.4)	0% (82.1)	0% (43.1)	0% (38.4)	82% (35.2)	2% (41.3)	16% (35.6)
	2009/10	0.45	100% (56.1)	0% (223.0)	0% (63.6)	0% (63.6)	27% (65.5)	0% (71.0)	73% (49.9)	0.49	100% (63.9)	0% (252.3)	0% (71.1)	0% (71.7)	24% (66.7)	1% (78.2)	74% (59.2)
West-coastal region	1993/94	0.20	100% (38.8)	0% (98.4)	1% (43.0)	0% (27.2)	36% (38.6)	57% (39.1)	6% (34.7)	0.35	100% (40.3)	0% (92.7)	1% (44.2)	3% (37.0)	55% (38.5)	32% (40.5)	8% (40.9)
	2009/10	0.45	100% (57.8)	0% (249.5)	0% (65.8)	0% (64.6)	9% (69.2)	43% (57.2)	48% (55.3)	0.59	100% (72.2)	1% (248.4)	2% (69.2)	6% (79.6)	29% (76.1)	26% (58.9)	36% (69.0)
All India	1993/94	0.23	100% (34.1)	1% (91.7)	4% (38.8)	46% (31.2)	28% (36.3)	3% (39.2)	18% (30.4)	0.34	100% (37.3)	2% (90.8)	8% (39.5)	32% (31.4)	42% (36.6)	4% (40.7)	13% (35.0)
	2009/10	0.41	100% (63.3)	0% (250.5)	0% (56.3)	0% (65.8)	9% (67.2)	43% (61.6)	48% (54.7)	0.53	100% (69.7)	1% (250.8)	2% (58.1)	6% (65.9)	29% (70.8)	26% (65.6)	36% (60.3)

Source: See Table 5.3.

Note: Figures in parentheses are nominal prices in rupee.

from 0.4 million tons in 1993–94 to 6.5 million tons in 2009–10. According to an estimate by Food and Agriculture Organization (FAO), the percentage of palm oil to the total edible oils consumption in India rose from 4 per cent in 1993 to 22 per cent in 2009 (FAO). The large-scale palm oil imports strongly affected farmers who had expanded their production of oil crops, especially in the southern parts of India in the 1980s and the beginning of the 1990s, after the government initiated various measures including technical support by the Technology Mission on Oilseeds and market intervention operations by the National Dairy Development Board (World Bank 1999; Chand 2004). However, examination to date has revealed that the huge amounts of imported palm oil enabled vulnerable people among the population to consume larger amounts of edible oils and avoid the severe deterioration of their diets while coping with stagnant income growth.

Consumption of Milk

The monthly per-capita consumption of milk in India swelled from 3.9 litres per month in 1993–94 to 4.1 litres in 2009–10 in rural areas and from 4.9 litres to 5.4 litres in urban areas. The increased consumption was apparent in all food regions in urban areas and four out of six regions in rural areas. The food regions showing decreased consumption in rural areas were the north-western region and the north-central region, both of which had already attained quite a high degree of milk consumption in 1993–94 and both of which reported a slight reduction between 2004–05 and 2009–10. Great inter-regional disparity prevails, but it has tended to shrink because of reduced consumption in the major consuming regions on the one hand and increased consumption in other regions on the other hand. Milk consumption also varies considerably among the MPCE classes. However, the differences have shown a tendency to decrease. The ratio of milk consumed in the households belonging to the fifth quintile of MPCE class to the first quintile respectively fell from 6.8 in 1993–94 to 4.7 in 2009–10 in rural areas and from 5.1 to 3.7 in urban areas.

Milk consumption has improved since the 1990s with respect to the enlarged consumption and the narrowed disparity among the MPCE classes. An important source of the improvement is expected to be a favourable movement of milk prices in real terms. Prices were quite stable between 1993–94 and 2009–10 in rural India with a growth rate of 1.5 per cent for the entire period. Prices dropped in urban India with a growth rate of −5.2 per cent. The reason underlying the stable or declining trends of milk prices in real terms has yet to be investigated. However, technological progress in milk production and the improvement of infrastructure, especially in urban areas, are likely factors in these developments.

Another aspect related to the improvement in milk consumption is the important role played by home-produced milk in rural household consumption. The supply of milk in rural areas is unique in that the substantial part is home-produced. The percentages of home-produced milk in households

Table 5.8 Percentage of home-produced milk in rural areas (for labour households)

Food region	Household type	1993/94	2004/05	2009/10
North-western region	Ag. labour	71	48	55
	Other labour	64	55	53
	Regional total	83	74	73
North-central region	Ag. labour	71	52	41
	Other labour	57	47	48
	Regional total	78	67	61
Eastern region	Ag. labour	48	29	34
	Other labour	48	28	21
	Regional total	62	48	42
Middle-western region	Ag. labour	49	38	21
	Other labour	22	23	23
	Regional total	57	50	41
Southern region	Ag. labour	28	21	12
	Other labour	17	7	3
	Regional total	41	32	20
West-coastal region	Ag. labour	33	30	20
	Other labour	19	14	14
	Regional total	39	25	21
All India	Ag. labour	59	40	35
	Other labour	51	42	40
	Regional total	74	63	59

Source: See Table 5.4.

that are self-employed in agriculture remained high in 2009–10, ranging from 42 per cent in the west-coast region to 90 per cent in the north-western region, but flagged considerably in all food regions between 1993–94 and 2009–10. It is not only the farming households but also rural labour households that depend on home-produced milk to a considerable degree, as shown in Table 5.8. The percentages of home-produced milk were 40 per cent to 50 per cent in 2009–10 for households employed in manual labour in the north-western region and the north-central region. Other regions aside from the southern region also reported considerably high shares of around 20 per cent. The home-produced milk greatly bolstered the diet and caloric intake of vulnerable people among the rural population, especially in the north-western region and the north-central region.

Conclusion

Newly emerging trends in the consumption of cereals, pulses, edible oils, and milk in low-income households can be summarized as presented below. Cereal consumption underwent profound changes attributable to the introduction of the PDS on a large scale. Cereals provided through it accounted for a substantial part of cereals consumed by poor people. Results show that the households engaged in manual work were deeply dependent on the PDS cereals in both rural and urban areas, especially in the southern states. Considering the large share of PDS cereals provided at an extremely low price, it is difficult to conclude that the decreased consumption of cereals in poorer households indicates saturation of the demand for cereals among those households. It is likely that further demand will arise for cereals among poorer people.

Pulse consumption has been decreasing continually in all MPCE classes in all food regions. The major reason for this is likely to be a price hike, which directly influences low-income households. The declining consumption of pulses suggests the vulnerability of the food system, which depends heavily on the market and which lacks effective measures to control the food supply such as PDS.

In the case of edible oils, the introduction of 'other edible oils' on a large scale transformed their consumption. The massive inflow of 'other edible oils' led to a steady increase in the total edible oil consumption in all the MPCE classes, including the poorest households. It changed the composition of this area of consumption by substituting groundnut oil, which had been the most important edible oil in the southern part of India until the 1990s. The context for the massive supply of 'other edible oils' is the import of palm oil, which has risen sharply since the trade liberalization implemented in the 1990s. The 'other edible oils' seems to have fulfilled the role the PDS has played in the supply of cereals.

Milk consumption has been increasing gradually, although it shows stark regional differences. Milk consumption in rural households engaged in labour work is characterized by a considerable share of home-produced milk, especially in the northern parts of India. The percentage of home-produced milk shows a tendency to decrease, but it still bolsters the diets of poor households in rural areas.

Economic growth in India, initiated in the 1990s, has not entirely benefitted poorer people. Faced with stagnant incomes, they have been depending increasingly on cereals provided through the PDS and the non-traditional edible oils mainly imported from Indonesia and Malaysia on a large scale under the liberalized trade regime. This study also revealed that home-produced milk has played an important role. The PDS, palm oil, and home-produced milk are apparently functioning as essential devices to keep the wage rates of labourers extremely low in both rural and urban areas. The food supply system, as presented in this report, can be seen as an indispensable sub-system to support the recent economic growth of India.

Notes

1 The average MPCE for the poorest 20 per cent was calculated by the author as a simple average of the corresponding state averages from NSSO (2011) and NSSO (2012a).
2 Kumar, Mruthynjaya and Dey (2007) and Gupta (2012) examined changes in food consumption patterns. Meenaksi and Ray (1999) and Mittal (2006) shed light on the food demand system in India. Atkin (2013) examined regional tastes in food consumption in India.

3 New NSS regions were formed by exchanging and merging the districts included in NSS regions. The data presented in Kumar and Somaanathan (2009) were fully utilized for the NSS region modification work. The number of NSS regions after modification by the author was 73. Out of 73, 11 NSS regions were omitted from the analysis because the survey was not conducted in these NSS regions.

4 NSS assigns five household types for rural households and four for urban households to be utilized in the analysis of occupation structure. The household types for rural households are 'self-employed in non-agriculture', 'agricultural labour', 'other labour', 'self-employed in agriculture', and 'others'. And those for urban households are 'self-employed', 'regular wage/salary earning', 'casual labour', and 'others'.

5 The food regions located in the southern part of India, i.e., the middle-western, the southern, and the west-coastal region, showed marked dependence on the PDS in 2009–10, with the share of PDS cereals of around 40 to 50 per cent. In contrast, the share was low in the north-western, the north-central, and the eastern regions, being around 20 per cent though the increasing dependency on the PDS was similarly shown in those regions, too.

6 The wealthiest 20 per cent in rural India ate 2.3 times as much in pulses per capita per month as the poorest 20 per cent in 1993–94; the ratio changed to 2.1 in 2009–10. In urban India, it changed from 2.2 to 2.0. The ratios did not differ much among the food regions in 1993–94 and 2009–10.

References

Atkin, David (2013) 'Trade, Taste, and Nutrition in India', *The American Economic Review* 103(5): 1629–1663.

Chand, Ramesh (2004) 'WTO and Oilseeds Sector: Challenges of Trade Liberalisation', *Economic and Political Weekly* 39(7): 533–537.

Drèze, Jean and Amartya Sen (2013), *An Uncertain Glory: India and Its Contradictions*, London: Penguin Book Ltd.

FAO, FAOSTAT «seurld>https://www.fao.org/faostat/en/#data/FBSH</seurld», viewed on February 26, 2022.

Gupta, Shline (2012) 'Food Expenditure and Intake in the NSS 66th Round', *Economic and Political Weekly* 47(2): 23–26.

Khera, Reetika (2011) 'Revival of the Public Distribution System: Evidence and Explanations', *Economic and Political Weekly* 46(44/45): 36–50.

Kumar, Praduman, Mruthynjaya, and Madan M. Dey (2007) 'Long-Term Changes in Indian Food Basket and Nutrition', *Economic and Political Weekly* 42(35): 3567–3572.

Kumar, Hemanshu and Rohini Somaanathan (2009) *Mapping Indian Districts across Census Years, 1971–2001*, Working Paper No. 176, Centre for Development Economics.

Meenakshi, J. V. and Ranjan Ray (1999) 'Regional Differences in India's Food Expenditure Pattern: A Complete Demand Systems Approach', *Journal of International Development* 11: 47–74.

Mittal, Surabhi (2006), *Structural Shift in Demand for Food: Projections for 2020*, Working Paper No. 184, Indian Council for Research on International Economic Relations.

NSSO (National Sample Survey Office) (2011), Household Consumer Expenditure 66th Round Type-1 (2009/10), released on the website of http://microdata.gov.in/nada43/index.php/home, viewed on August 15, 2022.

NSSO (2012a), Household Consumer Expenditure, NSS 50th Round: July 1993–June 1994, released on the website referred for NSSO (2011).

NSSO (2012b), Household Consumer Expenditure, NSS 61st Round: July 2004–June 2005, released on the website referred for NSSO (2011).

Usami, Yoshifumi (2011) 'A Note on Recent Trends in Wage Rates in Rural India', *Review of Agrarian Studies* 1(1): 149–182.

Usami, Yoshifumi (2012) 'Recent Trends in Wage Rates in Rural India: An Update', *Review of Agrarian Studies* 2(1): 171–181.

World Bank (1999), *The Indian Oilseed Complex: Capturing Market Opportunities*, New Delhi: Allied Publishers Ltd.

6 Dairy Industry Modernization and the Changing Rural Economy of India

Hideki Esho

The government started to liberalize the Indian economy in 1991 and it has been globalizing rapidly since. The historic change from a supply-constrained to a demand-led economy is progressing quickly. Symbolic of this transformation is the skyrocketing growth of ICT and ICT-enabling service industries along with the modernization of service industries, as exemplified by the emergence of modern retailing. In the past, the expansion of agricultural production had a decisive influence on general economic growth. However, that relative influence has ceased. Conversely, the growth rate of the service industry has started to exert a much greater influence. Analyzing such a transformation demands scrutiny of the effects of changing consumption patterns and behaviors of urban people on rural economy and society: research must particularly address the changing economy and society from the perspective of "from urban to rural" or "from consumption to production." Alternatively, in the words of Reardon and Gulati, we should seek to promote research of the food supply chain "from plate to plough" (Reardon and Gulati, 2008: 36).

This chapter specifically examines dairy products (milk and milk products), which are representative cases of demand-driven growth (Shah and Dave, 2010; World Bank, 2011). Dairy products are an indispensable part of the Indian diet. The Indian dairy industry has developed in a unique manner from its start after Independence. Since the 1970s, a modernization program for milk and milk products has been developed under the dairy cooperative society, well known as the "Amul model" or "Operation Flood." However, the economic liberalization of the 1990s also promoted liberalization of trade and foreign direct investment in the field of milk and milk products. Furthermore, an increase of per-capita income, urbanization, and the modernization of retail businesses has promoted investment in the dairy industry by the private sector. These are the key driving forces that have altered not only the dairy industry but also the rural economy and society of India.[1]

DOI: 10.4324/9781003311898-7

India Bovine Sector Characteristics and Changing Trends

India is the world leader in terms of its number of bovines. As of 2010, there was 210.2 million head of cattle, accounting for 14.7 per cent of the world total and ranking among the top countries alongside Brazil. Moreover, its 111.3 million buffaloes remarkably represent 57.3 per cent of the world total (DAHD, 2012: 131).

Figure 6.1 presents the changing numbers of cattle and buffaloes among all bovines for 1951–2019. During 1951–2019, the percentage of cattle decreased from 78.2 per cent to 63.7 per cent. In contrast, that of buffaloes increased from 21.8 per cent to 36.3 per cent. Table 6.1 presents male/female numbers of cattle and buffaloes for 1951–2012. In the case of cattle, the proportion of female cattle among all cattle risen from 35.0 per cent in 1951 to 40.2 per cent in 2012. Also in the case of buffaloes, the percentage of female buffaloes among total buffaloes has risen steadily from 48.4 per cent in 1951 to 52.1 per cent in 2007. All these figures indicate clearly that bovines, both cattle and buffaloes, are progressively concentrating their respective roles in milk production. Furthermore, the huge differences in female/male ratios between cattle and buffalo derive from the different social roles and recognition of the respective animals among Indians.

Traditionally in India, bullocks have been used for draught power in agriculture and transport. Cattle have remained an integral part of the agricultural production system. They provide not only draught power but also milk and milk products for household consumption, as well as manure for agriculture and fuel for cooking. In turn, for their sustenance, cattle obtain their fodder from crop residues and by-products. This synergistic relation between cattle and crop production is designated as a "mixed crop–livestock system" (Sharma, 2004; Birthal and Negi, 2012). Customarily, milk production has not been a primary concern for

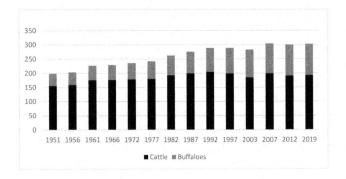

Figure 6.1 Number of cattle and buffaloes, 1951–2019 (in million).

Source: Department of Animal Husbandry, Dairying & Fisheries, Ministry of Agriculture, Basic Animal Husbandry Statistics, various years.

Table 6.1 Numbers and percentages of female cattle/female buffaloes in total cattle/buffaloes

Species	1951	1956	1961	1966	1972	1977	1982	1987	1992	1997	2003	2007	2012
(1) Cattle	155.3	158.7	175.6	176.2	178.3	180	192.5	199.7	204.6	198.9	185.2	199.1	190.9
(2) Adult female cattle	54.4	47.3	51	51.8	53.4	54.6	59.2	62.1	64.4	64.4	64.5	73	123
(3)=(2)/(1) (%)	-35	-29.8	-29.0	-29.4	-29.9	-30.3	-30.7	-31.1	-31.5	-32.4	-34.8	-36.6	-40.2
(4) Buffaloes	43.4	44.9	51.2	53	57.4	62	69.8	76	84.2	89.9	97.9	105.3	108.7
(5) Female buffaloes	21	21.7	24.3	25.4	28.6	31.3	32.5	39.1	43.8	46.8	51	54.5	92.6
(6)=(5)/(4) (%)	-48.4	-48.3	-47.5	-47.9	-49.8	-50.5	-46.6	-51.5	-52.0	-52.0	-52.1	-51.7	-52.1

Source: DAHD (2012); DAHD (2014).

farmers. Cows are regarded as a by-product of the process of securing outstanding bulls for draught power. Primarily for this reason, the male/female ratio of cattle has not significantly changed for a very long time. However, people do not expect buffaloes to be draught power. In India, they are mostly river-type buffaloes, which differ greatly from the swamp-type found in Southeast Asian countries and are unsuitable for laboring. Furthermore, a religious taboo has important effects; in India, cows are worshipped as "sacred." People dislike slaughtering cows and do not eat beef. Nevertheless, this taboo applies neither to bulls nor to non-milk-bearing cows nor to buffaloes with black hides. Another unique feature of Indian bovine husbandry is that many animals are reared by poor farmers. Bovine wealth is distributed more equitably compared to that of land. Furthermore, cattle have formed a major component of the poverty allevi-ation strategy of the Government of India (Chand and Raju, 2008; Kumar and Singh, 2008).

Table 6.2 presents the distribution of operational landholdings[2] and livestock for 1991–92, 2001–02, and 2005–06. The livestock holding ratio decreases concomitantly with increasing landholding size. It is true that livestock is much more equitably distributed than landholding. If one were to compare three periods of 1991–92, 2001–02, and 2005–06, they would find the following: (1) The percentages of landholdings of marginal and small-scale farmers increased from 15.3 per cent and 18.1 per cent in 1991–92 to 20.2 per cent and 20.9 per cent in 2005–06, although those of medium and large-scale farmers decreased from 27.1 per cent and 15.9 per cent each in 1991–92 to 23.1 per cent and 11.8 per cent each in 2005–06. (2) The percentage of livestock distribution of marginal farmers rose dra-matically from 36.9 per cent in 1991–92 to 50.1 per cent in 2005–06. However, the livestock distribution among small, semi–medium, medium, and large-scale farmers shrank during 1991–92 and 2005–06. This data was collected by the Department of Animal Husbandry, Dairying & Fisheries, Ministry of Agriculture. Although it is valuable, regrettably, there is no classification

Table 6.2 Distribution of operational holdings and livestock per household 1991–92, 2001–02, and 2005–06 (%)

Category of land holdings	Distribution of land holdings			Distribution of livestock		
	1991–92	*2001–02*	*2005–06*	*1991–92*	*2001–02*	*2005–06*
Marginal (below 1.00 ha)	15.3	18.3	20.2	36.9	46.5	50.1
Small (1.00 to 1.99 ha)	18.1	20.4	20.9	23.5	22.5	21.6
Semi-medium (2.00 to 3.99 ha)	23.6	24.3	23.9	20.2	17.5	15.9
Medium (4.00 to 9.99 ha)	27.1	24.5	23.1	14.7	10.6	9.6
Large (10.00 ha and above)	15.9	12.5	11.8	4.8	2.9	2.8
All sizes	100.0	100.0	100.0	100.0	100.0	100.0

Source: DAHD (2006, 2010, 2012).

Table 6.3 Changes in size distribution of household operational holdings (rural) (%)

Category of holdings	1960–61	1971–72	1981–82	1991–92	2002–03
Nil (operating no land or land of area 0.002 ha or less)	26.9	27.4	26.2	21.8	31.9
Marginal (0.002–1.00 ha)	30.7	32.9	41.1	48.3	47.1
Small (1.01–2.00 ha)	16.2	16.4	14.5	14.2	11.2
Semi-medium (2.01–4.00 ha)	13.8	12.9	10.6	9.7	6.2
Medium (4.01–10.00 ha)	9.4	8.1	6.3	4.9	2.9
Large (larger than 10.00 ha)	3.0	2.2	1.4	1.1	0.5
All sizes	100.0	100.0	100.0	100.0	100.0
Estimated number of household operational holdings (million)	52.9	56.88	69.4	93.39	101.75

Source: NSSO (2006).

of "landless laborers." The classification of "nil," which means "operating no land or land of 0.002 ha or less," the equivalent of a landless household, is included in the NSS 59th Round Survey Report "Livestock Ownership Across Operational Land Holding Classes in India, 2002–03" (NSS 2006). From NSS data, Table 6.3 shows the changes and distribution of household operational holdings (rural) from 1960–61 to 2002–03.

The NSS data classify categories of operational holdings as nil (operating no land or land area 0.002 ha or less), marginal (0.002–1.00 ha), small (1.01–2.00 ha), semi–medium (2.01–4.00 ha), medium (4.01–10.00 ha), and large (larger than 10.00 ha). From this, one can infer the following: (1) The percentage of landless laborers increased substantially from 22 to 27 per cent before 1991–92 to 31.9 per cent in 2002–03. Because these figures of 2002–03 are related only to the Kharif season, one cannot compare these figures with those of the previous period. Nevertheless, this growth is substantial. (2) The percentage of marginal farmers was 47.1 per cent in 2002–03, rising from 30.7 per cent in 1960–61. If one adds landless laborers to marginal farmers, their percentage accounts for 79 per cent of the total in 2002–03. (3) As the size of landholding increases, the share of each holding decreases: each of their shares diminishes from 1960–61 onward. The decreasing share of large-scale farmers is especially conspicuous: it fell from 3.0 per cent in 1960–61 to 0.5 per cent in 2002–03. (4) The absolute numbers and percentages of landless laborers and marginal farmers increased, which is the result of growing pressure of the expanding population on land and the consequent subdivision of holdings. Weakening of the joint family system and more nuclear families spur this tendency (Datta and Dadhich, 2007).

Table 6.4 presents the trend of the percentage change of "in-milk"[3] cattle and buffaloes per 100 households to respective total stocks from 1971–72

Table 6.4 Percentage of in-milk cattle and buffaloes to respective total stock (rural)

Bovine stock	1971–72	1981–82	1991–92	2002–03
1. Number of cattle per 100 households	216	172	143	104
2. Number of in-milk cattle per 100 households	34	20	26	19
3. % of in-milk cattle	16	12	18	18
4. Number of buffaloes per 100 households	62	68	59	51
5. Number of in-milk buffaloes per 100 households	20	17	20	17
6. % of in-milk buffaloes	32	25	34	33
7. % of buffaloes in in-milk stock	37	46	43	47

Source: NSSO (2006).

to 2002–03. The number of cattle per 100 households dropped from 216 in 1971–72 to 104 in 2002–03: a 51 per cent decrease. During that period, the number of buffaloes also dropped from 62 to 51: an 18 per cent decrease. In addition, the number of in-milk cattle declined from 34 to 19, but no change occurred in the number of in-milk buffaloes because buffaloes yield higher returns than cattle stock. Still, the decrease of in-milk cattle numbers is conspicuous because of the rapid shift from indigenous cattle to crossbred cattle that has taken place to maintain and increase milk production (Datta and Dadhich, 2007). The number of crossbred cattle increased from about 20 million in 1997 to almost 50.4 million in 2019. Their percentage of the total number of cattle also went up from 10.1 per cent to 26.2 per cent (Figure 6.2).

Table 6.5 presents changes in the stock of in-milk cattle and buffaloes per 100 households by category of operational holdings in rural areas. In the case of marginal and small-scale farmers, the in-milk cattle are more

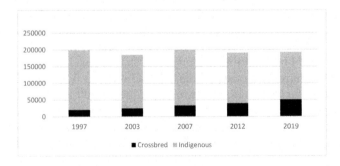

Figure 6.2 Number of crossbred and indigenous cattle, 1997–2019 (in thousand).

Source: Department of Animal Husbandry, Dairying & Fisheries, Ministry of Agriculture, Basic Animal Husbandry Statistics, various years.

Table 6.5 Changes in the stock of in-milk cattle and buffaloes per 100 household operational holdings (rural)

Category of landholdings	1971–72			1981–82			1991–92			2002–03		
	In-milk bovines	In-milk cattle	In-milk buffaloes	In-milk bovines	In-milk cattle	In-milk buffaloes	In-milk bovines	In-milk cattle	In-milk buffaloes	In-milk bovines	In-milk cattle	In-milk buffaloes
Nil (less than 0.002 ha)	16	9	7	7	3	4	6	3	3	0	0	0
Marginal (0.002–1.00 ha)	33	23	10	28	15	13	41	25	16	40	22	18
Small (1.01–2.00 ha)	64	41	23	48	26	22	69	38	31	63	31	32
Semi-medium (2.01–4.00 ha)	93	58	35	74	40	34	80	39	41	84	42	42
Medium (4.01–10.00 ha)	142	86	56	106	54	51	102	43	59	126	59	67
Large (larger than 10.00 ha)	225	140	85	153	86	67	130	43	87	208	111	97
All	54	34	20	37	20	17	46	26	20	36	19	17

Source: NSSO (2006).

numerous than in-milk buffaloes during 1971–72 and 2002–03, although the opposite is true for medium and large-scale farmers: The number of in–milk buffaloes is greater than that of in-milk cattle. A more remarkable phenomenon is that the number of in-milk bovines held by landless laborers decreased continually from 16 in 1971–72 to zero in 2002–03. In the case of larger than marginal-scale farmers, the number of in-milk bovines fell substantially in 1981–82. Furthermore, in 1991–92, for marginal, small, and semi-medium-scale farmers, the number of in-milk bovines increased slightly. However, it decreased further in the case of medium and large-scale farmers. In 2002–03, for marginal and small-scale farmers, the number of in-milk bovines declined, but in the case of semi-medium, medium, and large-scale farmers, the numbers grew. The increase was particularly notable for large-scale farmers: 130 in 1991–92 to 208 in 2002–03. From these data, we can indicate first that landless laborers withdrew completely from milk husbandry by 2002. Shah and Dave pointed out that, for landless laborers, dairy husbandry was "an occupation involving high risk and little safety mechanism to absorb the uncertainty in the milk production enterprises." Furthermore, they suggest that, for landless laborers, returns from dairy farming might be unfavorable compared to the opportunity costs of labor in a rural area because the Mahatma Gandhi National Rural Employment Guarantee Act (MGNREGA) might have given rise to such exit from dairying (Shah and Dave, 2010; Birthal and Negi, 2012). Secondly, large and medium-scale farmers seem to aggressively enter commercial dairy farming by 2002.

Figure 6.3 shows the trend of the share agriculture and livestock sector in GDP/GVA at constant prices.[4] The share of agriculture in all GDP/GVA declined consistently after Independence. Its share declined from 34.7 per cent in 1980–81 to 8.7 per cent in 2017–18. However, if one extracts the share

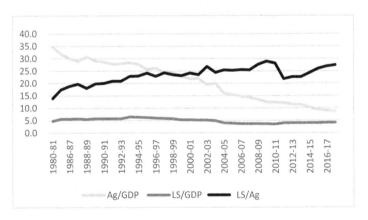

Figure 6.3 Share of agriculture and livestock sector in GDP/GVA at constant prices from 1980–81 to 2017–18.

Source: Department of Animal Husbandry & Dairying, Ministry of Fisheries, Animal Husbandry & Dairying, Basic Animal Husbandry Statistics 2019.

of the livestock sector, it increased from 4.8 per cent in 1980–81 to 6.5 per cent in 1993–94. Then it fell from 1994–95 to 3.5 per cent in 2011–12. Then it remains stable at around 4 per cent since 2011–12 onward. As a result, the share of livestock sector GDP in agricultural GDP surprisingly rose from 13.9 per cent in 1980–81 to 27.4 per cent in 2017–18, almost doubling.

India Dairy Industry Characteristics and Their Changing Trends

Milk Production

India produces more milk than any other country. As of 2010, total milk production in India was 117 million tons, accounting for 16.2 per cent of the world's total. India surpassed the USA in 1999 and has retained its top position since then. Nevertheless, per-capita availability of milk in India is 252 g/day, less than the world average of 279 g/day (DAHD, 2012: 126–130). Furthermore, surprisingly, bovine milk productivity is extremely low. For example, the average milk yield of a cow was 1,230 kg/annum in 2009–10: 781 kg/annum for indigenous cows and 2,508 kg/annum for crossbred cows. This is about half of the world average (Birthal and Negi, 2012). The main reason is that the rearing patterns in India differ greatly from those of the US, Europe, and Japan. A severe problem is the shortage of feed and fodder, especially green fodder.[5] There is insufficient grassland in most parts of India, so most cows are reared only in cow sheds throughout their lives.

About 55 per cent of total milk production comes from buffaloes. Such a high degree of dependence on buffalo milk is common in India and Pakistan but very peculiar from a global perspective. Consequently, although the world share of India's cow milk is around 7–8 per cent, its share of buffalo milk amounts to almost 70 per cent of the total (Table 6.6).

The growth rate of milk production since Independence is remarkable (Table 6.7). It was 17 million tons in 1950–51 immediately after the

Table 6.6 World estimates of cow and buffalo milk production and India (million tons)

Year	Cow			Buffalo		
	World	India	Percentage share to the world total	World	India	Percentage share to the world total
2000	491.2	34.0	6.9	67.4	44.4	65.9
2001	497.6	35.6	7.2	70.4	46.6	66.2
2002	508.9	36.2	7.1	72.3	48.0	66.4
2003	518.5	36.5	7.0	75.5	50.1	66.3
2004	523.4	37.5	7.2	76.5	50.7	66.3
2007	569.6	43.5	7.6	83.9	55.9	66.9
2008	578.7	44.1	7.6	89.6	60.9	68.2
2009	580.5	45.1	7.7	90.3	59.2	66.9
2010	599.6	50.3	8.4	92.5	62.4	67.5

Source: DAHD (2006, 2010, 2012).

Table 6.7 Estimates of production and per-capita availability of milk

Year	Production (million tons)	Per-capita availability (g/day)
1950–51	17.0	124
1955–56	19.0	124
1960–61	20.0	124
1968–69	21.2	112
1973–74	23.2	112
1979–80	30.4	127
1980–81	31.6	128
1981–82	34.3	136
1982–83	35.8	139
1983–84	38.8	147
1984–85	41.5	154
1985–86	44.0	160
1986–87	46.1	164
1987–88	46.7	163
1988–89	48.4	166
1989–90	51.4	173
1990–91	53.9	176
1991–92	55.7	178
1992–93	58.0	182
1993–94	60.6	187
1994–95	63.8	194
1995–96	66.2	197
1996–97	69.1	202
1997–98	72.1	207
1998–99	75.4	213
1999–00	78.3	217
2000–01	80.6	220
2001–02	84.4	225
2002–03	86.2	230
2003–04	88.1	231
2004–05	92.5	233
2005–06	97.1	241
2006–07	100.9	251
2007–08	104.8	260
2008–09	112.5	266
2009–10	116.2	273
2020–11	121.8	281
2011–12	127.9	290
2012–13	132.4	299
2013–14	137.7	307
2014–15	146.3	322
2015–16	155.5	337
2016–17	165.4	355
2017–18	176.3	375
2018–19	187.7	394

Source: DAHD (2019).

Independence. This amount had doubled to 34 million tons by 1981–82, taking 30 years. The doubling of 34.3 million tons in 1981–82 to 68.6 million tons was achieved in 1996–97, taking only 15 years. And then it kept almost the same growth rates up to 2018–19 when the production was 187.7 million tons. It is apparent that milk production accelerated year by year. Furthermore, per-capita availability increased from 124 g/day in 1950–51 to 394 g/day in 2018–19.

Table 6.8 presents milk production data by state. In 2018–19, the top 5 states accounted for 53.1 per cent of the total; the top 10 states accounted for 81.4 per cent of the total. The most productive state by far is Uttar Pradesh,

Table 6.8 Estimates of milk production by state

States	1997–98 Production ('000 tons)	Ranking	2005–06 Production ('000 tons)	Ranking	2018–19 Production ('000 tons)	Ranking	Share to the total (%)
All India	72,128		97,066		1,87,749		100.0
Andhra Pradesh	4,473	7	7,624	4	15,044	4	8.0
Arunachal Pradesh	43		48		55		
Assam	719		747		882		
Bihar	3,420	11	5,060	10	9,818	9	5.2
Chhattisgarh	–		839		1,567		
Goa	38		56		57		
Gujarat	4,913	6	6,960	5	14,493	5	7.7
Haryana	4,373	8	5,299	9	10,726	8	5.7
Himachal Pradesh	714		869		1,460		
Jammu & Kashmir	1,167		1,400		2,540		
Jharkhand	–		1,335		2,183		
Karnataka	3,970	10	4,022	11	7,901		
Kerala	2,343		2,063		2,548		
Madhya Pradesh	5,377	4	6,283	7	15,911	3	8.5
Maharashtra	5,193	5	6,769	6	11,655	7	6.2
Manipur	62		77		86		
Meghalaya	59		73		87		
Mizoram	17		15		26		
Nagaland	46		74		73		
Odisha	672		1,342		2,311		
Punjab	7,165	2	8,909	2	12,599	6	6.7
Rajasthan	6,487	3	8,713	3	23,668	2	12.6
Sikkim	35		48		61		
Tamil Nadu	4,061	9	5,474	8	8,362	10	4.5
Telangana (included in Andhra Pradesh till 2013–14)	–		–		5,416		
Tripura	57		87		185		
Uttar Pradesh	12,934	1	17,356	1	30,519	1	16.3
Uttarakhand	–		1,206		1,792		
West Bengal	3,415	12	3,891	12	5,606		
Others	374		427		117		

Source: DAHD (2006, 2014, 2019).

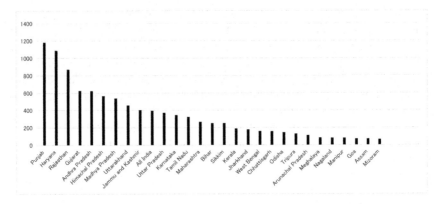

Figure 6.4 Per-capita availability of milk by states, 2018–19 (g/day).

Source: Department of Animal Husbandry & Dairying, Ministry of Fisheries, Animal Husbandry & Dairying, Basic Animal Husbandry Statistics 2019.

followed in descending order of production volume by Rajasthan, Madhya Pradesh, Andhra Pradesh, Gujarat, Punjab, Maharashtra, Haryana, Bihar, and Tamil Nadu. If one compares the ranking of 2018–19 to those of 1997–98, it has changed a bit. Andhra Pradesh, Rajasthan, Bihar, Gujarat, and Madhya Pradesh have ascended the ranking, although Punjab, Maharashtra, Tamil Nadu, and Karnataka have moved lower.

Figure 6.4 shows the per-capita availability of milk by state. The national average per-capita availability of milk was 394 g/day in 2018–19. Only nine states exceeded this figure: two outstanding states are Punjab (1,181 g/day) and Haryana (1,087 g/day), followed by Rajasthan (870 g/day), Gujarat (626 g/day), Andhra Pradesh (623 g/day), Himachal Pradesh (565/day), Madhya Pradesh (538 g/day), Uttarakhand (455 g/day), and Jammu and Kashmir (401 g/day).

Milk and Milk Product Demand

Regarding the demand side of milk production, Table 6.9 shows the changes of percentage values of milk and milk products and food items during 30 days (All India) from 1977–78 to 2011–12. During this period, the percentage of expenditure spent on food declined continually from 64.4 per cent to 48.3 per cent in rural areas and from 60.0 per cent to 37.3 per cent in urban areas. However, if one single out the percentage of milk and milk products from all expenditures in rural areas, it increased from 7.7 per cent in 1977–78 to 10.0 per cent in 1997 and then declined to 7.8 per cent in 2008. However, it rose again from 2010. In urban areas too, it increased from 9.5 per cent in 1977–78 to 10.7 per cent in 1993. Then it shrank to 7.5 per cent in 2012. However, if one examines the percentages of milk and milk products in all food expenditures, it went from 11.9 per cent in 1977–78

Table 6.9 Percentage of consumption of milk and milk production and food items for a period of 30 days in total expenditure: All India (%)

NSS Round	Year	Percentage of milk and milk products expenditure in total expenditure (%)		Percentage of food expenditure in total expenditure (%)		Percentage of expenditure of milk and milk products in total food expenditure (%)	
		Rural	Urban	Rural	Urban	Rural	Urban
32nd	1977–78	7.7	9.5	64.4	60.0	11.9	15.9
38th	1982	7.5	9.2	65.6	58.6	11.5	15.8
42nd	1986–87	9.6	10.5	65.7	57.9	14.6	18.1
43rd	1987–88	8.6	9.5	63.8	55.9	13.5	17.0
44th	1988–89	8.9	10	63.9	57.1	14.0	17.5
45th	1989–90	9.7	9.9	64.3	55.5	15.1	17.9
46th	1990–91	9.4	9.9	66.0	56.9	14.3	17.4
47th	July 1991–Dec.1991	9.0	10.0	63.1	56.1	14.3	17.9
48th	Jan. 1992–Dec. 1992	9.4	10.4	65.0	56.0	14.5	18.6
49th	Jan. 1993–June 1993	9.4	10.7	65.2	57.6	14.4	18.6
50th	July 1993–June 1994	9.5	9.8	63.2	54.7	15.0	17.9
51st	July 1994–June 1995	8.9	9.7	61.0	53.4	14.6	15.9
52nd	July 1995–June 1996	9.4	9.4	60.3	50.1	15.6	18.8
53rd	Jan. 1997–Dec. 1997	10.0	9.7	58.7	49.6	16.9	19.6
54th	Jan. 1998–June 1998	9.6	9.5	60.8	49.6	15.7	19.0
55th	July 1999–June 2000	8.8	8.7	59.4	48.1	14.8	18.1
56th	July 2000–June 2001	8.7	8.3	56.3	43.8	15.5	19.0
57th	July 2001–June 2002	8.4	8.1	55.5	43.1	15.1	18.8
58th	July 2002–Dec. 2002	8.5	7.7	55.0	42.5	15.5	18.1
59th	Jan. 2003–Dec.2003	8.0	7.8	54.0	42.0	14.8	18.6
60th	Jan. 2004–June 2004	8.4	7.8	53.9	41.6	15.6	18.8
61st	July 2004–June 2005	8.5	7.9	55.1	42.5	15.4	18.6
62nd	July 2005–June 2006	8.2	7.3	53.3	40.0	15.4	18.3
63rd	July 2006–June 2007	8.1	7.4	52.3	39.4	15.5	18.8
64th	July 2007–June 2008	7.8	7.3	52.4	39.6	14.9	18.4
66th	July 2009–June 2010	8.6	7.8	53.6	40.7	16.1	19.1
68th	July 2011–June 2012	9.0	7.5	48.3	37.3	18.7	20.2

Source: DAHD (2014); NSSO (2014).

to around 15 per cent from 1989–90 up to 2007–08, and increased sharply from 2009–10 in rural areas. In urban areas too, it stabilizes around 17–19 per cent from 1986–87. In short, although the percentage of milk and milk products in all expenditures shows a declining trend, the percentage of milk and milk products in all food expenditures is growing steadily up to nearly 19 per cent in rural areas and 20 per cent in urban areas.

Table 6.10 shows a percentage breakdown of monthly per capita consumption expenditures (MPCE) by item group for households in different

Table 6.10 Percentage break-up of monthly per-capita consumption expenditure (MPCE) by item group for households in different fractile classes of MPCE in 2011–12 (%)

Item group	Percentage share in total consumption expenditure in each fractile class of MPCE (%)										
	0–10	10–20	20–30	30–40	40–50	50–60	60–70	70–80	80–90	90–100	All classes
Rural											
1. Milk and milk products	4.41	6.05	6.77	8.58	8.95	9.34	10.06	10.20	10.78	9.24	9.02
2. Total food	57.13	56.55	55.47	55.14	54.19	53.05	51.50	49.73	46.38	36.73	48.32
3. Total expenditure	100.00	100.00	100.00	100.00	100.00	100.00	100.00	100.00	100.00	100.00	100.00
4. Share of milk and milk products in total food expenditure (%)	7.73	10.69	12.20	14.55	16.52	17.60	19.53	20.52	23.00	25.16	18.67
Urban											
1. Milk and milk products	6.87	8.60	8.68	9.08	9.00	9.27	8.78	8.39	7.74	5.30	7.53
2. Total food	56.99	52.3	49.7	47.56	45.71	43.52	41.15	38.57	34.78	25.25	37.26
3. Total expenditure	100.00	100.00	100.00	100.00	100.00	100.00	100.00	100.00	100.00	100.00	100.00
4. Share of milk and milk products in total food expenditure (%)	12.16	16.45	17.45	19.09	19.70	21.30	21.33	21.76	22.26	21.00	20.20

Source: NSSO (2014).

fractile classes of MPCE in 2011–12. In both rural and urban areas, the percentage of milk and milk product consumption among all expenditures first increases and then decreases as income rises. In rural areas, the percentage of consumption for milk and milk products in all expenditures peaks at 10.78 per cent at the 80–90 per cent income class. In urban areas, it peaks at 9.27 per cent at 50–60 per cent income class, then declines. Furthermore, if we take the percentage of milk and milk products expenditure among all food expenditures, it continually rises from 7.73 per cent in the bottom 10 per cent income class to 25.16 per cent in the top 10 per cent income class in rural areas. In urban areas, it goes from 12.18 per cent in the bottom 10 per cent income class to 22.26 per cent in the 80–90 per cent income class. Then it finally falls slightly to 21.00 per cent in the top income class. We infer that, in both rural and urban areas, the percentage of milk and milk products of the total food expenditure increases as income rises up to around 25 per cent in rural areas and 22 per cent in urban areas.

Milk Industry Liberalization

Milk Industrial Policy

Dairy and animal husbandry programs were initiated under the Key Village Development Program of the Second Five Year Plan of the Agricultural Ministry, which commenced in 1956. With the growth of the dairy sector, the government created two separate ministries: the Ministry of Food Processing Industries (MFPI) and the Department of Animal Husbandry and Dairying (DAHD). The Indian dairy sector has been protected from foreign competition to achieve the socioeconomic object of alleviating poverty. To develop the domestic livestock and dairy industry, the imports and exports of milk and milk products were strictly regulated by high tariffs, quantitative restrictions, and canalization by the Indian Dairy Corporation, a government agency. Only small-scale enterprises and cooperative societies were eligible to participate in the production and processing of milk. Furthermore, competition among organized sectors was regulated by license. New entry into the dairy sector was prohibited. The development of dairy businesses has been recognized as a measure to create additional income and employment for small and marginal-scale farmers and landless households.

However, de-licensing of the dairy sector in 1991 and the Uruguay Round Agreement on Agriculture of WTO in 1995 turned the Government's approach to the dairy sector from protection to liberalization. De-licensing of the dairy sector in 1991 encouraged private investment.[6] Within a year of de-licensing, over 100 new dairy processing plants arose in the private sector (Sharma, 2004). Faced with a rush of entry by private companies, the Government of India (GOI) promulgated the Milk and Milk Products Order (MMPO) in 1992 under the Essential Commodities Act of 1955 to strengthen regulation again by reason of excess capacity and the sale of contaminated or substandard quality of milk. The MMPO required no permission for units handling less than 10,000 liters of milk per day or milk solids up to 500 tons per annum. Furthermore, MMPO prescribed state registration to plants producing 10,000–75,000 liters of milk per day or manufacturing milk products containing between 500 and 3,750 tons of milk solids per year. Furthermore, plants producing over 75,000 liters of milk per day or more than 3,750 tons of milk solids per year must be registered with the Central Government. These measures restricted new investments from private enterprises and MNCs. Moreover, most manufacturing activities of private companies were restricted to value-added milk products such as baby foods, dairy whitener, and condensed milk. Since then, the GOI amended MMPO from time to time to make it more liberal. Finally, it made a major amendment in March 2002, when restrictions on setting up milk processing and milk products were removed and the concept of the milk shed was also abolished. In addition, restrictions on imports and exports of most livestock products were removed (Sharma, 2004).

The "Amul Model" and "Operation Flood"

The Indian dairy industry has three main characteristics: the ratio of buffalo milk is high; the dairy sector has developed mainly under the cooperative dairy society; and it has tropical dairies. Among these three characteristics, the development of the dairy industry under the cooperative dairy society has been recognized worldwide as a big success story of India's "White Revolution." That is the story of the "Amul Model" or "Operation Flood"[7] (Chandra and Tirupati, 2003).

Table 6.11 presents basic data related to dairy cooperatives, who produce the majority of liquid milk. The number of dairy cooperative societies (DCS) increased rapidly, from 13,284 at the end of fiscal 1981 to 140,227 at the end of 2010. The number of cooperative members also swiftly rose from 17,50,000 at the end of fiscal 1981 to 1,40,71,000 at the end of 2010. The quantity of rural milk procurement increased from 20,070 kg/day at the end of fiscal 2005 to 25,865 kg/day at the end of 2010. The amount of liquid milk sales grew from 1,56,28,000 liters per day to 1,86,14,000 liters per day during the same period. However, huge regional differences are apparent among states.[8] At the end of 2010, the states in which the number of DCS is beyond 20,000 are Maharashtra and Uttar Pradesh. Those with DCS in excess of 10,000 are Rajasthan, Gujarat, Karnataka, and Tamil Nadu. In terms of the number of farmers, Gujarat is at the top, followed by Tamil Nadu, Karnataka, and Maharashtra, by far exceed the totals of the other states. In terms of the quantity of milk procurement at the end of 2010, Gujarat is overwhelming other states: its procurement is 9,054 kg/day, followed in order by Karnataka, Maharashtra, Tamil Nadu, Rajasthan, and Andhra Pradesh. Finally, in terms of the quantity of liquid milk sales, the leading state is again Gujarat, followed by Delhi, Karnataka, and Maharashtra.

Table 6.11 Achievement of some of the key components of dairy development in different states under cooperative sector

States/UT	DCS organized (No.)			Farmer members ('000)			Rural milk procurement ('000 kg/day)			Liquid milk sale ('000 liter/day)	
	As on 30 3.1981	As on 30 3.2005	As on 31 12.201	As on 30 3.1981	As on 30 3.2005	As on 31 12.201	As on 30 3.1981	As on 30 3.2005	As on 31 12.201	As on 30 3.2005	As on 31 12.201
Andhra Pradesh		4,561	4,911		762	842		1,055	1,443	1,028	1,414
Assam		66	66		3	3		4	5	7	12
Bihar		5,023	8,299		254	441		482	736	293	437
Chhattisgarh		445	751		20	31		18	24	30	35
Delhi		–	–		–			–		2,103	3,047
Goa		174	179		19	19		51	36	90	75
Gujarat		11,615	13,890		2,428	2,809		5,857	9,054	2,226	3,204
Haryana		5,172	6,881		239	312		367	522	214	384
Himachal Pradesh		387	795		20	32		28	55	16	18
Jharkhand		80	50		2	1		6	5	173	240
Karnataka		9,619	11,902		1,809	2,052		2,700	3,565	1,597	2,468
Kerala		3,238	3,632		733	775		669	769	801	1,067
Madhya Pradesh		4,815	5,729		239	266		392	525	304	447
Maharashtra		19,192	22,217		1,621	1,845		2,698	3,151	2,595	1,881
Nagaland		76	47		3	2		3	9	4	3
Orissa		1,896	3,203		130	181		164	241	151	264
Pondicherry		100	101		32	39		51	48	59	87
Punjab		6,893	6,904		409	381		780	952	501	723
Rajasthan		10,852	15,956		565	670		1,470	1,654	874	1,365
Sikkim		194	287		7	10		7	12	7	14
Tamil Nadu		8,031	10,038		1,998	2,174		1,981	2,277	1,329	976
Tripura		84	84		4	6		3	2	9	13
Uttar Pradesh		18,272	21,343		845	971		958	518	425	402
West Bengal		2,367	2,962		184	210		326	262	792	38
Total	13,284	1,13,152	1,40,227	1,750	12,326	14,071	940	20,070	25,865	15,628	18,614

Source: DAHD (2006, 2010); Birthal (2008).

Dairy Industry Development Since Liberalization

Table 6.12 shows the numbers and capacities of dairy plants registered under the MMPO (both under the central authority and state registering authorities) as of the end of fiscal 2011 by state and organization. Among the total 1,065 plants, the number of cooperative plants was 263 (24.7 per cent), private plants were 765 (71.8 per cent), and government plants were 37 (3.5 per cent). Furthermore, of the total capacity of 120,548 thousand liters/day, that of cooperatives was 4,32,51,000 liters/day (35.9 per cent), that of the private sector was 7,32,52,000 liters/day (60.8 per cent), and that of the government sector was 40,46,000 liters/day (3.4 per cent). Both in numbers and in capacity, the private sector figure far exceeded those of cooperatives. One can infer that today the dairy cooperatives are no more outshining all other actors, but rather private companies, including foreign capital, is more prevalent.

However, here again, there are huge differences among states. The capacity of the states/UT in which the percentage of the cooperative society exceed the national average of 35.9 per cent were Chhattisgarh (100 per cent), Puducherry (100 per cent), Tripura (100 per cent), Gujarat (90.9 per cent), Karnataka (89.9 per cent), Orissa (87.5 per cent), Kerala (76.6 per cent), Bihar (63.6 per cent), Tamil Nadu (43.2 per cent), Rajasthan (41.9 per cent), and West Bengal (41.6 per cent). The states/UT in which the percentage of the private sector exceeds the national average of 60.8 per cent were Jammu and Kashmir (100.0 per cent), Goa (95.7 per cent), Himachal Pradesh (90.1 per cent), Uttar Pradesh (90.1 per cent), Delhi (87.5 per cent), Haryana (82.0 per cent), Madhya Pradesh (80.1 per cent), Punjab (78.2 per cent), and Andhra Pradesh (72.6 per cent).

Table 6.13 presents a comparison of rankings of state-wise milk procurement by dairy cooperatives and milk production in 2010–11. The ranking of milk procurement by dairy cooperatives and that of milk production differs considerably. If one selects the top 12 states in milk procurement by dairy cooperatives, the states in which the percentage of milk procurement in all procurement exceeds the percentage of milk production in all milk production are Gujarat (+12.9 per cent), Karnataka (+10.3 per cent), Tamil Nadu (+9.4 per cent), Maharashtra (+6.2 per cent), and Kerala (+3.7 per cent). The figures in parentheses denote the percentage figure of milk procurement minus the percentage figure of milk production. In all these states, dairy cooperatives are active. However, the states where the percentage of milk procurement by dairy cooperatives was less than that of milk production were Uttar Pradesh (−10.5 per cent), Rajasthan (−6.3 per cent), Punjab (−5.0 per cent), Madhya Pradesh (−4.3 per cent), Andhra Pradesh (−3.4 per cent), Haryana (−2.9 per cent), West Bengal (−2.2 per cent), and Bihar (−1.7 per cent). Among these states, Uttar Pradesh, Punjab, Madhya Pradesh, Haryana, and Andhra Pradesh have active private dairies. In the states where both the activities of dairy cooperatives are weak and milk production high, private companies tend to enter the market positively.

Table 6.12 Number of dairy plants registered under milk and milk products ordinance (1992) as on March 31, 2011 (Capacity: '000 liter/day)

States/UT	Cooperative			Private			Government			Total		
	No.	Capacity	(%)	No.	Capacity	(%)	No.	Capacity	(%)	No.	Capacity	(%)
Andhra Pradesh	9	2,150	27.4	39	5,693	72.6	0	0	0.0	48	7,843	100.0
Bihar	10	700	63.6	2	400	36.4	0	0	0.0	12	1,100	100.0
Chhattisgarh	1	100	100.0	0	0	0.0	0	0	0.0	1	100	100.0
Delhi	0	0	0.0	1	3,500	87.5	1	500	12.5	2	4,000	100.0
Goa	1	30	4.3	3	670	95.7	0	0	0.0	4	700	100.0
Gujarat	33	13,160	90.9	15	917	6.3	2	400	2.8	50	14,477	100.0
Haryana	5	470	15.9	31	2,417	82.0	1	60	2.0	37	2,947	100.0
Himachal Pradesh	3	60	9.9	4	545	90.1	0	0	0.0	7	605	100.0
Jammu & Kashmir	0	0	0.0	1	30	100.0	0	0	0.0	1	30	100.0
Karnataka	16	4,323	89.9	8	485	10.1	0	0	0.0	24	4,808	100.0
Kerala	15	1,223	76.6	10	373	23.4	0	0	0.0	25	1,596	100.0
Madhya Pradesh	5	1,000	19.9	35	4,013	80.1	0	0	0.0	40	5,013	100.0
Maharashtra	86	7,865	29.6	276	15,641	58.8	33	3,086	11.6	395	26,592	100.0
Orissa	13	523	87.5	2	75	12.5	0	0	0.0	15	598	100.0
Puducherry	1	50	100.0	0	0	0.0	0	0	0.0	1	50	100.0
Punjab	13	1,820	21.8	64	6,529	78.2	0	0	0.0	77	8,349	100.0
Rajasthan	18	2,420	41.9	20	3,361	58.1	0	0	0.0	38	5,781	100.0
Sikkim	1	25	100.0	0	0	0.0	0	0	0.0	1	25	100.0
Tamil Nadu	11	4,030	43.2	26	5,289	56.8	0	0	0.0	37	9,319	100.0
Tripura	1	10	100.0	0	0	0.0	0	0	0.0	1	10	100.0
Uttar Pradesh	35	2,476	9.9	216	22,569	90.1	0	0	0.0	251	25,045	100.0
West Bengal	3	816	41.6	12	1,145	58.4	0	0	0.0	15	1,961	100.0
Total	263	43,251	35.9	765	73,252	60.8	37	4,046	3.4	1065	1,20,548	100.0

Source: DAHD (2012).

Table 6.13 Activities of dairy cooperative society and production of milk by state in 2010–11

States/UT	Activities of dairy cooperative society				Milk production			
	Numbers	Rural milk procurement			('000 tons)	Ranking	(2) Share to the total (%)	(1)–(2) (%)
		('000 kg/day)	Ranking	(1) Share to the total (%)				
All India	1,44,246	14,461		100.0	1,21,848		100.0	
Andhra Pradesh	4,964	846	7	5.8	11,203	3	9.2	−3.4
Assam	145	4			790			
Bihar	9,425	523	9	3.6	6,517	9	5.3	−1.7
Chhattisgarh	757	31			1,029			
Goa	178	19			60			
Gujarat	14,347	2,970	1	20.5	9,321	5	7.6	12.9
Haryana	7,019	313	11	2.2	6,267	10	5.1	−2.9
Himachal Pradesh	803	33			1,102			
Jharkhand	53	1			1,555			
Karnataka	12,273	2,091	3	14.5	5,114	11	4.2	10.3
Kerala	3,666	851	6	5.9	2,645	13	2.2	3.7
Madhya Pradesh	6,216	271	12	1.9	7,514	7	6.2	−4.3
Maharashtra	22,378	1,845	4	12.8	8,044	6	6.6	6.2
Nagaland	49	2			76			
Orissa	3,256	187			1,671			
Punjab	7,069	386	10	2.7	9,423	4	7.7	−5.0
Rajasthan	16,290	670	8	4.6	13,234	2	10.9	−6.3
Sikkim	287	10			43			
Tamil Nadu	10,079	2,176	2	15.0	6,831	8	5.6	9.4
Tripura	84	6			104			
Uttar Pradesh	21,793	977	5	6.8	21,031	1	17.3	−10.5
West Bengal	3,012	213	13	1.5	4,471	12	3.7	−2.2

Source: DAHD (2012).

Among private dairy companies, there are nine large companies with handling capacity greater than 100 million liters per day. These are Nestle India (Gurgaon, Haryana), Milkfood Ltd. (Patiala, Punjab), Hatsun Agro (Chennai, Tamil Nadu), Heritage Foods (Hyderabad, Telangana), Tirumala Milk Products (Chennai, Tamil Nadu), Paras Dairy (Sahibabad, Uttar Pradesh), Sterling Agro Industries (New Delhi), Dynamix Dairy Industries (Mumbai, Maharashtra), and Bhole Baba Dairy Industries (Agra, Uttar Pradesh). Out of these nine companies, only Nestle India was established before 1992, when milk businesses were de-licensed. The first dairy plant of Nestle India was established in 1961 in Moga, a backward area of Punjab. The other eight companies are new entrants after de-licensing. In addition, there are some private dairy companies with milk handling capacity between 50 and 100 million liters per day, such as Parag Milk Foods (Pune, Maharashtra), Prabhat Dairy (Ahmednagar, Maharashtra), Chitale Dairy (Sangli, Maharashtra), Dodla Dairy (Hyderabad, Telangana), Creamline Dairy Products (Hyderabad, Telangana), SMC Foods (Saharanpur, Uttar Pradesh), and Gopaljee Dairy Foods (Noida, Uttar Pradesh) (Chandramogan, 2013). Among these large private dairy companies, the largest is Hatsun Agro Product Ltd. based in Chennai. It was founded by R. G. Chandramogan in 1986. They collect milk from 320,000 farmers at 5,600 "Hatsun Milk Banks" covering over 9,500 villages. 320,000 liters milk per day is procured. Furthermore, they have 87 chilling centers and more than 1,348 contract vehicles (http://www.hatsun.com). A remarkable aspect of the growth of private dairies is that it has come about with no subsidies or support from the Operation Flood program.

Among these big private dairy processing companies, Nestle India and Dynamix Dairy Industries have adopted a dairy contract farming system.[9] Nestle India is now the largest private dairy company in Punjab. They collected from nearly 100,000 farmers through 1,700 collection centers in 2005–06. Nestle India gives special support to large-scale farmers: "In addition to management techniques, it provides milk cans to large-scale farmers, chilling tanks at the farm gate and milking machines at low cost and credit to even larger ones" (The World Bank, 2011: 77).

Management Innovation at Amul and Mother Dairy

As described above, after the liberalization of the dairy industry, many private companies entered the dairy sector, where they compete with dairy cooperatives. Under such circumstances, an important issue for the future of the dairy industry in India is how dairy cooperatives respond to such competition (Rangasamy and Dhaka, 2007; Singh, 2007; World Bank, 2011: 78–80). Faced with these new situations, the most successfully and aggressively responding ones are a dairy cooperative Amul and a government dairy company Mother Dairy.

After the liberalization of the dairy industry, Amul (GCMMF) hastened the pace of its management innovation. In 1995, they introduced ICT technology integration as a strategic thrust: automatic milk collection systems called Automatic Milk Collection Unit Systems (AMCUS), e-mail and internet connectivity at the village level, customized enterprise resource planning for manufacturing units, cyber-shops throughout India and in some parts of the USA, Singapore, and Dubai, and geographical information systems (GIS) with digital city maps at major cities implemented for distribution planning were introduced. Furthermore, all sales offices spread throughout the country have e-mail connectivity and send daily reports related to sales and inventory to Anand (Bowonder, Prasad, and Kotla, 2005; Operational Flood & Amul India Story, 2007). Today Amul is the largest food brand in India. The member farmers amount to 2.35 million, and the number of village cooperative societies amounts to 11,400. They produce milk, milk powder, butter, ghee, cheese, chocolate, ice cream, pizza, sweets, flavored milk, and soup. The 3,000 dealers sell to 5,00,000 retail shops. "Amul Baby" of Amul is a well-known mascot image in India.

On the other hand, Mother Dairy based in Delhi is a wholly owned subsidiary of NDDB under the OP Program 1974. They buy all liquid milk from dairy cooperative societies through the State Federation of Dairy Cooperatives. Furthermore, they buy vegetables and fruits from farmers and the federation of producers. They buy oil seeds from oil seed farmers' cooperatives and sell "Dhara" brand edible oil nationwide. In 1988, NDDB set up a fruit and vegetable project and started to sell products under the "Safal" brand. In April 2004, Mother Dairy Fruit & Vegetable Pvt. Ltd. (MDFVL) was established, integrating its milk department and fruits and vegetable department. Later, MDFVL became a holding company of Mother Dairy India Ltd. (MDIL) as a sales company and Mother Dairy Processing Ltd. (MDFP) as a production company. MDFP has various units across India. Mother Dairy (Delhi) is a unit of MFDP. Since its founding in 1974, Mother Dairy sold only liquid milk for 22 years. However, in 1966 they started to manufacture ice cream. Since then, they have produced curd, flavored milk, lassi, mishti dahi, butter, ghee, long-life milk, cheese, and milk with vitamin A as a social contribution. Furthermore, under the Safal brand, they produce frozen vegetables, fruit juices, and so on.

In the National Capital Region (NCR) of Delhi, the strongest rival of Mother Dairy is Amul, GCMMF. It is interesting that the two organizations under NDDB are each other's strongest rivals. Turnover of GCMMF is 2.5 times greater than that of Mother Dairy in the national market. The fundamental difference from Amul is that MDFLV is registered under company law. NDDB promotes the conversion of the dairy cooperative society to a company. Here, "economic trust" more than "social trust" is regarded as important. Under company law, milk producers are recognized as company members. This move is a measure freed from oft-repeated political interventions in dairy cooperative societies and responding to fierce market competition.

Emergence of Commercial Dairy Farming

Alongside the mushrooming development of private dairy companies, another notable new development is the emergence of commercial dairy farming. One representative type of the latter is the commercial dairy farms run by the so-called "progressive dairy farmers." The progressive dairy farmers' movement started in Punjab. The Progressive Dairy Farmers Association (PDFA) was established in 1972 based in Ludhiana, Punjab under the technical support of Punjab Agricultural University. The main objectives of PDFA are to procure better milk procurement prices for member farmers tying up with MILKFED Punjab[10] and to provide better technical and medical support to member farmers. Today the member farmers of PDFA are about 6,000. Average farm size varies from 10 to 500 high-yielding crossbred cows. Furthermore, the production of milk by these farms is about 1.2–1.5 million liters per day (in total, nearly 800,000 liters per day). The average yield of a cow is nearly 8,000 liters in a lactation cycle, against the national average of 1,500 liters. Therefore, this is sometimes designated as a "Second White Revolution." About 80 per cent of the members are between 22 and 45 years of age and educated youths. Most members have machine milking, with open and well-ventilated sheds that are especially constructed to suit the needs of crossbred cows, provisions for silage making, total mix ration (TMR) wagons, and other provisions designed to maximize profit. Furthermore, PDFA incorporated Progressive Dairy Solutions (PDS) Pvt. Ltd. to introduce consumers to high-quality milk, an own brand milk named "La Pure," which they produce.

PDFA set up the All India Dairy Farmers Association in 2012 to replicate its success in other states. Its main objectives are to provide dairy farmers with the technical know-how in setting up commercial dairies and other relevant information. Today, we can find PDFAs in Andhra Pradesh, Gujarat, and Madhya Pradesh, and more PDFAs will appear in Haryana and Chhattisgarh. On top of members of PDFA, there are many commercial dairy farms across India.[11]

One notable trend among commercial dairy farmers is the preference for cow milk over buffalo milk (Chand, Singh, and Singh, 2002). "La Pure," produced by PDFA, is one brand. Another interesting case is the production of organic milk. Parag Milk Foods at Pune is the pioneer company producing organic farm-fresh milk under the brand name "Pride of Cows." Parag Milk Foods have Bhagyalaxmi Dairy Farm in Manchar, Maharashtra, where they rear 4,000 cows. It follows Sarda Farms in Nasik, Landmark Dairy in Gurgaon, and so on. It is interesting that all the founders of these commercial dairy farmers and producers of milk (all of them use farm-to-home delivery systems) come from outside of agriculture. For example, Sarda Farms has 700 cows on 20 acres and another 30 acres of open land. The Landmark Group has 1,200 cows on 250 acres of land (*The Telegraph*, "The New Milky Way").[12]

Conclusion: Effects of Demand-Led Growth on Indian Rural Society

With the promotion of economic liberalization starting in 1991, the globalization of the Indian economy has been expanding quickly. The dairy industry, which used to be a typical import-substituting industry, is not an exception. Here again, a policy shifts to de-license and liberalize private companies has occurred. Furthermore, with the development of economic liberalization, the per-capita income is rising, urbanization is progressing, the population of young people is growing, and the modernization of Indian society in all aspects of life is rapidly taking place. An especially notable phenomenon is the changing lifestyle of the urban population: the increase of nuclear families, modernization of transport, increased use of credit cards, increased social activities of women, and the market penetration of electronic goods such as refrigerators and ovens. These changes in lifestyle accompany a sweeping change in consumption patterns in urban as well as rural areas, especially in the former. Demand for the food service industry and high value-added foods is rising. Among high value-added foods, the most conspicuously increasing consumption goods are milk and milk products, poultry, and eggs.

In the dairy industry, on top of dairy cooperative societies, many private companies have participated in milk processing industries. Because of this, modernization of the distribution system and commercialization of the milk processing industry started to change. Management innovation depending on ICT technology is accelerated, market infrastructure is under construction, and market access is improving. The basic idea or philosophy of the "development of dairy industry for eradicating poverty" is also changing to "development of market-oriented modern dairy business."

These various new movements in the dairy industry, led by the consumption revolution, are also changing rural society. The most notable change is the breakdown of the mixed crop–livestock system. It is a well-known fact that the number of bullocks had been decreasing with the advancement of mechanization under the "Green Revolution" that started in the late 1960s. Furthermore, the "White Revolution," initiated in the 1970s, further decreased the number of bullocks. Then specialization in milk cattle for the dairy industry started. Liberalization of the dairy industry, which began in the 1990s, is accelerating this movement. The "Second White Revolution" is occurring, although large regional differences exist. Today, private milk processing companies are competing with dairy cooperatives. Moreover, private commercial dairy farms are quickly increasing in number. The commercial dairy farms have nothing to do with the traditional crop–livestock system. Because of this movement, the breakdown of the traditional crop–livestock system is accelerating. Furthermore, landless households are exiting from livestock activity, whereas farmers with more than small landholdings are further specializing in milk production or converting to "progressive dairy farmers." Today these trends remain confined to some states, but they are expected to continue intensifying, along with a stark division of labor between agriculture and livestock and development of modern commercial dairies that have no relation to the traditional crop–livestock system.

Notes

1 However, one must remain aware that only 24 per cent of the total milk output in India is consumed through formal chains. It is estimated that about 40 per cent of milk output is consumed by the producers themselves and that 60 per cent is marketed, of which 36 per cent passes through informal chains and 24 per cent passes through formal chains managed by cooperatives, the private sector, and government parastatals (World Bank, 2011: 70).

2 NSSO defines "operational landholding" as "a techno-economic unit that is wholly or partially for agricultural production and operated by one person alone or with the assistance of others, without regard to title, size, or location."

3 Among the cattle and buffaloes, those which were in milk on the day of the survey were counted as "in-milk" class. Those which had calved at least once and were not in milk on the date of survey but which had the potential of coming in milk in the future were counted as "dry." The combined class of in-milk and dry cattle and buffaloes is called "milch" animals.

4 GVA (Gross Value Added) is used after 2011–12.

5 The country is reported to be in deficit in dry fodder by 11 per cent, in green fodder by 35 per cent, and in concentrate feed by 28 per cent (Birthal and Negi, 2012).

6 But no foreign capital has newly entered India.

7 Operation Flood means "to fulfil all around India with a flood of milk."

8 This mixed record of dairy cooperatives arises from differences of management of dairy cooperatives. Lack of competition, deviation from the Anand model, political intervention, and poor delivery of inputs and services are some reasons for the inefficiencies that are prevalent among some dairy cooperatives (World Bank, 2011: 73).

9 Contract farming of milk in Jaipur and Sikar, Rajasthan, is explained well by Birthal, Jha, Tiongco, and Narrod (2009).

10 MILLFED Punjab is a popular name of The Punjab State Cooperative Milk Producer's Federation Limited. It is a state-level cooperative federation like GCMMF in Gujarat. MILKFED Punjab was established in 1973 under the company law like Mother Dairy. Its producer members are more than 409,000. It has 6,893 village dairy cooperative societies, 11 District Unions, and 13 dairy plants. The brand name of its products is "Verka" (World Bank, 2011: 84).

11 For a discussion of commercial dairy farms of Bikaner, Rajasthan, good information is provided by Chand, Singh and Singh (2002). Regarding those of Ahmednagar district of Maharashtra, a study by Ghule, Verma, Cahuhan, and Sawale (2012) is helpful.

12 Many of such cases might be designated as "semi-formal chains" (The World Bank, 2011: 82–83). The author visited A Dairy (pseudonym) based in Chennai on January 6, 2016. They deliver farm-fresh milk directly from their farm to homes. Their number of customers is 1,600. They have 85 crossbred cows (i.e., HF and Jersey) on farmland in Ponthavakkam village, about 70 km from Chennai. The cows are fed with green fodders cultivated in their own farm

of eight acres. They sell "raw cow milk," which means "not processed," i.e., neither pasteurized nor homogenized. Their fresh milk in one liter glass bottles costs Rs. 75, which is much more expensive than normal processed milk that costs about Rs. 40 per liter. A Dairy was established in 2012. They were a textile exporter but converted their business to a commercial dairy.

References

Birthal, P. S. (2008) "Linking Smallholder Livestock Producers to Markets: Issues and Approaches," *Indian Journal of Agricultural Economics*, 63(1): 19–37.

Birthal, P. S., Jha, A. K., Tiongco, M. M., and Narrod, C. (2009) "Farm-Level Impacts of Vertical Coordination of the Food Supply Chains: Evidence from Contract Farming of Milk in India," *Indian Journal of Agricultural Economics*, 64(3): 481–96.

Birthal, P. S. and Negi, D. S. (2012) "Livestock for Higher, Sustainable and Inclusive Agricultural Growth," *Economic and Political Weekly*, 47(26/27): 89–99.

Bowonder, B., Prasad, B. R. R. and Kotla, A. (2005) "ITC Application in a Dairy Industry: The e-Experience of Amul," *International Journal of Services Technology and Management*, 6(3/4/5). (https://www.semanticscholar, Access: August 13, 2022).

Chand, R. and Raju, S. S. (2008) "Livestock Sector Composition and Factors affecting Its Growth," *Indian Journal of Agricultural Economics*, 63(2): 198–210.

Chand, K., Singh, K. and Singh R. V. (2002) "Economic Analysis of Commercial Dairy Herds in Arid Region of Rajasthan," *Indian Journal of Agricultural Economics*, 57(2): 224–33.

Chandra, P., and Tirupati, D. (2003) Business Strategies for Managing Complex Supply Chains in Large Emerging Economies: The Story of AMUL, Indian Institute Management, Ahmedabad, April 2003 (www.iimb.emet.in/~chandra/AMULpaper2.pdf, Access: January 25, 2016).

Chandramogan, R. G. (2013) "Private Sector's White Revolution," *Business Line*, January 17 (https://www.thehindubusinessline.com, Access: August 14, 2022).

DAHD (Department of Animal Husbandry, Dairying & Fisheries, Ministry of Agriculture) (2006) *Basic Animal Husbandry Statistics 2006*. AHS Series 10.

DAHD (Department of Animal Husbandry, Dairying & Fisheries, Ministry of Agriculture) (2010) *Basic Animal Husbandry Statistics 2010*. AHS Series 12.

DAHD (Department of Animal Husbandry, Dairying & Fisheries, Ministry of Agriculture) (2012) *Basic Animal Husbandry Statistics 2012*. AHS Series 13.

DAHD (Department of Animal Husbandry, Dairying & Fisheries, Ministry of Agriculture) (2014) *Basic Animal Husbandry & Fisheries Statistics 2014*. AHS Series 15.

DAHD (Department of Animal Husbandry and Dairying, Ministry of Fisheries, Animal Husbandry & Dairying) (2019) *Basic Animal Husbandry Statistics 2019*.

Datta, T. N. and Dadhich, C. L. (2007) "Operational Land Holdings and Ownership of Dairy Animal in India," *Sarvekshana*, 92nd Issue, 27(3/4).

Ghule, A. K., Verma, N. K., Cahuhan, A. K. and Sawale, P. (2012) "An Economic Analysis of Investment Pattern, Cost of Milk Production and Profitability of Commercial Dairy Farms in Maharashtra," *Indian Journal of Dairy Science*, 65(4): 329–36.

Kumar, A. and Singh, D. K. (2008) "Livestock Production Systems in India: An Appraisal across Agro-Ecological Regions," *Indian Journal of Agricultural Economics*, 63(4): 577–97.

NSSO (2006) *Livestock Ownership Across Operational Land Holding Classes in India, 2002–03*, NSS 59th Round (January–December 2003).

NSSO (2014) *Level and Pattern of Consumer Expenditure, 2011–12*, NSS 68th Round (July 2011–June 2012).

Operational Flood & Amul India Story (2007) *"Symposium on Trade Networking for Cooperatives*, International *Cooperative Alliance*," June 26 (http://www.docstec.com/docs/65904925/Amul-Branding-Strategy#, Access: January 25, 2015).

Rangasamy, N. and Dhaka, J. P. (2007) "Milk Procurement Cost for Co-operative and Private Dairy Plants in Tamil Nadu — A Comparison," *Indian Journal of Agricultural Economics*, 62(2): 679–93.

Reardon, T. and Gulati, A. (2008) *The Rise of Supermarkets and their Development Implications: International Experience Relevant for India*, February 2008, IFPRI Discussion Paper 00752. New Delhi Office.

Shah, J. and Dave, D. (2010) "A Shift from Crop-Mixed Traditional Dairying to Market-Oriented Organised Dairy Farming–Plausible Factors Responsible for Structural Transformation in Indian Dairy Sector," *Indian Journal of Agricultural Economics*, 65(2): 298–307.

Sharma, V. P. (2004) "Livestock Economy of India: Current Status, Emerging issues and Long-Term Prospects," *Indian Journal of Agricultural Economics*, 59(3): 512–54.

Singh, S. (2007) "Marketing of Liquid Milk: A Case Study of Ahmedabad Milk Market," *Indian Journal of Agricultural Economics*, 62(3): 440–47.

The Telegraph (2014) "The New Milky Way" (http://www.telegraphindia.com/1140119/jsp/graphiti/17782776.jsp)

World Bank (2011) *Demand-led Transformation of the Livestock Sector in India: Achievements, Challenges, and Opportunities*, Washington D.C.: The World Bank.

7 Disparities in Convergence

Rural–Urban Child Welfare in India

Kazuya Wada

In India, large populations live in rural areas, but that situation is changing gradually. The rural populace, which accounted for 74.3 per cent of the population in 1991, decreased to 72.2 per cent in 2001 and 68.8 per cent in 2011, suggesting a rising importance of urban population. Although the fact remains that rural areas are crucial residential regions, urban areas are steadily gaining in prominence in the context of India's remarkable economic growth. Rural areas cannot help but be affected by this sweeping socioeconomic change. This chapter, presenting an overview of household data in India, specifically examines people's lives in the middle 2000s, how differences between rural and urban areas have changed, and the nature of remaining problems.

The Indian socioeconomy has experienced considerable change since the 1980s, bringing about great improvements in infrastructure such as electricity, drinking water plumbing, sewage systems, and communication. According to household surveys, the prevalence of electricity was 59 per cent in 1992–93, 67 per cent in 1998–99, and 79 per cent in 2005–06. Although the number of fixed telephones increased moderately, it is noteworthy that mobile phone usage has spread rapidly among all Indian people. The International Telecommunication Union reported that there were 3.6 million mobile phone subscriptions in 2000, 13 million in 2002, and 166 million in 2006. This figure rose to 865 million in 2012, reflecting a remarkable rate of increase. This explosive growth of mobile telephony suggests a brisk economy, although it is apparent not only in India but in every economically developing country.

In addition, the quality of people's lives in India is transforming too. For example, child mortality is an important index that represents the quality of life (QOL) of individuals, as shown in the fourth goal of the Millennium Development Goals. The child mortality rate in India was historically quite high. The Census of India shows that it exceeded 200 in many districts in 1981. Fortunately, circumstances have improved radically. The child mortality rate decreased steadily to 109.3 in 1992–93, 94.9 in 1998–99, and 74.3 in 2005–06, implying the promotion of health-related knowledge and improvements in sanitary infrastructure. Educational surroundings have also improved. The

DOI: 10.4324/9781003311898-8

literacy rate, which was 36 per cent in 1981, increased to 55 per cent in 2001, reflecting the markedly enhanced educational infrastructure.

As presented above, socioeconomic changes are salient in today's India. However, it is noteworthy that they were not always homogeneous throughout the country. They vary from region to region, and rural–urban differences demand attention. These persistent characteristics have been pointed out and monitored over many years in studies. For example, the prevalence of electricity in 2005–06 was 96 per cent in Punjab, but no more than 28 per cent in Bihar; 93 per cent in urban areas and 56 per cent in rural areas. Similarly, the child mortality rate was 52 ‰ in Punjab, but it was no less than 85 ‰ in Bihar; 52 ‰ in urban areas, and 82 ‰ in rural areas. One can readily observe remarkable regional diversity and wide rural–urban disparity. In spite of those figures, it is possible that the recent socioeconomic changes had no small effect on regional diversity and reduced the rural–urban difference. This might alter the stereotypes that many people foster in their image of India.

In the next section onwards, the regional diversity and the rural–urban differences, especially in child mortality, are studied using household data. This chapter examines the effects of "living in urban areas" and "living in rural areas" on the QOL and the factors producing inter-state differences.

Differences in Rural–Urban Child Mortality

Through an examination of National Family Health Survey (NFHS) information, one can outline the environment of people's lives in India. The NFHS, a large sample survey, mainly examines the health conditions of married women and children and includes information related to household member characteristics, household economic status, and the surroundings of households. The NFHS was administered in 1992–93 (NFHS-1), 1998–99 (NFHS-2), and 2005–06 (NFHS-3).[1] To outline and assess the 1990s and the 2000s, this study uses NFHS-1 and NFHS-3. In addition, 14 states that account for more than 90 per cent of India's population receive specific attention.[2] In 1992–93 NFHS (NFHS-1), interviews were conducted across 24 states and the National Capital Territory of Delhi with a nationally representative sample of 89,777 currently or previously married (ever-married) women aged 13–49 years. The 2005–06 NFHS (NFHS-3) was conducted in all states and assessed married women aged 15–49 years. The number of observations was 124,385.

Table 7.1 presents the child mortality rate trend[3] between 1992–93 and 2005–06. In 1992–93, the child mortality rate in India was 109.3 ‰, but it decreased greatly to 74.3 ‰ in 2005–06, suggesting that QOL had improved by about one-third during that period. Although the improvement is expected to be conspicuous, there is room for additional improvement, considering that the figure is less than 10 ‰ in economically developed countries. Differences among states also deserve attention.

Table 7.1 Child mortality rate (‰)

	1992–93 (NFHS-1)	2005–06 (NFHS-3)
Punjab	68.0	52.0
Uttarakhand	–	56.8
Haryana	98.7	52.3
Rajasthan	102.6	85.4
Uttar Pradesh	141.3	96.4
Bihar	127.5	84.8
West Bengal	99.3	59.6
Jharkhand	–	93.0
Orissa	131.0	90.6
Chhattisgarh	–	90.3
Madhya Pradesh	130.3	94.2
Gujarat	104.0	60.9
Maharashtra	70.3	46.7
Andhra Pradesh	91.2	63.2
Karnataka	87.3	54.7
Kerala	32.0	16.3
Tamil Nadu	86.5	35.5
India	109.3	74.3

Source: IIPS (1995: 221) and IIPS (2006: 187).

Uttar Pradesh had the highest child mortality rate in 1992–93 (141.3 ‰); Kerala had the lowest (32.0 ‰). In 2005–05, as in 1992–93, the highest child mortality rate was found in Uttar Pradesh (96.4 ‰); the lowest was found in Kerala (16.3 ‰). Kerala also achieved the greatest drop in child mortality, to 49 per cent of its earlier value. In Uttar Pradesh, the child mortality rate fell by 32 per cent. The greatest rate decrease was achieved in Tamil Nadu, where it shrank by 51 per cent from 86.5 ‰ to 35.5 ‰. Regarding large decreases in the child mortality rate, Haryana (47 per cent) and Gujarat (41 per cent) are noteworthy. The smallest decrease was 17 per cent in Rajasthan. The child mortality rate there was close to that of Uttar Pradesh.[4] The decline was slight in Punjab (23 per cent) and Madhya Pradesh (28 per cent). On average, India has attained improvement in the child mortality rate during these periods, but inter-state diversity remained large.

Table 7.2 presents crude death rates for children under five years old[5] in urban and rural areas in 1992–93 and 2005–06. In urban areas, 1992–93, the crude death rate was the highest in Orissa (87.3 ‰) and the lowest in Kerala (9.6 ‰). In rural areas, too, Orissa was the highest (121.1 ‰) and Kerala the lowest (32.5 ‰). Compared with urban areas, rural areas show high crude death rates, with considerable variation between states. The rural area of Kerala had a crude death rate more than three times higher than the urban area. In Madhya Pradesh and Uttar Pradesh, the corresponding rates of rural areas were about twice as high as those of urban areas. Karnataka, for example, shows almost identical figures for urban and rural areas. In

Table 7.2 Crude death rate (‰)

1992–93 (NFHS-1)	Total	Urban	Rural	2005–06 (NFHS-3)	Total	Urban	Rural
Punjab	61.7	47.2	66.2	Punjab	46.5	46.1	46.7
Uttarakhand	–	–	–	Uttarakhand	52.8	34.6	59.3
Haryana	80.8	57.3	91.2	Haryana	47.4	17.5	55.7
Rajasthan	86.2	69.6	89.4	Rajasthan	76.6	75.2	77.1
Uttar Pradesh	108.1	60.2	118.1	Uttar Pradesh	80.0	67.6	86.3
Bihar	100.2	77.2	105.8	Bihar	69.1	61.3	72.7
West Bengal	79.9	58.5	84.1	West Bengal	52.3	46.2	56.4
Jharkhand	–	–	–	Jharkhand	75.5	51.4	85.1
Orissa	112.3	87.3	121.1	Orissa	68.3	41.2	77.1
Chhattisgarh	–	–	–	Chhattisgarh	73.6	52.1	80.7
Madhya Pradesh	96.1	51.5	108.2	Madhya Pradesh	73.9	52.1	89.6
Gujarat	86.0	69.9	93.1	Gujarat	58.5	39.5	69.4
Maharashtra	57.9	40.7	68.6	Maharashtra	43.8	37.6	55.4
Andhra Pradesh	76.7	54.6	84.1	Andhra Pradesh	41.4	27.7	64.7
Karnataka	69.0	64.2	71.0	Karnataka	50.6	41.5	55.5
Kerala	26.7	9.6	32.5	Kerala	19.1	16.3	20.5
Tamil Nadu	67.8	56.1	74.1	Tamil Nadu	34.7	28.3	41.3
India	80.5	58.9	88.6	India	57.1	45.1	64.3

Source: Calculated by the author from NFHS-1 and NFHS-3 using data of children born during the five-year periods preceding the survey.

2005–06, rural areas displayed higher rates than urban areas. Regarding urban areas, the lowest rate was achieved in Haryana (17.5 ‰), although the highest was in Rajasthan (75.2 ‰). Among rural areas, Madhya Pradesh had the highest rate (89.6 ‰), although Kerala had the lowest (20.5 ‰). As was true for 1992–93, the regional diversity is noteworthy. In Haryana, the crude death rate in rural areas was about three times that in urban areas, although Punjab and Rajasthan had almost identical figures in both types of areas.

The crude death rate in urban areas in India decreased from 58.9 ‰ in 1992–93 to 45.1 ‰ in 2005–06. In rural areas, it fell from 88.6 ‰ to 64.3 ‰. Their respective decreases over that time were 23.4 per cent and 27.4 per cent. The rate of rural areas is higher than that of urban areas, implying that the discrepancies between urban and rural areas were gradually redressed. The rate of decline in urban areas was the highest in Haryana (69 per cent), although Kerala, Rajasthan, Uttar Pradesh, and Madhya Pradesh showed increased crude death rates. Some states, such as Punjab, exhibited a reduction in the crude death rate and higher rates of decrease in rural areas than in urban areas. Urban areas improved at higher rates than rural areas in other states, such as Tamil Nadu. Children residing in rural areas and those in urban areas certainly showed improved survival, but variation between states persisted in the 2000s. The next section examines factors affecting rural–urban differences in child welfare.

Empirical Analysis

Effects of Rural Dummy and State Dummies

This section, employing NFHS-1 and NFHS-3, conducts empirical analyses to explore what factors generate differences in child welfare. The dependent variable is the index that takes 1 if the child who was born in the five-year periods preceding the survey died younger than five years old and 0 otherwise. The independent variables are parents' age and schooling years, the number of children ever born, wealth index,[6] electricity dummy,[7] rural dummy, state dummies,[8] and caste/religion dummies.[9]

Table 7.3 presents the results of probit regression. In the context of progress in developing countries, the strong effects of the mother's schooling years are particularly deserving of attention. If the mother's schooling years increase by one year, then the probability that a child dies at younger than five years old decreases by 0.16 per cent in 1992–93 and by 0.11 per cent in 2005–06. The father's schooling years exhibited significantly favorable effects on child welfare in 1992–93, but they were not significant in 2005–06. The effects of the wealth index and electricity dummy show a tendency similar to the father's schooling years: the consistent effect of mother's schooling years is pronounced.

The effect of the rural dummy is significant and positive in 1992–93, indicating the probability that a child under five years old dies increases by 0.7 per cent if the family lives in rural areas. In 2005–06, however, the effect of the rural dummy is not significant. As presented in Tables 7.1 and 7.2, differences between urban and rural areas were ameliorated gradually, suggesting that rural areas were viewed as a world apart a generation ago, but such areas are now regarded as living spaces that are roughly comparable to those of urban areas.

The empirical analyses include 13 state dummies, where Uttar Pradesh is the reference. In 1992–93, many state dummies have significant negative effects, suggesting that the likelihood of children dying younger than five years old apparently decreases if the family lives in a state other than Uttar Pradesh. For example, a child residing in Kerala is less likely to die under five years old than those residing in Uttar Pradesh. Of 13 state dummies, nine state dummies show significant negative effects. In 2005–06, the number of state dummies that show significant negative effects is seven. In addition, the effect of the Kerala state dummy attenuated from –6.9 per cent in 1992–93 to –2.8 per cent, which implies that differences in crude death rates among states have diminished gradually. Then, in 1992–93, what does "living in rural areas" mean? Even in 2005–06, differences among states remain, although they were alleviated gradually. What explains variation between states? The next section investigates this.

Table 7.3 Estimations of child death (all households)

1992–93 (NFHS-1)	dy/dx	z-value	2005–06 (NFHS-3)	dy/dx	z-value
Mother's age	−0.0045	(−10.94)***	Mother's age	−0.0038	(−9.88)***
Father's age	−0.0005	(−1.77)*	Father's age	−0.0007	(−2.39)**
Mother's schooling years	−0.0016	(−3.05)***	Mother's schooling years	−0.0011	(−3.15)***
Father's schooling years	−0.0014	(−4.16)***	Father's schooling years	−0.0004	(−1.26)
Children ever born	0.0161	(16.76)***	Children ever born	0.0156	(18.5)***
Wealth index	−0.0085	(−2.53)**	Wealth index	0.0000	(−1.4)
Electricity	−0.0085	(−2.09)**	Electricity	−0.0010	(−0.31)
Rural dummy	0.0073	(1.77)*	Rural dummy	0.0017	(0.56)
State dummy: Punjab	−0.0205	(−2.7)***	State dummy: Punjab	−0.0088	(−1.26)
State dummy: Haryana	−0.0099	(−1.47)	State dummy: Haryana	−0.0156	(−2.27)**
State dummy: Rajasthan	−0.0181	(−3.32)***	State dummy: Rajasthan	−0.0017	(−0.34)
State dummy: Bihar	−0.0076	(−1.63)	State dummy: Bihar	−0.0064	(−1.66)*
State dummy: West Bengal	−0.0273	(−4.16)***	State dummy: West Bengal	−0.0083	(−1.55)
State dummy: Orissa	0.0057	(1.05)	State dummy: Orissa	0.0039	(0.71)
State dummy: Madhya Pradesh	−0.0111	(−2.17)**	State dummy: Madhya Pradesh	0.0012	(0.31)
State dummy: Gujarat	−0.0058	(−0.93)	State dummy: Gujarat	−0.0061	(−1.03)
State dummy: Maharashtra	−0.0412	(−5.92)***	State dummy: Maharashtra	−0.0104	(−2.05)**
State dummy: Andhra Pradesh	−0.0259	(−3.73)***	State dummy: Andhra Pradesh	−0.0174	(−3.04)***
State dummy: Karnataka	−0.0304	(−4.78)***	State dummy: Karnataka	−0.0108	(−1.98)**
State dummy: Kerala	−0.0689	(−6.67)***	State dummy: Kerala	−0.0279	(−2.78)***
State dummy: Tamil Nadu	−0.0176	(−2.29)**	State dummy: Tamil Nadu	−0.0183	(−2.8)***
Caste/religion dummies	yes		Caste/Religion dummies	yes	
NOB	45,524		NOB	46,049	
Log-likelihood	−12,824.65		Log-likelihood	−10,042.71	

Note: * Significant at 10%; ** significant at 5%; *** significant at 1%.

QOL in Rural Areas and Differences Among States

The former sections have suggested that the state diversity was large. Then, this section presents an exploration of the effect of "living in rural areas," devoting attention to differences between states. Table 7.4 is the result of Probit regression using only rural households. The effects of state dummies show whether some distinctions exist compared with rural households in Uttar Pradesh. In 1992–93, of 13 state dummies, 11 dummies were found to be significant and negative. However, in 2005–06, the number of states showing significant effects decreased to only two. In short, great differences were found in rural areas among states in the early 1990s, but these had attenuated by the mid-2000s.

Table 7.5 presents the effects of the rural dummy from the results of probit regression for each state.[10] Its effects differ somewhat from those expected from Table 7.3. In Table 7.3, the rural dummy has a significant effect in 1992–93, but it was not significant in 2005–06. Table 7.4, however, shows that the impact of the rural dummy diverges greatly from state to state both in 1992–93 and in 2005–06. Substantial effects are observed in some states not only in 1992–93 but also in 2005–06. In addition, some results are discrepant with what is expected by "living in rural areas." In Haryana, Madhya Pradesh, and Kerala in 1992–93, and in Haryana, Orissa, and Andhra Pradesh in 2005–06, the rural dummy has a noteworthy positive effect. In contrast, in Karnataka in 1993–93 and Rajasthan in 2005–06, a significant negative effect was found. For example, in Karnataka in 1992–93, a child residing in a rural area has a 2.6 per cent lower probability of dying when younger than five years old than a child residing in an urban area. Consequently, the meaning of "living in rural areas" is not homogeneous from state to state.

What causes the differences? Another probit regression was conducted using rural household data with additional dummy variables: "Government hospital in village" and "private hospital in village." However, it is noteworthy that these variables are somewhat different for NFHS-1 and NFHS-3. For that reason, the results cannot be compared as they are.[11] The impact of the two additional variables is quite diverse by state. For example, "government hospital in village" in 1992–93 had a significant and negative effect on the probability that a child under five years old would die in Karnataka or Kerala. However, no other state shows the same effect. In 2005–06, in Punjab and Uttar Pradesh, "government hospital in village" indicates a significant and negative effect on the probability of child survival, but the other states show no such effect. It is possible that some difference in the quality of medical facilities exists among states.[12]

The effects of other variables should command more attention. In the context of development in economically developing countries, again, the effects of mother's schooling years should be examined specifically.[13] Tables 7.3 and 7.4 show that the mother's schooling years consistently have a significant negative effect on child survival, but the effect of mother's schooling years is not always significant and negative from state to state, both in 1992–93 and in 2005–06, according to Table 7.6. The states in which the

Table 7.4 Estimations of child death (rural households)

1992–93 (NFHS-1)	dy/dx	z-value	2005–06 (NFHS-3)	dy/dx	z-value
Mother's age	−0.0049	(−10.06)***	Mother's age	−0.0045	(−8.84)***
Father's age	−0.0004	(−1.5)	Father's age	−0.0009	(−2.39)**
Mother's schooling years	−0.0012	(−1.8)*	Mother's schooling years	−0.0011	(−2.15)**
Father's schooling years	−0.0018	(−4.42)***	Father's schooling years	−0.0004	(−0.92)
Children ever born	0.0171	(15.02)***	Children ever born	0.0177	(15.77)***
Wealth index	−0.0063	(−1.38)	Wealth index	0.0000	(−1.89)*
Electricity	−0.0092	(−1.86)*	Electricity	−0.0036	(−0.91)
State dummy: Punjab	−0.0276	(−2.98)***	State dummy: Punjab	−0.0074	(−0.76)
State dummy: Haryana	−0.0109	(−1.3)	State dummy: Haryana	−0.0083	(−0.98)
State dummy: Rajasthan	−0.0238	(−3.75)***	State dummy: Rajasthan	−0.0052	(−0.81)
State dummy: Bihar	−0.0114	(−2.08)**	State dummy: Bihar	−0.0074	(−1.44)
State dummy: West Bengal	−0.0353	(−4.6)***	State dummy: West Bengal	−0.0172	(−2.29)**
State dummy: Orissa	0.0044	(0.67)	State dummy: Orissa	0.0120	(1.73)*
State dummy: Madhya Pradesh	−0.0111	(−1.85)*	State dummy: Madhya Pradesh	0.0049	(0.94)
State dummy: Gujarat	−0.0121	(−1.54)	State dummy: Gujarat	0.0015	(0.19)
State dummy: Maharashtra	−0.0483	(−5.44)***	State dummy: Maharashtra	−0.0101	(−1.21)
State dummy: Andhra Pradesh	−0.0329	(−3.92)***	State dummy: Andhra Pradesh	−0.0004	(−0.05)
State dummy: Karnataka	−0.0447	(−5.63)***	State dummy: Karnataka	−0.0107	(−1.45)
State dummy: Kerala	−0.0748	(−6.05)***	State dummy: Kerala	−0.0313	(−2.29)**
State dummy: Tamil Nadu	−0.0288	(−2.92)***	State dummy: Tamil Nadu	−0.0121	(−1.25)
Caste/religion dummies	yes		Caste/Religion dummies	yes	
NOB	34,849		NOB	28,650	
Log-likelihood	−10,566.31		Log-likelihood	−6,954.50	

Note: * Significant at 10%; ** significant at 5%; *** significant at 1%.

Table 7.5 Estimations of rural dummy by states

1992–93 (NFHS-1)	dy/dx	z-value	2005–06 (NFHS-3)	dy/dx	z-value
Punjab	0.0001	(0.01)	Punjab	−0.0083	(−0.70)
Haryana	0.0310	(1.95)*	Haryana	0.0362	(1.96)*
Rajasthan	−0.0001	(−0.01)	Rajasthan	−0.0326	(−1.99)**
Uttar Pradesh	0.0196	(1.56)	Uttar Pradesh	−0.0062	(−0.83)
Bihar	−0.0062	(−0.44)	Bihar	0.0037	(0.37)
West Bengal	0.0066	(0.36)	West Bengal	−0.0041	(−0.32)
Orissa	0.0089	(0.55)	Orissa	0.0382	(2.23)**
Madhya Pradesh	0.0331	(1.92)*	Madhya Pradesh	−0.0060	(−0.57)
Gujarat	−0.0113	(−0.72)	Gujarat	0.0061	(0.43)
Maharashtra	−0.0073	(−0.58)	Maharashtra	0.0000	(0.00)
Andhra Pradesh	0.0194	(1.03)	Andhra Pradesh	0.0324	(3.45)***
Karnataka	−0.0263	(−2.04)**	Karnataka	−0.0101	(−0.97)
Kerala	0.0182	(1.74)*	Kerala	0.0030	(0.35)
Tamil Nadu	−0.0117	(−0.76)	Tamil Nadu	0.0023	(0.25)

Note: * Significant at 10%; ** significant at 5%; *** significant at 1%. To save space, the results of the other independent variables are not reported.

mother's schooling years show a notable negative effect are Uttar Pradesh, Madhya Pradesh, and Kerala in 1992–93, and Bihar, West Bengal, Gujarat, and Maharashtra in 2005–06. Although this result might be somewhat surprising to development policymakers, it might mean that the contents and quality of education differ among states. Therefore, the heterogeneous effects of education among states are noteworthy. Differences among states, although decreased, might emerge from these complicated surroundings because of the mixed effects of different factors.

QOL in Urban Areas

Table 7.7 presents the results of probit regression using urban household data. Unlike Table 7.4, which shows the results of the analysis using rural household data, it seems that variation between states increased from the early 1990s to the mid-2000s. Only two state dummies show a significant effect for NFHS-1, but six do so for NFHS-3. The diversity of environments for child survival in urban areas apparently changed and increased among states, which is a completely different result from that found in rural areas.

What happened to the environment for child survival in urban areas in 2005–06? NFHS-3 includes data for eight large cities: Delhi, Meerut (Uttar Pradesh), Kolkata (West Bengal), Indore (Madhya Pradesh), Mumbai (Maharashtra), Nagpur (Maharashtra), Hyderabad (Karnataka), and Chennai (Tamil Nadu). It includes information related to the slums of the eight large cities. Therefore, this section presents an examination of this data and explores the QOL in urban areas. Although definitions of slums are various, this chapter employs the definition used for the Census of India

Table 7.6(A) Estimations of child death by state: Northern and eastern regions (rural households)

1992–93 (NFHS-1)	Punjab		Haryana		Rajasthan		Uttar Pradesh		Bihar		West Bengal		Orissa	
	dy/dx	z-value	dy/dx	z-value	dy/dx	z-value	dy/dx	z-value	dy/dx	z-value	dy/dx	z-value	dy/dx	z-value
Mother's age	-0.0017	(-0.73)	-0.0081	(-3.03)***	-0.0062	(-3.49)***	-0.0067	(-5.81)***	-0.0050	(-3.27)***	-0.0014	(-0.71)	-0.0022	(-0.54)
Father's age	-0.0035	(-1.95)*	-0.0009	(-0.49)	-0.0007	(-0.59)	0.0000	(-0.04)	0.0007	(0.72)	0.0023	(1.89)*	-0.0047	(-1.35)
Mother's schooling years	0.0014	(0.62)	0.0003	(0.11)	0.0023	(0.79)	-0.0039	(-2.27)**	0.0005	(0.20)	0.0016	(0.55)	0.0048	(0.88)
Father's schooling years	0.0005	(0.25)	-0.0038	(-1.87)*	-0.0002	(-0.18)	-0.0016	(-1.86)*	-0.0023	(-1.85)*	-0.0034	(-1.62)	-0.0075	(-1.76)*
Children ever born	0.0199	(3.53)***	0.0227	(3.58)***	0.0201	(5.26)***	0.0187	(7.19)***	0.0180	(4.9)***	0.0053	(1.20)	0.0299	(3.26)***
Wealth index	-0.0194	(-1.21)	0.0180	(0.95)	0.0098	(0.68)	-0.0161	(-1.37)	-0.0231	(-1.24)	-0.0111	(-0.51)	-0.0674	(-1.45)
Electricity	-0.0157	(-0.65)	-0.0371	(-1.58)	-0.0277	(-1.73)*	-0.0145	(-1.13)	-0.0133	(-0.49)	0.0106	(0.36)	0.1200	(2.39)**
Government hospital in village	0.0155	(1.07)	0.0038	(0.22)	0.0061	(0.36)	0.0059	(0.30)	-0.0228	(-0.80)	-0.0053	(-0.26)	-0.0151	(-0.28)
Private hospital in village	0.0293	(1.98)**	-0.0023	(-0.13)	-0.0129	(-1.07)	-0.0027	(-0.35)	0.0037	(0.34)	-0.0202	(-1.3)	-0.0777	(-2.34)**
Caste/religion dummies	yes		yes		yes		yes		yes		yes		yes	
NOB	1,485		1,483		2,696		7,432		3,699		1,928		643	
Log-likelihood	-350.09		-438.58		-792.37		-2,602.37		-1,206.98		-535.93		-203.78	

(Continued)

Table 7.6(A) Estimations of child death by state: Northern and eastern regions (rural households) (Continued)

2005–06 (NFHS-3)	Punjab dy/dx	Punjab z-value	Haryana dy/dx	Haryana z-value	Rajasthan dy/dx	Rajasthan z-value	Uttar Pradesh dy/dx	Uttar Pradesh z-value	Bihar dy/dx	Bihar z-value	West Bengal dy/dx	West Bengal z-value	Orissa dy/dx	Orissa z-value
Mother's age	-0.0061	(-2.35)**	-0.0038	(-1.41)	-0.0047	(-1.88)*	-0.0061	(-5.41)***	-0.0021	(-1.48)	-0.0024	(-1.17)	-0.0055	(-2.51)**
Father's age	0.0025	(1.30)	-0.0011	(-0.56)	-0.0024	(-1.24)	-0.0005	(-0.57)	-0.0012	(-1.08)	-0.0025	(-1.62)	0.0007	(0.44)
Mother's schooling years	0.0008	(0.39)	0.0001	(0.05)	-0.0018	(-0.63)	-0.0015	(-1.42)	-0.0038	(-2.10)**	-0.0049	(-2.22)**	-0.0032	(-1.30)
Father's schooling years	0.0001	(0.13)	0.0007	(0.54)	-0.0010	(-0.87)	0.0001	(0.32)	0.0001	(0.37)	0.0003	(0.68)	-0.0016	(-1.27)
Children ever born	0.0288	(4.38)***	0.0189	(3.41)***	0.0194	(4.46)***	0.0214	(9.34)***	0.0111	(3.51)***	0.0137	(2.97)***	0.0182	(3.35)***
Wealth index	0.0000	(0.88)	0.0000	(-0.03)	0.0000	(-0.59)	0.0000	(-1.83)*	0.0000	(-0.16)	0.0000	(1.29)	0.0000	(0.11)
Electricity	-0.0134	(-0.44)	-0.0008	(-0.04)	0.0063	(0.39)	0.0053	(0.61)	-0.0080	(-0.58)	-0.0313	(-1.96)**	0.0097	(0.52)
Government hospital in village	-0.0410	(-1.69)*	0.0003	(0.01)	0.0013	(0.05)	-0.0430	(-2.27)**	0.0281	(1.34)	0.0542	(3.57)***	-0.0155	(-0.77)
Private hospital in village	-0.0201	(-1.31)	0.0209	(1.18)	0.0050	(0.35)	-0.0039	(-0.57)	-0.0015	(-0.15)	0.0137	(0.80)	-0.0246	(-1.06)
Caste/religion dummies	yes		yes		yes		yes		yes		yes		yes	
NOB	1,040		1,214		1,843		6,885		3,545		1,679		1,589	
Log-likelihood	-181.07		-253.16		-480.04		-1,851.69		-944.26		-342.36		-417.48	

Note: * Significant at 10%; ** significant at 5%; *** significant at 1%.

Table 7.6(B) Estimations of child death by state: Southern and western regions (rural households)

1992–93 (NFHS-1)	Madhya Pradesh		Gujarat		Maharashtra		Andhra Pradesh		Karnataka		Kerala		Tamil Nadu	
	dy/dx	z-value	dy/dx	z-value	dy/dx	z-value	dy/dx	z-value	dy/dx	z-value	dy/dx	z-value	dy/dx	z-value
Mother's age	−0.0043	(−2.18)**	−0.0052	(−1.71)*	−0.0068	(−3.01)***	−0.0028	(−1.27)	−0.0075	(−3.98)***	0.0011	(0.77)	−0.0046	(−2.20)**
Father's age	−0.0022	(−1.86)*	−0.0033	(−1.34)	−0.0010	(−0.78)	0.0006	(0.48)	0.0003	(0.36)	−0.0008	(−0.70)	−0.0002	(−0.24)
Mother's schooling years	−0.0055	(−1.86)*	−0.0028	(−0.96)	0.0004	(0.17)	0.0014	(0.42)	0.0036	(1.55)	−0.0036	(−1.90)*	0.0036	(1.32)
Father's schooling years	−0.0018	(−1.11)	−0.0016	(−0.77)	−0.0023	(−1.26)	−0.0039	(−1.64)	−0.0027	(−1.48)	−0.0005	(−0.26)	−0.0036	(−1.52)
Children ever born	0.0183	(4.29)***	0.0221	(3.64)***	0.0200	(3.75)***	0.0137	(2.61)***	0.0186	(4.13)***	0.0012	(0.36)	0.0273	(3.90)***
Wealth index	0.0173	(0.93)	−0.0222	(−1.17)	0.0025	(0.16)	0.0157	(0.75)	−0.0128	(−0.72)	−0.0216	(−1.63)	−0.0174	(−0.80)
Electricity	−0.0030	(−0.19)	0.0079	(0.39)	−0.0225	(−1.30)	−0.0154	(−0.80)	−0.0009	(−0.06)	0.0143	(0.98)	−0.0195	(−0.93)
Government hospital in village	−0.0152	(−0.66)	0.0166	(0.84)	0.0109	(0.55)	−0.0071	(−0.33)	−0.0307	(−1.68)*	−0.0251	(−1.87)*	−0.0146	(−0.66)
Private hospital in village	−0.0006	(−0.05)	−0.0044	(−0.29)	−0.0217	(−1.21)	0.0101	(0.49)	−0.0183	(−1.29)	0.0036(0.35)		0.0146	(0.72)
Caste/religion dummies	yes		yes		yes		yes		yes		yes		yes	
NOB	3,006		1,591		1,515		1,520		1,878		1,225		1,162	
Log-likelihood	−1,009.71		−481.58		−354.57		−426.33		−464.00		−145.17		−286.33	

(Continued)

Table 7.6(B) Estimations of child death by state: Southern and western regions (rural households) (Continued)

2005–06 (NFHS-3)	Madhya Pradesh		Gujarat		Maharashtra		Andhra Pradesh		Karnataka		Kerala		Tamil Nadu	
	dy/dx	z-value	dy/dx	z-value	dy/dx	z-value	dy/dx	z-value	dy/dx	z-value	dy/dx	z-value	dy/dx	z-value
Mother's age	-0.0057	(-3.53)***	-0.0016	(-0.59)	-0.0051	(-2.58)**	-0.0096	(-2.97)***	-0.0026	(-1.48)	-0.0028	(-1.51)	-0.0020	(-0.88)
Father's age	-0.0014	(-1.24)	-0.0010	(-0.45)	0.0014	(1.08)	0.0007	(0.33)	-0.0030	(-2.14)**	0.0013	(0.91)	-0.0015	(-0.93)
Mother's schooling years	0.0018	(1.12)	-0.0066	(-2.62)***	-0.0035	(-1.97)**	0.0006	(0.24)	0.0023	(1.43)	-0.0010	(-0.50)	0.0002	(0.14)
Father's schooling years	-0.0006	(-0.78)	-0.0002	(-0.18)	0.0002	(0.18)	-0.0050	(-2.47)**	-0.0001	(-0.14)	0.0000	(0.02)	0.0027	(1.54)
Children ever born	0.0178	(5.24)***	0.0081	(1.28)	0.0124	(2.16)**	0.0308	(3.64)***	0.0247	(5.12)***	0.0110	(2.23)**	0.0252	(3.93)***
Wealth index	0.0000	(-3.31)***	0.0000	(0.11)	0.0000	(0.03)	0.0000	(1.63)	0.0000	(-0.47)	0.0000	(-0.22)	0.0000	(-1.01)
Electricity	0.0090	(0.85)	-0.0233	(-1.18)	-0.0255	(-1.60)	-0.0121	(-0.52)	0.0090	(0.52)	0.0005	(0.03)	-0.0050	(-0.27)
Government hospital in village	-0.0108	(-0.56)	-0.0119	(-0.40)	0.0063	(0.29)	-0.0169	(-0.69)	-0.0234	(-1.22)	0.0051	(0.44)	-0.0025	(-0.16)
Private hospital in village	0.0045	(0.46)	-0.0187	(-1.19)	0.0140	(0.96)	0.0019	(0.10)	-0.0012	(-0.11)	-0.0087	(-0.67)	0.0001	(0.01)
Caste/religion dummies	yes		yes		yes		yes		yes		yes		yes	
NOB	3,733		1,195		1,277		1,029		1,814		908		1,090	
Log-likelihood	-1,058.25		-289.57		-246.68		-222.11		-372.46		-84.82		-181.80	

Note: * Significant at 10%; ** significant at 5%; *** significant at 1%.

Table 7.7 Estimations of child death (urban households)

1992–93 (NFHS-1)	dy/dx	z-value	2005–06 (NFHS-3)	dy/dx	z-value
Mother's age	−0.0033	(−4.40)***	Mother's age	−0.0027	(−4.89)***
Father's age	−0.0004	(−0.83)	Father's age	−0.0003	(−0.58)
Mother's schooling years	−0.0020	(−2.67)***	Mother's schooling years	−0.0010	(−2.19)**
Father's schooling years	−0.0006	(−0.92)	Father's schooling years	−0.0003	(−0.73)
Children ever born	0.0134	(7.59)***	Children ever born	0.0133	(10.32)***
Wealth index	−0.0072	(−1.58)	Wealth index	0.0000	(−0.60)
Electricity	−0.0079	(−1.10)	Electricity	0.0073	(1.23)
State dummy: Punjab	−0.0086	(−0.68)	State dummy: Punjab	−0.0074	(−0.80)
State dummy: Haryana	−0.0116	(−1.08)	State dummy: Haryana	−0.0460	(−2.93)***
State dummy: Rajasthan	0.0001	(0.01)	State dummy: Rajasthan	0.0083	(1.05)
State dummy: Bihar	−0.0010	(−0.10)	State dummy: Bihar	−0.0096	(−1.60)
State dummy: West Bengal	−0.0143	(−1.09)	State dummy: West Bengal	−0.0058	(−0.80)
State dummy: Orissa	0.0061	(0.65)	State dummy: Orissa	−0.0153	(−1.50)
State dummy: Madhya Pradesh	−0.0121	(−1.23)	State dummy: Madhya Pradesh	−0.0049	(−0.90)
State dummy: Gujarat	0.0070	(0.71)	State dummy: Gujarat	−0.0194	(−2.16)**
State dummy: Maharashtra	−0.0217	(−2.15)**	State dummy: Maharashtra	−0.0120	(−2.1)**
State dummy: Andhra Pradesh	−0.0066	(−0.56)	State dummy: Andhra Pradesh	−0.0268	(−3.94)***
State dummy: Karnataka	0.0013	(0.13)	State dummy: Karnataka	−0.0091	(−1.17)
State dummy: Kerala	−0.0702	(−3.44)***	State dummy: Kerala	−0.0255	(−1.72)*
State dummy: Tamil Nadu	0.0044	−0.4	State dummy: Tamil Nadu	−0.0224	(−2.75)***
Caste/religion dummies		yes	Caste/religion dummies		yes
NOB		10,675	NOB		17,399
Log-likelihood		−2238.54	Log-likelihood		−3,053.28

Note: * Significant at 10%; ** significant at 5%; *** significant at 1%.

2001.[14] According to Gupta, Arnold, and Lhungdim (2009), the definition is the following:

i   All specified areas in a town or city are notified as "Slum" by State/ Local Government and Union Territory Administration under any Act including a "Slum Act."
ii All areas recognized as "Slum" by State/Local Government and Union Territory Administration, Housing and Slum Boards which may have not been formally notified as slums under any act.
iii A compact area of at least 300 population or about 60–70 households of poorly built congested tenements, in unhygienic environments, usually with inadequate infrastructure and lacking in proper sanitary and drinking water facilities.

Table 7.8 presents the crude death rate of children under five years old in eight large cities. In Delhi, Meerut, Indore, Nagpur, and Chennai, children under five years old residing in slums have a higher probability of dying than those residing in non-slums. In contrast, the figures for slums in Kolkata, Mumbai, and Hyderabad are somewhat discrepant with what might be expected for the QOL in slums: Child survival in non-slums is worse than that in slums. However, these figures are likely to include some effects of various factors. Therefore, probit regression was conducted using the large city data, particularly addressing the effects of "living in slums." The results are presented in Table 7.9.[15] Results of the regression analysis indicate that in Indore, the environment for child survival when residing in slums is significantly worse than in non-slums. In contrast, children under five years old residing in slums in Kolkata have a significantly lower probability of dying than those residing in non-slums. When it comes to "living in slums," poor QOL can be inferred. The environment for child survival in slums is expected to be worse than that in non-slums. The reality, however, is different.

To clarify matters, probit regression is conducted using only the data of households that had resided in slums in Kolkata for more than five years.

Table 7.8 Crude death rate in eight large cities (‰)

	Slums	Non-slums
Delhi	53.0	34.9
Meerut	72.2	57.7
Kolkata	41.1	63.9
Indore	61.5	38.0
Mumbai	36.9	39.3
Nagpur	42.4	39.4
Hyderabad	19.9	25.2
Chennai	31.4	21.1

Source: Calculated by the author from NFHS-3 using data of children born during the five-year periods preceding the survey.

Table 7.9 Estimations of slum dummy by city

	NOB	dy/dx	z-value
Delhi	1,406	−0.0082	(−0.62)
Meerut	1,436	−0.0040	(−0.28)
Kolkata	608	−0.0567	(−2.65)***
Indore	1,007	0.0350	(2.40)**
Mumbai	751	−0.0092	(−0.61)
Nagpur	920	−0.0142	(−1.04)
Hyderabad	1,194	−0.0079	(−0.88)
Chennai	533	−0.0086	(−0.49)

Note: * Significant at 10%; ** significant at 5%; *** significant at 1%.
To save space, results of other independent variables are not reported.

Results show that "living in slums" has no significant effect.[16] What does this mean? If the data for the analysis is limited to households that had resided in slums for more than five years, the recent migrants to urban areas in Kolkata are excluded from the analyses. In fact, of 202 households excluded because of the short residence, 90 households are headed by migrants from rural areas. This fact implies the likelihood that the significant negative effect of "living in slums" is attributed mostly to the QOL of recent migrants to slums in Kolkata. In addition, this implies the likelihood that the QOL of migrants from rural areas was better than that of urban people in West Bengal. Table 7.2 shows that the environment for child survival in rural areas has been greatly ameliorated, implying that some rural people with good health migrated to urban areas.

According to Table 7.4, the differences of rural areas between states decreased from the early 1990s to the mid-2000s. In addition, Table 7.7 shows that the difference of urban areas among states increased for the same periods. Tables 7.2, 7.4, 7.6, and 7.7 imply that the QOL in rural areas greatly improved, although that in urban areas did not improve so much. Then, the QOL in slums in Kolkata improved because many migrants with good health moved from rural areas. However, it is noteworthy that this does not mean that the QOL in slums improved substantively.[17]

Conclusion

The analyses explained in this chapter present trends in child survival as a proxy for the QOL from the early 1990s to the mid-2000s in India, with an examination of what effect "living in rural areas" and "living in urban areas" have on child survival. In addition, the causes of the differences among states are given some attention. Employing NFHS-1 and NFHS-3, empirical analyses were conducted. The results are summarized below.

Rural–urban differences in India decreased on average because improvements were greater in rural areas than in urban areas. In addition, rural differences among states attenuated, but it is noteworthy that the situation is not homogeneous depending on the state. In contrast, urban differences among states increased. Moreover, in one of the eight large cities, the environment for child survival in non-slums was worse than that in slums, which might be mostly attributable to the QOL of migrants from rural areas to slums being better in the mid-2000s. Therefore, it is striking that these facts do not necessarily mean that the QOL in slums improved to a marked degree.

Some problems remain. An important difficulty is a causality problem of the empirical analysis, such as the relation between child survival and medical facilities. It is possible that medical facilities were established more frequently in poor performance states, inducing a so-called reverse causality problem. This point demands further examination. Another possible shortcoming is that these analyses did not explore all causes of differences among states, despite suggesting some possibilities. These shortcomings should be resolved in future studies.

Notes

1 In addition, the survey was conducted as 2015–16 NFHS (NFHS-4).
2 The 14 states are those in the Census of India 1991: Punjab, Haryana, Rajasthan, Uttar Pradesh, Bihar, West Bengal, Orissa, Madhya Pradesh, Gujarat, Maharashtra, Andhra Pradesh, Karnataka, Kerala, and Tamil Nadu.
3 In NFHS, the child mortality rate (under five mortality rate) is calculated using the data of children born in the five-year periods preceding the survey.
4 In 2005–06, the figure for Uttar Pradesh did not include Uttarakhand. Therefore, it is noteworthy that the figure would be less than 96.4 ‰ if Uttarakhand were included in Uttar Pradesh and calculated.
5 The crude death rate shows the proportion of children under five years old who died among children who were born during the five-year periods preceding the survey.
6 NFHS provides a wealth index which is calculated using a principal component analysis of household items. See Filmer and Pritchett (2001) for details.
7 This variable is used as a representative of household living standards.
8 To compare NFHS-3 with NFHS-1, states divided of NFHS-3 were integrated: Bihar and Jharkhand are integrated into Bihar, Madhya Pradesh, and Chhattisgarh into Madhya Pradesh and Uttar Pradesh and Uttarakhand into Uttar Pradesh.
9 To save space, results for caste/religion dummies are not reported.
10 The specifications of regression are the same as those for empirical analysis in the previous section, aside from the exclusion of the state dummies.
11 NFHS-1 includes a village questionnaire. Therefore, village data can be used. In this case, the empirical analysis in this paper uses a proxy that takes 1 if there is a facility in the village. NFHS-3 does not include a village questionnaire. For NFHS-3, a household question about access to any medical facility is used. This chapter uses a proxy that takes a value of 1 if the household has access to a medical facility in the village.
12 "Government hospital in village" and "private hospital in village" show significant positive effects in some cases. For "government hospital in village," a significant positive effect can be observed in West Bengal in 2005–06. For "private hospital in village," a significant positive effect can be observed in Punjab in 1992–93. This result is against what is expected

intuitively. This might be a reverse causality problem, but this problem is not examined herein because of space. This problem should be resolved in a future study.

13 Many development studies have pointed out this problem. For example, see Rosenzweig and Schultz (1982), Murthi, Guio, and Dreze (1995), Sen (1999), and Anderson and Eswaran (2009).

14 For instance, the National Sample Survey Organization considers a cluster as a slum if there is a lack of basic services and at least 20 households reside in the area (Gupta, Arnold, and Lhungdim, 2009). In addition to the definition of the census, NFHS-3 includes an alternative definition of slums in the eight designated cities as identified by the interviewing team supervisor at the time of the fieldwork. However, this chapter uses the definition of the census because the empirical analysis in the latter part of this chapter is qualitatively equivalent irrespective of the definition.

15 The specification of regression is the same as Table 7.5 for rural areas. Most results of the regression are not reported to save space.

16 The number of observations is 502. Dy/dx and z-value of "living in slums" are −0.0385 and −1.63, respectively. Results of the other variables are not reported to save space. If households that had lived in slums in Kolkata for more than four years, then "living in slums" shows a significant negative effect: dy/dx and z-value are − 0.0384 and −1.76, respectively. NOB is 538.

17 It would be worth noting other possibilities. For example, because NFHS-3 conforms the definition of the Census of India 2001 for identifying slums, it might be inadequate to use the definition at the time of 2005–06. This problem should be explored further in a future study.

References

Anderson, S. and Eswaran, M. (2009) "What Determines Female Autonomy? Evidence from Bangladesh," *Journal of Development Economics* 90(2): 179–191.

Filmer, D. and Pritchett, L.H. (2001) "Estimating Wealth Effects without Expenditure Data-or Tears: An Application to Educational Enrollments in States of India," *Demography* 38(1): 115–132.

Gupta, K., Arnold, F. and Lhungdim, H. (2009) *Health and Living Conditions in Eight Indian Cities*. National Family Health Survey (NFHS-3), India, 2005–06. Mumbai: International Institute for Population Sciences; Calverton, Maryland, USA: ICF Macro.

IIPS (International Institute for Population Sciences) (1995) *National Family Health Survey (MCH and Family Planning) India 1992–93*. Mumbai: International Institute for Population Sciences.

IIPS (International Institute for Population Sciences) (2007) *National Family Health Survey (NFHS-3), 2005-06: India: Volume I*. Mumbai: International Institute for Population Sciences.

Murthi, M., Guio, A.C. and Dreze, J. (1995) "Mortality, Fertility, and Gender Bias in India: A District-Level Analysis," *Population and Development Review* 21(4): 745–782.

Rosenzweig, M.R. and Schultz, T.P. (1982) "Market Opportunities, Genetic Endowments, and Intrafamily Resource Distribution: Child Survival in Rural India," *American Economic Review* 72(4): 803–815.

Sen, Amartya (1999) *Development as Freedom*, Oxford: Oxford University Press.

8 Environmental Problems of Food Production and Consumption

A District-Level Analysis of Nitrogen Flow

Ippei Sekido

The supplying of food to support its increasing population is a principal problem for India. An increased nitrogen fertilizer input has contributed toward solving this problem by raising crop yields. However, nitrogen that is not absorbed by crops causes severe difficulties related to environmental pollution, including groundwater pollution, river and wetland eutrophication, and red tide outbreaks. Regarded from the perspective of food consumption, nitrogen absorbed into crops can also cause environmental problems through humans and their excrement if not treated with appropriate systems. Population concentration and increased protein consumption, along with economic development and urbanization, are factors strongly affecting nitrogen pollution in urban areas. For these reasons, nitrogen flow is a helpful index to assess the environmental pollution caused by food production and consumption.

Numerous studies of nitrogen flow have been conducted in India and Asia. From the perspective of the global nitrogen cycle, Galloway (2000) showed that Asia is a hotspot for nitrogen mobilization, primarily because of intensive food production. Seitzinger and Kroeze (1998) examined N_2O emissions from aquatic environments across the globe and estimated that China and India account for about 50 per cent of the N_2O emissions from rivers and estuaries. Velmurugan et al. (2008) estimated the nitrogen cycle for the Indian agro-ecosystem.

This current study specifically examines nitrogen inflow and outflow around farmland ('nitrogen balance on farmland') and the nitrogen contained in human excrement ('nitrogen load from humans') to assess the environmental impact of food production and consumption. The former is used as an index of the rural environmental load of food production. The latter is used as an index of the urban environmental load of food consumption. District-level statistical data related to population, food production, cropped area, nitrogen fertilizer input, livestock, and other aspects which are necessary to estimate the two indices above are available. Including the work of Pathak et al. (2010), most earlier studies of nitrogen flow have been conducted on the state or river basin level. District-level analysis can support our evaluation of the environmental effects of migration from rural to urban areas. Moreover, we can clarify the contrast between rural and urban environmental problems. In

DOI: 10.4324/9781003311898-9

addition to elucidating recent changes, two datasets were used, respectively emphasizing 2000 and 2010. The administrative boundaries of districts have changed in some parts of India, but the boundaries in 2000 were used to track the changes in divided districts. The analyses conducted for this study did not include Jammu and Kashmir because of a lack of data.

The composition of this study was set as follows. The nitrogen flow model and the nitrogen flow for the entirety of India are explained in the first section based on the results of earlier studies. The second section presents estimates of the nitrogen balance on farmland at a district level and clarifies characteristics of the geographical distribution of the environmental load caused by food production. In the next two sections, the total future population and inter-district immigration are estimated. As one might expect, the population is the most important variable used to estimate food demand and nitrogen load from humans. In the fifth section, Indian dietary characteristics and their changes are analyzed, particularly addressing protein intake per person. Finally, future prospects and measures to reduce environmental problems caused by food production and consumption are discussed.

Nitrogen Flow in India

This section explains the nitrogen flow model in relation to those of previous studies. In addition, nitrogen flow characteristics in India are discussed in comparison with Japan and China.

Shindo (2012) estimated nitrogen balance changes in agriculture for 13 Asian countries using the nitrogen flow model shown in Figure 8.1. Nitrogen

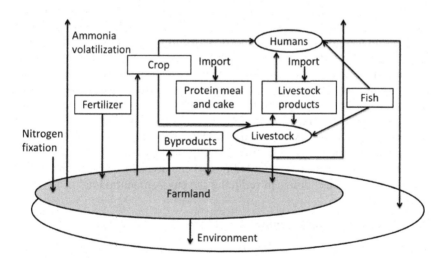

Figure 8.1 Nitrogen flow model.

Source: Shindo (2012), omitted partially by the author for space.

is introduced into this system by the importation of food, fish, fertilizer, and nitrogen fixation. It circulates through humans, crops, and livestock. Regarded from the perspective of farmland: nitrogen inflows into farmland from fertilizer, nitrogen fixation, and livestock, but nitrogen outflows from farmland to crops and via ammonia volatilization into the environment (groundwater and rivers). It was assumed that all nitrogen taken in by humans is excreted because the amount of nitrogen in the human body remains relatively constant.

The characteristics of nitrogen flow estimated by Shindo et al. (2006, 2009), and Shindo (2012) are summarized as follows. The nitrogen flow through crops is much stronger than that through livestock: most nitrogen that people consume comes from crops. Calculated annual per-capita nitrogen flows show that for every 12.4 kg of nitrogen fertilizer used, 8.4 kg of nitrogen flows from farmland to the environment. Also, 3.4 kg of nitrogen is supplied to humans. The total nitrogen load to the environment, when calculated as the sum of surplus nitrogen from farmland, nitrogen from humans, and ammonia volatilization, was estimated as 13.1 kg per person. In China, all nitrogen flows were larger than those in India. Particularly, the amount of nitrogen fertilizer used was roughly five times larger, and the surplus nitrogen on farmland was roughly double. The total nitrogen load to the environment was also approximately double. In Japan, the nitrogen flow from crops is small, but the flow from livestock is as large as that of China. As a result, the surplus nitrogen on farmland was 6.8 kg per person, which is lower than that of India despite the higher nitrogen supply to humans. In addition, the total nitrogen load to the environment slightly exceeded that of India (14.4 kg). Regarding the low surplus nitrogen on farmland in Japan, although Japan supplies sufficient protein for its people, the food supply mainly depends on imports from foreign countries. Japan imports nitrogen contained in wheat, livestock products, and feed crops, which accounts for 53 per cent of all nitrogen inflow to the system. However, there is little importation of food and feed to India and China. In recent years, India has become a nitrogen exporting country. High-protein feed, mainly soy meal, contributes the largest share of exported nitrogen. In addition, rice is an important export item in terms of quantity: 4 million tons have been exported since 1995 (FAOSTAT). The export of livestock products also slightly exceeds imports. However, food and feed trade only contributes 2.9 per cent of all nitrogen inflows. The import of agricultural products in Japan was not intended to prevent environmental pollution, but it is expected to be effective in reducing the environmental load.

Nitrogen Balance on Farmland by District Level Analysis

The nitrogen balance on farmland was evaluated using the following formula.

$$NB = Nf + Nl + Nfix - Ncrop - NNH3v$$

In that equation, the following variables are used: *NB*, nitrogen balance; *Nf*, nitrogen fertilizer input; *Nl*, nitrogen load from livestock; *Nfix*, nitrogen fixation; *Ncrop*, nitrogen contained in crops; and *NNH3v*, ammonia volatilization.

Nitrogen Fertilizer Input

Map 8.1 shows the nitrogen fertilizer input by total district land area in 2010. The input of nitrogen fertilizer differed greatly among regions, the districts in Punjab and Haryana contributed the largest amount of nitrogen fertilizer per area. In this region, the Green revolution spread earliest in India, and agriculture used large amounts of nitrogen fertilizer to attain high yields while double cropping both rice and wheat. The area from this region to the entire Ganges Basin also uses a large amount of nitrogen fertilizer because of the very high ratio of cultivated area to the total land areas in this district. In addition, multiple cropping is common and nitrogenous fertilizer input per cropped area is high. On the other hand, the nitrogen fertilizer input per area was small in Rajasthan, Madhya Pradesh, Orissa, Jharkhand, and the northeast states because of the large cropped area of pulses and coarse cereals, which do not need much nitrogen fertilizer. In

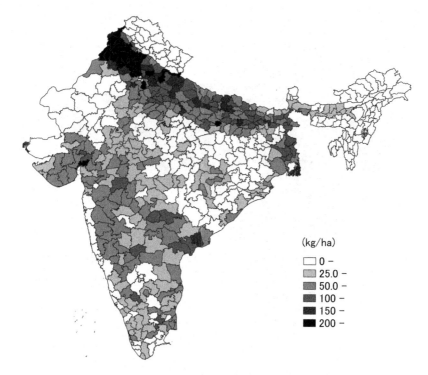

(kg/ha)
- 0 –
- 25.0 –
- 50.0 –
- 100 –
- 150 –
- 200 –

Map 8.1 Nitrogen fertilizer input per total district land area in 2010.

Source: Calculated by the author from data of The Fertilizer Association of India (2009).

some districts of Rajasthan, the nitrogen fertilizer input per area was low because of the low ratio of cultivated area to the total land area. In southern India, large amounts of nitrogen fertilizer were input into the Godavari River Basin, especially in East Godavari, West Godavari, Krishna, and Guntur districts. These were the top four districts for rice production in Andhra Pradesh in 2009. In addition, the large irrigated area that spreads in a fan shape from Tiruchirappalli to Thanjavur in Tamil Nadu practices rice cultivation using large amounts of nitrogen fertilizer.

Regional differences in nitrogen fertilizer input are large. The distribution resembles the respective distributions of rice and wheat production. Farmers improved the rice and wheat yields to meet demand. As a result, they also increased the nitrogen load.

Nitrogen fertilizer inputs increased in most districts, especially in districts located in places that were remote from the large cities of Uttar Pradesh, Punjab, Maharashtra, and Haryana (Map 8.2). In addition, the increase in nitrogen fertilizer input was especially large in the Kathiawar Peninsula of Gujarat. In this area, wheat production has been spreading in recent years. For example, in Junagadh, which is located on the Kathiawar Peninsula, the

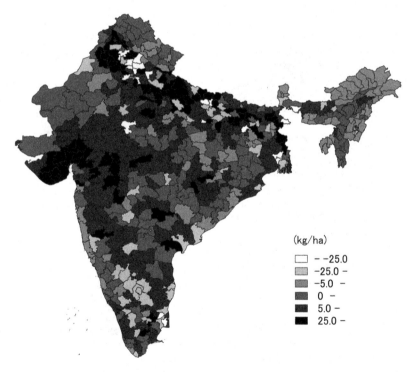

(kg/ha)
☐ – –25.0
▨ –25.0 –
▩ –5.0 –
▦ 0 –
▪ 5.0 –
■ 25.0 –

Map 8.2 Changes in nitrogen fertilizer during 2000–2010.

Source: Calculated by the author from data of The Fertilizer Association of India (2001) and (2009).

wheat cropped area increased from 70,000 ha in 1998 to 210,000 ha in 2009. Nitrogen fertilizer input increased along with this expanded wheat production. On the other hand, some districts located near large cities decreased their nitrogen fertilizer inputs because of land conversion from farmland to urban use. For example, the decrease was remarkable in districts around Delhi, Kolkata, and Bangalore. Farmers are giving up agriculture around the cities as a result of urban expansion.

Livestock

Regarding macro nitrogen flow, nitrogen does not outflow into the environment merely by livestock animals eating the grass around them (excluding ammonia volatilization). There is more than one billion head of livestock in India, but cereal consumption for feed is extremely low. Therefore, the ratio of the contribution of the nitrogen load from livestock to whole nitrogen flow is low.

According to the *Livestock Census* (2014), the total number of livestock is constantly increasing (Figure 8.2). Growth in poultry accounts for most of the growth in the total heads of livestock after 1972. Particularly since 1997, the number of poultry proliferated following the rising demand for eggs and chicken. However, cattle and buffalo, which are symbolic Indian animals, did not increase very much. The number of cattle peaked at 205 million in 1992. Viewed at the district level, the number of cattle and buffalo decreased slightly in almost all districts. No regional differences were observed.

Regional differences are extremely large in the case of poultry. Map 8.3 shows that the number of poultry is increasing greatly in districts located 100–200 km

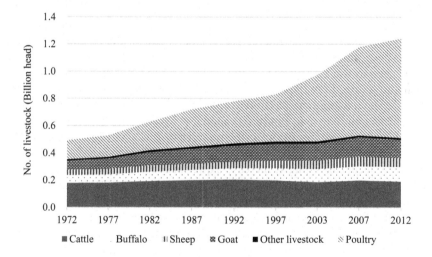

Figure 8.2 Number of livestock.

Source: Department of Animal Husbandry, Dairying & Fisheries, Ministry of Agriculture, Government of India (2014), *Livestock Census 2012.*

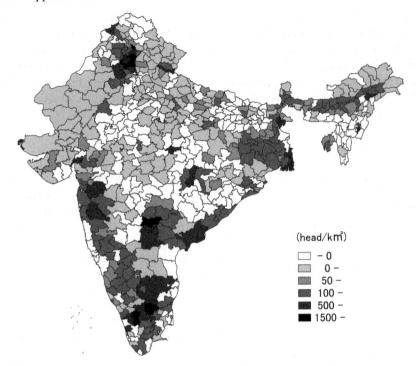

Map 8.3 Change in number of poultry during 1997–2012.

Source: Calculated by the author from data from the Department of Animal Husbandry, Dairying
    & Fisheries, Ministry of Agriculture, Government of India (2014), *Livestock Census 2012.*

from large cities. This is the result of increasing chicken production to meet the demand for chicken in large cities. In contrast to the cultivation of rice and wheat, poultry farming requires no large areas of land. Therefore, there is little need to run a business in a remote location that is distant from the large demand source. In India, where the cold chain is insufficiently developed, being situated near a large city has important benefits. It is thought that the demand for chicken and eggs will continue to increase. Meeting this demand will necessitate a continued expansion of the number of poultry. Therefore, the local nitrogen load caused by intensive poultry farming, which uses large amounts of cereal feed, can similarly increase. Appropriate treatment of the excreta is, therefore, necessary to prevent nitrogen from leaking to the environment.

Because no district-level data related to the production of livestock products and consumption of feed crops is available, it is not easy to estimate the nitrogen load from livestock precisely. The present study used a rough method to estimate the whole nitrogen load from livestock using data from FAOSTAT (FAO) (1.85 million tons), which was then distributed to each district in proportion to the number of livestock. Regarding nitrogen flow, ten fowl, three heads of sheep, goats, or pigs, and a single head of cattle or buffalo are assumed as equivalent.

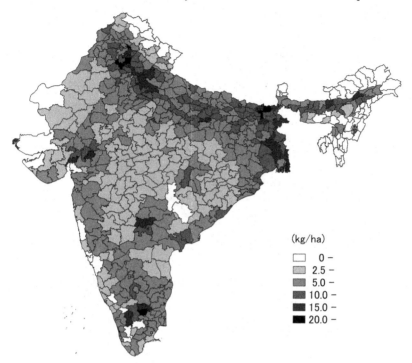

Map 8.4 Nitrogen load from livestock.

Source: Calculated by the author.

Map 8.4 presents estimate results of the nitrogen load from livestock. Comparison with Map 8.2 clarifies that the nitrogen load from live- stock was quite low. As with nitrogen fertilizer, a high nitrogen load was observed in the Ganges Basin. In the districts of West Bengal and the east side of Bihar, the nitrogen load from livestock was estimated as the highest because of the large number of cattle and buffalo. In addition, in the western districts of Uttar Pradesh, around Delhi, and in some districts around Hyderabad and Bangalore, large numbers of livestock are bred to produce livestock products for people living in these urban areas. Unlike areas with nitrogenous fertilizer input, Punjab had a small nitrogen load. As cattle and buffalo are distributed over all districts, regional differences in nitrogen load from livestock are smaller than those of nitrogen fertilizer input.

Nitrogen Balance on Farmland

Map 8.5 presents results of the estimated nitrogen balance on farmland using values analyzed in earlier sections. These include nitrogen fixa- tion, nitrogen contained in crops, and ammonia volatilization, which

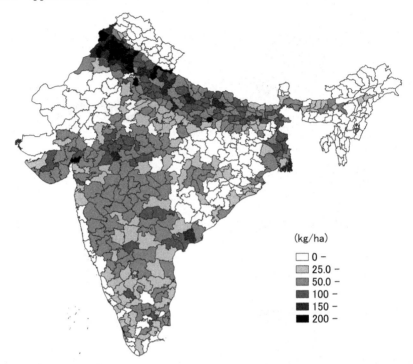

(kg/ha)

☐ 0 –
▨ 25.0 –
▨ 50.0 –
▨ 100 –
▨ 150 –
■ 200 –

Map 8.5 Nitrogen balance on farmland.

Source: Calculated by the author.

were determined in reference to Shindo (2013) and *District-Wise Crop Production Statistics*. Because nitrogen fertilizer input accounts for a large share of the nitrogen flow, the distribution was similar to the distribution of nitrogen fertilizer input. However, in the southwestern section of Madhya Pradesh and the inland districts of Maharashtra, the nitrogen balance was high despite the low nitrogen fertilizer input because the crop area accounted for by pulses, which have nitrogen-fixation capabilities, was large in these regions. Large consumption of pulses is a characteristic of the food culture in India, but pulse crops are greatly concentrated. For example, Madhya Pradesh alone accounts for 50 per cent of soybean production.

Nitrogen fertilizer inputs account for a large share of the nitrogen balance on farmland. Despite the high nitrogen fertilizer input, rice and wheat yields are low in Uttar Pradesh and Bihar. If more nitrogen fertilizer comes to be used in these two states to raise yields, the nitrogen load will similarly rise. By contrast, the nitrogen load from livestock accounts only for a small share. However, the enlarged nitrogen load from poultry following the increasing demand for eggs and chicken might cause local environmental problems.

Demographic Features and Population Projections

Population increase is the fundamental factor affecting environmental problems. *World Population Prospects the 2015 revision* estimates that the population of India will exceed the population of China in 2022 to become the most populated country. In this section, after clarifying the characteristics of population dynamics after 2000, the future population of India was projected. In addition, based on an analysis of changes in the total fertility rate (TFR), the estimation of the United Nations (UN) was critically reassessed.

Total Population

The population of India increased from 1.05 billion in 2000 to 1.23 billion in 2010. The average annual population growth rate during these ten years was 1.57 per cent. The population growth rate peaked at 2.30 per cent in 1974. According to *World Population Prospects the 2015 revision*, the annual population growth is also declining from the peak of 18.6 million in 1999 to 15.8 million in 2014. The period of population explosion experienced in the late 20th century has ended. The medium variant of the UN estimates suggests that the population will grow to 1.71 billion in 2050 and reach a peak at 1.75 billion in 2068. The UN projection is used as the most basic figure for projections by many fields. It is important to review this estimate carefully. The most important assumption of this estimation is the fertility rate. Consequently, the change in fertility rate in India must be analyzed.

Fertility

Figure 8.3 presents changes of TFR in selected states. The pace of decline in TFR for the whole of India was extremely slow until the early 1980s, but it accelerated a little and maintained a constant pace after the late 1980s. The TFR differs substantially by state: higher in the north and lower in the south. In Tamil Nadu and Kerala, the TFR declined below 2.30 before 1990. However, the TFR in less-developed states such as Bihar and Uttar Pradesh were above 4.00 until 2006 and 2008, respectively. The slow pace of decline in the TFR in these two states had a dampening effect on the drop in the average TFR of India. It is noteworthy that the TFR in Uttar Pradesh and Bihar was almost stable from the 1990s to the early 2000s when the TFR in most states decreased at a stable rate. However, after 2005, the reduction in TFR appeared to accelerate in these two states. It is reasonable to assume that the TFR will continue falling in Uttar Pradesh and Bihar because no state shows a TFR declining that halted before it fell below 2.00. The drop in TFR in the most-populated states is favorable for controlling population growth in India. The tendency for the TFR to stop falling has been observed in some states where the TFR is less than 2.00. It appears to be stable around 1.7–1.8 in Andhra Pradesh, Kerala, and Tamil Nadu. The rate

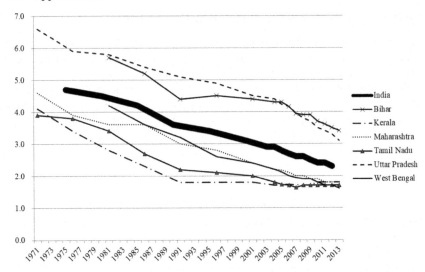

Figure 8.3 Total fertility rate by state.

Source: Office of the Registrar General & Census Commissioner, India, Ministry of Home
Affairs, Government of India (2014), *SRS Statistical Report 2013*.

continues to shrink in West Bengal, Punjab, Maharashtra, and Delhi, even
after dropping below 2.0.

The UN estimate includes the assumption that the drop in fertility rate
will greatly slow going forward. For example, the TFR is estimated as less
than 2.00 in 2035–2040. If the rate of TFR decrease in recent years continues, it will fall below 2.00 by 2020–2025 at the latest. Consequently, the
fertility rates assumed by the UN are too high.

Future population

A cohort component method was used to estimate the future population. This
study assumed the future TFR based on the analysis presented above (Table 8.1).
The mortality rate, international migration rate, sex ratio at birth, and infant
mortality rate are assumed to be the same as the medium variant in the UN
estimation. The total population was estimated to peak at 1.58 billion in 2050.
This study estimated the population to be 130 million fewer in 2050 than the
medium variant estimated by the UN. There will only be a 19 per cent population increase from 2015. The decline in the natural growth of the population
means that there will be a larger influence of inter-district migrants on the
district population: this point is analyzed in the next section.

Aged India

Estimating the age structure based on the TFR assumed in this study
reveals that the population aged 65 years or older will exceed 15 per cent and

Table 8.1 TFR assumptions

Year	UN medium variant	This study
2005–2010	2.80	2.80
2010–2015	2.48	2.48
2015–2020	2.34	2.23
2020–2025	2.23	2.00
2025–2030	2.14	1.80
2030–2035	2.06	1.60
2035–2040	1.99	1.50
2040–2045	1.94	1.50
2045–2050	1.89	1.50

reach the standard for an 'aged society' in 2050. As the cost of social welfare increases in an aged society, it is probable that it will become difficult to allocate large budgets to infrastructure for the environment. The current pace of infrastructure improvement will be too slow to accommodate the aging population in India.

Estimate of Migrants by District

Methodology of Estimation

It is necessary to estimate the scale of migration to predict the future population at the district level. For example, in Gurgaon in the suburbs of Delhi, the population increased by 57 per cent during 2000–2010, mainly because of in-migration from other districts. However, it is difficult to ascertain the actual situation in inter-district migration. Migration statistics have not been collected systematically. Therefore, this study was conducted to estimate inter-district migration during 2000–2010 using the method described below.

The closed population was defined as the estimated population without inter-district migration. This study compared this closed population and the actual population to calculate inter-district migration. First, using a cohort component method, the closed population by district in 2010 was calculated from the population by district in the 2000 Census, the fertility rate, and the death rate. Then the difference between the closed population and the actual population in the 2010 census was assumed to be the net migration. For example, when the closed population of a rural district with 1,000 people in the 2000 Census was calculated as 1,080 in 2010, the actual population was 1,050 in the 2010 Census. It can be inferred that the net number of out-migrants during 2000–2010 was 30. In contrast, the actual population in the 2010 Census exceeds the closed population. The difference is assumed to be the net number of migrations.

Estimation Accuracy

The TFR and mortality rate used in the calculation were state-level data from the Sample Registration System (2014). This method presents difficulties related to accuracy. In reality, the urban–rural statistics from the Sample Registration System show clearly that both the fertility rate and mortality rate in urban districts were lower than those in rural districts. Based on the described method, the numbers of births and deaths in urban districts were estimated as higher. However, errors in the numbers of births and deaths are mutually offsetting. Therefore, this method can retain a degree of accuracy regarding migration. Yet, if the population is considered based on age group, then in the case of urban districts, the number of children born and adults who die are estimated as larger, which causes a non-negligible error in the age structure. Therefore, only the net migration number will be considered.

Results

Maps 8.6 and 8.7 present the results of the estimation of the net migration between districts. Considering the accuracy of the estimation, only districts that had 50,000 and more people who in-migrated or out-migrated are shown.

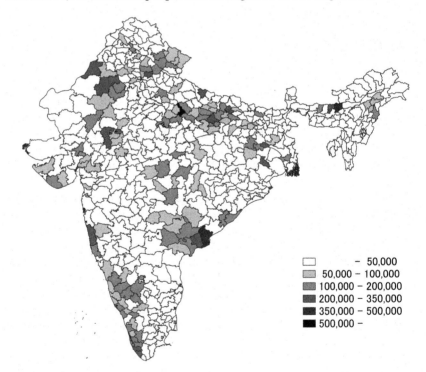

☐	– 50,000
▨	50,000 – 100,000
▨	100,000 – 200,000
■	200,000 – 350,000
■	350,000 – 500,000
■	500,000 –

Map 8.6 Estimated out-migration.

Source: Calculated by the author.

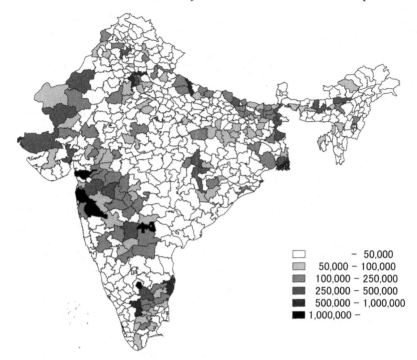

☐	− 50,000
▨	50,000 − 100,000
▤	100,000 − 250,000
▦	250,000 − 500,000
▬	500,000 − 1,000,000
■	1,000,000 −

Map 8.7 Estimated in-migration.

Source: Calculated by the author.

The out-migration from rural areas such as the northern region of Rajasthan, the central and eastern regions of Uttar Pradesh, and the Godavari River Basin area in Andhra Pradesh stand out. This out-migration reflects circumstances in which the rural population migrates to urban areas looking for job opportunities. It is also important that Lucknow, the state capital of Uttar Pradesh, did not accumulate more migrants. In-migration might be underestimated because the actual TFR in Lucknow is much lower than the state average. However, considering the fact that Ghaziabad, an urban district near Delhi in Uttar Pradesh, gained 600,000 people, probably there is weak in-migration to Lucknow. Because the population density in Lucknow and Ghaziabad are almost identical, it is difficult to say that it is only Lucknow's high population density that prevents in-migration. Delhi might be more attractive than Lucknow for inter-district migrants.

It was estimated that people out-migrated from Kerala and the coastal areas of Maharashtra. Actually, Kerala is famous for its many workers going abroad. The large number of out-migrants and the low TFR in this area will engender a population decrease over the next decade.

Looking at the districts to which people are in-migrating, these tend to be suburbs in metropolitan areas. However, it is estimated that people have migrated out of central parts of large cities such as Delhi Central, New Delhi, Mumbai, Kolkata, Hyderabad, and Chennai. In particular, 530,000 people left Kolkata, which is the largest out-migration among all districts in the current calculation. The estimated number might be excessive because the birth rate in Kolkata is much lower than the average rate for West Bengal, which was used for the estimation of Kolkata. However, even if the TFR of Kolkata was 1.0 and the death rate was the same as the average rate for the state, out-migration would still be estimated as 300,000, which indicates that these large cities had been overpopulated and that the current infrastructure capacity has reached its limit. This situation leads to an expanding metropolitan area and people in-migrating into the surrounding districts. A notable exception is Bangalore, which has a large area but is not presently observed in-migration to the neighboring prefectures. Instead, the in-migration to Bangalore is so intense that it was estimated as 2,000,000 in ten years: the largest volume of in-migration to one district. Bangalore's population density was 4,400 persons per square kilometer in 2010. One can infer that the room for new in-migrants is now small: in the future, surrounding districts might start to gather in-migrating people.

Districts that border Delhi, Gurgaon, Faridabad, Gautam Budh Nagar, and Ghaziabad gathered 3.3 million in-migrants. The populations of these areas increased from 22.2 million in 2000 to 28.5 million in 2010; net in-migration accounts for 52 per cent of the population increase. Such population concentration has a severe impact on the environment.

Some districts near Pakistan, such as Rajasthan and Gujarat, experienced net in-migrants. This might be caused by the Mangala oilfield, which began operating in 2005 and is now among the largest oilfields in India. It was estimated that 300,000 people in-migrated into the Barmer district, which is located in the center of Mangala oilfield. Development of the oil industry and other related industries is expected to have caused this population inflow.

Protein Consumption and Nitrogen Load From Humans

Protein Consumption

This section explains protein consumption as analyzed by state. For two reasons, clarifying the characteristics of food consumption with respect to protein intake is important for the analysis of nitrogen flow. One reason is that per-capita nitrogen load from humans depends on the per-capita intake of protein. The other reason is that future food production and nitrogen fertilizer input can be estimated roughly from food consumption because heavily populated developing countries such as India try to attain sufficient food to support themselves to the extent that resources permit. The next section presents a discussion of future food demand based on an analysis of the regional differences in protein intake and associated changes in recent

Table 8.2 Protein intake by state (g/day)

State	2009–2010 Rural	2009–2010 Urban	1999–2000 Rural	1999–2000 Urban	Change in 10 years Rural	Change in 10 years Urban
Andhra Pradesh	56.9	58.8	49.4	50.8	7.5	8
Assam	54.4	58.8	47.7	56.5	6.7	2.3
Bihar	57.6	62.4	58.7	61	−1.1	1.4
Delhi	58.1	56.9	52.7	61.4	5.4	−4.5
Gujarat	56	56.4	54.2	54.7	1.8	1.7
Haryana	70.7	64.5	75.3	62.5	−4.6	2
Himachal Pradesh	71.8	69.7	73.1	75	−1.3	−5.3
Karnataka	53.4	56.3	54.2	53.5	−0.8	2.8
Kerala	59	59.9	52.4	55.2	6.6	4.7
Madhya Pradesh	62.7	59	58.2	60.6	4.5	−1.6
Maharashtra	60.2	58.8	56.5	55.9	3.7	2.9
Orissa	54.5	58	49.9	57.8	4.6	0.2
Punjab	67.2	64.4	71.7	64.8	−4.5	−0.4
Rajasthan	71.4	63.7	76.9	70.4	−5.5	−6.7
Tamil Nadu	52	55.5	44.9	51.7	7.1	3.8
Uttar Pradesh	63.3	60.1	69.7	62	−6.4	−1.9
West Bengal	53.3	55.5	51.6	55.5	1.7	0
India	59.3	58.8	59.1	58.5	0.2	0.3

Source: Calculated by the author from National Sample Survey Office (2001), (2007), and (2012), Nutritional Intake in India 1999–2000, 2004–2005, 2009–2010.

years. In addition, the influence of population concentration in cities on nitrogen flow is discussed by explaining the differences in protein intake between rural and urban areas.

Based on data from *Nutritional Intake in India* (55th round (1999–2000) and 66th round (2009–2010)), protein intake per person for each state is presented in Table 8.2. Chhattisgarh, Jharkhand, and Uttarakhand, which separated from one another after 1999, are excluded.

During the decade from 1999–2000 to 2009–2010, the change in protein intake seen at the national level for India was not seen for both urban and rural areas as presented in Table 8.3. Protein intake in urban areas was slightly smaller than that in rural areas. In most countries of the world, protein intake tends to increase with economic development and urbanization. A remarkable characteristic of the food culture in India is that protein intake has risen only slightly over the observed decade.

Protein intake from eggs, meat, and fish is famously very low in India. All Indian states are classifiable into three groups: 'Group 1' states, including Kerala, West Bengal, and Assam, consume greater amounts of eggs, meat, and fish; 'Group 2' states, including Haryana, Punjab, Rajasthan, and Gujarat, consume protein disproportionately from milk and dairy products; all other states are 'Group 3' states. Sources of animal protein differ greatly among regions, but with respect to total protein intake, cereals (mainly rice and wheat) are the most important

Ippei Sekido

Table 8.3 Protein intake by source in 2010 (g/day)

State	Group	Rural					Urban				
		Cereal	Pulses	Milk, milk products	Egg, meat, fish	Others	Cereal	Pulses	Milk, milk products	Egg, meat, fish	Others
Haryana	1	38.2(−5.8)	4.9(−2.8)	17.7(−1.2)	0.7(0.2)	9.2(5.1)	34.2(−1.5)	5.8(−2.0)	12.9(0.3)	1.9(1.1)	9.7(4.2)
Punjab		36.3(−5.2)	6.0(−2.1)	15.5(−0.5)	0.7(−0.1)	8.1(2.6)	32.8(−2.4)	7.1(−1.9)	14.2(0.9)	1.3(0.1)	9.0(2.8)
Rajasthan		45.0(−9.4)	3.6(−1.5)	12.9(−0.4)	0.7(0.0)	9.3(5.7)	38.9(−6.5)	3.8(−3.7)	10.8(0.0)	1.3(0.2)	8.9(3.3)
Gujarat		32.5(−2.4)	5.0(−2.0)	8.4(1.1)	1.1(0.5)	9.0(4.6)	29.3(−0.9)	6.8(−1.1)	9.0(−0.2)	1.1(−0.1)	10.2(3.9)
Kerala	2	23.6(−2.4)	4.1(0.0)	4.1(0.0)	14.2(3.3)	12.4(5.2)	22.2(−2.6)	5.4(0.1)	5.4(0.1)	14.4(2.1)	13.2(5.6)
Assam		32.6(0.1)	4.4(0.1)	2.2(0.3)	6.5(2.1)	8.7(4.1)	31.2(−1.1)	5.3(−0.9)	2.9(−3.0)	9.4(3.0)	9.4(3.7)
West Bengal		30.4(−5.2)	3.2(−0.7)	2.1(0.2)	7.5(2.7)	10.7(5.2)	26.6(−5.2)	3.9(−1.0)	3.9(−0.4)	10.0(2.7)	11.1(3.9)
Andhra Pradesh	3	29.6(−2.8)	5.1(−0.4)	4.6(0.6)	5.7(2.3)	11.9(7.8)	26.5(−2.2)	6.5(−0.2)	6.5(0.3)	6.5(3.2)	12.9(6.9)
Bihar		39.2(−3.8)	4.0(−2.2)	3.5(0.1)	2.3(0.9)	7.5(2.7)	39.3(−1.5)	5.0(−2.3)	5.6(0.8)	3.1(0.8)	9.4(3.6)
Karnataka		28.3(−5.0)	5.3(−2.2)	5.3(0.0)	4.3(0.0)	10.7(6.9)	25.9(−2.9)	6.2(−1.6)	6.8(−0.3)	5.1(1.3)	11.8(5.8)
Madhya Pradesh		42.0(−1.1)	5.6(−1.1)	5.6(1.9)	1.3(0.5)	8.8(4.9)	34.8(−4.3)	5.9(−1.7)	6.5(0.4)	1.8(0.3)	9.4(3.1)
Maharashtra		34.3(−3.3)	6.6(−0.9)	4.2(0.2)	2.4(0.7)	12.6(7.0)	28.2(−3.1)	7.1(−0.6)	7.1(0.5)	4.7(1.3)	12.3(5.5)
Orissa		35.4(−3.1)	3.8(0.2)	1.6(0.4)	3.3(1.1)	9.8(5.5)	33.6(−5.7)	4.6(−1.0)	3.5(0.3)	4.6(1.1)	11.0(5.0)
Tamil Nadu		26.0(−1.1)	6.2(0.0)	4.2(0.8)	5.2(1.9)	10.4(5.5)	24.4(−0.9)	7.2(−0.5)	6.7(−0.1)	5.6(1.0)	11.1(3.7)
Uttar Pradesh		41.8(−6.2)	5.7(−2.3)	6.3(−0.1)	1.3(−0.4)	8.2(2.6)	36.1(−2.6)	5.4(−2.1)	7.2(−0.1)	1.8(−0.5)	9.0(2.7)
India		35.6(−4.3)	4.7(−1.7)	5.3(−0.1)	3.6(1.2)	9.5(4.5)	30.0(−3.4)	5.9(−1.8)	7.6(0.4)	4.7(1.2)	10.6(3.9)

Source: See Table 8.2.
Note: Parenthesis shows change from 2000.

protein source for Indian people. As a result, the total protein intake is high in states where the level of cereals is high. Protein intake from cereals across the whole of India fell during 1999–2000 through 2009–2010, and in almost all states, especially in Haryana, Punjab, and Rajasthan, where large amounts of protein are consumed from wheat. This might explain why local differences in all protein intake decreased during 1999–2000 through 2009–2010.

The consumption of milk and dairy products did not increase, although the consumption of eggs, meat, and fish did in 'Group 1'. However, the consumption of milk and dairy products declined slightly in 'Group 2', and the consumption of eggs, meat, and fish did not increase. As a result, regional differences remained mostly unchanged.

It is remarkable that protein intake from other food sources increased greatly in all states. Among items classified as other foods, nuts, and prepared meals (served in restaurants or food shops) contain high concentrations of protein. Increased consumption of these foods suggests diversification and development of diet. Substances included in prepared meals are important elements that indicate how dietary habits change along with economic development. However, it is difficult to obtain detailed data related to prepared meals. Importantly, the National Sample Survey estimated that prepared meals contain 25 g of protein per meal: an amount that accounted for 42 per cent of the average daily intake of protein in urban areas in 2009–2010. Consequently, it can be said that the National Sample Survey estimation appears to assume that prepared meals contain the same amount of protein as that consumed in the typical daily diet. This suggests that protein intake does not increase, even if people have the money to spare for eating out. In contrast, in most countries, it is the case that prepared meals contain more protein than the daily diet. These characteristics of the changes in Indian dietary habits appear in the estimations of the National Sample Survey. Overall, the food culture in India is conservative.

Food culture in India varies. Particularly, sources of animal protein vary in different states. However, in terms of total protein intake, there is little regional variance. These differences become even smaller with the advancement of urbanization. Because of small differences in all protein intake between rural and urban areas, migration from rural to urban areas does not affect per-capita protein consumption. Population concentration is the only factor that increases nitrogen load in urban areas, whereas in most developing countries, per-capita protein increases concomitantly with the progress of urbanization. Consequently, this is probably a unique characteristic of nitrogen flow in India.

The trend whereby the intake of protein from cereals decreases and that from animals gradually increases will continue in the future. It is an important fact that the per-capita consumption of cereals has fallen in terms of both nitrogen load and agricultural production. Assuming that India will produce rice and wheat to meet domestic demand, the required growth rate of rice and wheat production is expected to be less than the growth rate of the population. Conversely, the increased demand for animal protein will cause increased feed demand. Yet, the growth of consumption of animal protein is slow, and the more popular livestock products are milk, eggs, and chicken, which require less feed resources than either beef or pork. Given this fact, the feed demand is not expected to grow by a large amount.

Results show that stable dietary habits have a positive effect on the environment in India. In addition, the declining population growth rate contributes to easing of stress on food production to satisfy demand. However, it is necessary to increase nitrogen fertilizer inputs by a small amount as population growth continues for at least the next 30 years. Consequently, the slow increase in nitrogen load from fertilizers is expected to continue for a few decades.

Nitrogen Load from Humans

The nitrogen load from humans was calculated using the following formula.

$$NLh = Pop \times PI/PCF$$

In that formula, the following variables are used: NLh, Nitrogen load from humans; Pop, Population by districts; PI, Protein intake by states; PCF, Protein conversion factor = 6.25.

Maps 8.5 and 8.8 have the same legends. Map 8.8 shows estimates of quite a light nitrogen load because the nitrogen load from humans is extremely concentrated in urban districts. Because the regional differences in protein intake per person do not reach 1.4 times at the maximum, the nitrogen load distribution from humans closely resembles the population distribution. Therefore, an extremely high nitrogen load is estimated for large cities, which have high population densities. The highest nitrogen load per area is observed in the North East district of Delhi with 1,100 kg/ha, followed in order by Chennai, Delhi East, Kolkata, Delhi Central, the Mumbai Suburbs, and Mumbai. This value is higher than the nitrogen load for current Japanese prefectures, which have been estimated using the same methodology. It is thought that severe pollution occurs locally in these cities. Large-scale sewers and sewerage treatment facilities are necessary to prevent environmental pollution and to cope with the nitrogen load. According to the 12th Five-Year Plan, the government used a 420 billion rupee budget (including 140 billion rupees for sewer projects) for sewage maintenance and a project for wastewater management during 2005–2011 through the Jawaharlal Nehru National Urban Renewal Mission. However, according to the High Powered Expert Committee, an investment of 7.5 trillion rupees will be required in the next 20 years to develop infrastructure for water supply, which includes sewage systems and rainwater management.

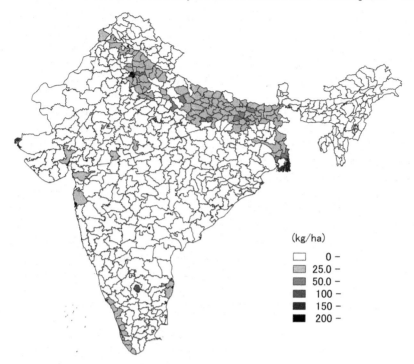

Map 8.8 Nitrogen load from humans per area.

Source: Calculated by the author.

Assuming this estimation is correct, the government must accelerate the pace of investment under the Jawaharlal Nehru National Urban Renewal Mission scheme. It is a great challenge for the urban development of India to improve the sewer infrastructure while the population continues to be so concentrated.

Discussion

The districts in the Ganga River Basin and Punjab, where both the nitrogen balance on farmland and the nitrogen load from humans are large, are regarded as having severe environmental problems caused by food production and consumption. The total nitrogen load (the sum of the nitrogen balance on farmland and the nitrogen load from humans) exceeds 200 kg/ha in most districts in Punjab and 100 kg/ha in most districts in the Ganga River Basin. Although these figures cannot be readily associated with other environmental indices such as water quality, nitrogen concentrations that exceed the allowable limits for drinking water set by the government were observed at 8 of 12 observation stations in Punjab, according to the Central Pollution Control Board (2011). Similar levels of nitrogen pollution are thought to have spread throughout the whole Ganga River Basin. Nitrogen fertilizer input accounts for the largest share of total nitrogen load in this area. This fertilizer input cannot decrease to meet food demand. However, because rice and wheat consumption per person did not increase (it even decreased) and because feed demand grew slowly, the nitrogen balance on farmland is not expected to deteriorate substantially in the future. Yet, it is a difficult problem to improve the present level of environmental pollution because it is widespread. Moreover, no direct method exists to remove surplus nitrogen from farmland. One measure that might address widespread nitrogen pollution is the diffusion of appropriate fertilization management to improve nitrogen efficiency, but this is no silver bullet.

In addition, although the magnitude of the nitrogen load from livestock to the total nitrogen load is small, the number of poultry in some districts near large cities is increasing sharply. Because the demand for eggs and chicken is rising slowly but constantly, the nitrogen load from poultry farming is expected to become an important difficulty at the local level. However, it is possible to prevent the nitrogen load from leaking from intensive poultry farms. Gathering up excrement and using it as fertilizer is one effective measure. Consequently, a monitoring system for poultry farming is necessary.

However, substantial nitrogen pollution as a result of population concentration is observed in city districts. The nitrogen load from humans in Delhi was estimated as 1,100 kg/ha. Furthermore, as was estimated above, the population concentration is geographically spreading to districts around large cities. The nitrogen load in these districts will continue to increase rapidly. Unlike widespread nitrogen pollution as a result of the nitrogen balance on farms, the pollution as a result of the nitrogen load from humans is controllable. The government of India is pushing forward, constricting wastewater infrastructure with a large budget. Judging from the experiences of Japan, improvement of sewage systems requires both a large budget and substantial time. This is a great challenge to be tackled in the long term with a large amount of effort.

In terms of nitrogen flow, the environmental problems of food production and consumption are divisible into two types: widespread pollution and local pollution. The nitrogen load on farmland causes the former. Pollution of this type is a severe problem that is difficult to alleviate. However, the conditions are unlikely to deteriorate to a much greater extent in the future. Population concentration and land-intensive livestock farming with feed crops are sources of local pollution. This type of pollution can be extremely high in some areas. It is expected to become a more severe difficulty in the future. However, measures exist to control the nitrogen load to prevent it from leaking into the environment. The improvement of sewage treatment systems depends on the government. It can be predicted that the challenges and responsibilities faced by the Indian government will increase.

References

Central Pollution Control Board, Basin Wise Water Quality Data 2011, http://cpcb. nic.in/data_statics.php. Accessed in Jul. 2013.

Department of Agriculture, Cooperation and Farmers Welfare, Ministry of Agriculture and Farmers Welfare, Government of India 2015, *District Wise Crop Production Statistics*, http://apy.dacnet.nic.in/cps.aspx/. Accessed Dec. 2015.

Department of Animal Husbandry, Dairying & Fisheries, Ministry of Agriculture, Government of India, 2014, *Livestock Census 2012*, New Delhi.

FAO 2011 FAOSTAT. http://faostat.fao.org/. Accessed Jan. 2013.

Galloway, J.N. (2000) 'Nitrogen mobilization in Asia', *Nutrient Cycling in Agroecosystems* 57: 1–12.

National Sample Survey Organization, Ministry of Statistics & Programme Implementation, Government of India (2001) *Nutritional Intake in India 1999–2000*, New Delhi.

National Sample Survey Organization, Ministry of Statistics & Programme Implementation, Government of India (2007) *Nutritional Intake in India 2004–2005*, New Delhi.

National Sample Survey Organization, Ministry of Statistics & Programme Implementation, Government of India (2012) *Nutritional Intake in India 2009–2010*, New Delhi.

Office of the Registrar General & Census Commissioner, India, Ministry of Home Affairs, Government of India (2014) *SRS Statistical Report 2013*, New Delhi.

Pathak, H., Mohanty, S., Jain, N. and Bhatia, A. (2010) 'Nitrogen, phosphorus, and potassium budgets in Indian agriculture', *Nutrient Cycling in Agroecosystems*, 86: 287–99.

Seitzinger, S.P. and Kroeze, C. (1998) 'Global distribution in nitrous oxide production and N inputs in freshwater and coastal marine ecosystems', *Global Biogeochemical Cycles*, 12: 93–113.

Shindo, J. (2012) 'Changes in the nitrogen balance in agricultural land in Japan and 12 other Asian Countries based on a nitrogen-flow model', *Nutrient Cycling in Agroecosystems*, 94: 47–61.

Shindo, J., Okamoto, K. and Kawashima, H. (2006) 'Prediction of the environmental effects of excess nitrogen caused by increasing food demand with rapid economic growth in eastern Asian countries, 1961–2020', *Ecological Modelling*, 193: 703–20.

Shindo, J., Okamoto, K. Kawashima, H. and Konohira, E. (2009) 'Nitrogen flow associated with food production and consumption and its effect on water quality in Japan from 1961 to 2005', *Soil Science and Plant Nutrition*, 55: 532–45.

The Fertilizer Association of India (2001) *Fertilizer and Agriculture Statistics 2000–2001*, New Delhi.

The Fertilizer Association of India (2009) *Fertilizer and Agriculture Statistics 2008–2009*, New Delhi.

United Nations Department of Economic and Social Affairs Population Division, *World Population Prospects: The 2015 Revision*, http://esa.un.org. Accessed Dec. 2015.

Velmurugan, A., Dadhwal, V.K. and Abrol, Y.P. (2008) 'Regional nitrogen cycle: An Indian perspective', *Current Science*, 94(11): 1455–68.

9 Power Sector Reform and Blackouts in India

Atsushi Fukumi

India has become an attractive destination for investment as a huge market with rich potential. Now that the Chinese economy is showing signs of decline, India is expected to play an increasingly important role as the engine pulling the world economy forward. That promise notwithstanding, looking ahead to India's further industrialization and economic growth in the coming years, the country's underdeveloped infrastructure presents a clear threat. It has the potential to act as a bottleneck constraining the dynamism of private investment. Given the direct role of power in business and industry, especially in the manufacturing sector, India's underdeveloped power infrastructure is perceived as the most important obstacle.

The State Electricity Boards (SEBs) were established as vertically integrated power utilities after Independence and bear much of the responsibility for the current difficulties. Although they have contributed to industrialization to some degree, their dwindling incentive to perform well as commercial entities is related to their weakened financial status. Tight fiscal constraints have hampered investment in the establishment, operation, and maintenance of facilities, which have, in turn, produced a poor power supply service. The core of the power sector reform started in the early 1990s and emphasized the reconstruction of state power utilities through drastic changes in their governance of them and the entire power sector. Two key steps were taken toward this end: (a) the establishment of the State Electricity Regulatory Commissions (SERCs) and (b) the unbundling of the SEBs into generation, transmission, and distribution corporations. Since the enforcement of the Electricity Act 2003 in June 2003, the reforms have been fundamentally completed. Several studies, such as those by Ruet (2005) and Tongia (2007), have revealed that the reforms were implemented merely as a matter of form. They have failed to alter the internal circumstances of some states.

This chapter explores the effects of power sector reform on power outages. The literature in this area includes the World Bank evaluation of the progress of corporate reform and regulatory governance, which is based on quantitative and qualitative information concerning the state power utilities and state regulatory commission. Pargal and Mayer (2014) advanced

DOI: 10.4324/9781003311898-10

the first study to use these indexes to quantitatively examine the progress of reform and to assess its effects empirically. Their regression results from state and utility level analyses show that these indexes are positively related to the financial and operational performance of the power utilities. Based on these earlier investigations, we explore the effects of governance reform on the private sector using firm-level data from a World Bank enterprise survey on commercial losses caused by power outages as a proxy for power supply quality. Our estimates demonstrate that shortcomings in the quality of the corporate governance of the utilities and regulatory governance of the SERCs exert important adverse effects on commercial losses attributable to power outages. Consequently, it is safe to conclude that governance reform has a considerable impact on the quality of customer service.

The first section presents a brief outline of issues facing the Indian power sector, with an exploration of the relevant background factors. The second section presents a description of the key aspects of power sector reform. The third section empirically assesses how corporate and regulatory governance affect the quality of the power supply.

Indian Power Sector: Challenges and Background

Quality and Quantity of Power Supply

The Indian power sector is a concurrent subject under Article 246 of the Indian Constitution, which assigns major roles to state governments related to power supply activities. For more than five decades leading up to the mid-2000s, the Indian power sector consisted mainly of SEBs. The central government fundamentally assumed responsibility for the interstate power supply through the agency of the National Corporations. From Figure 9.1,

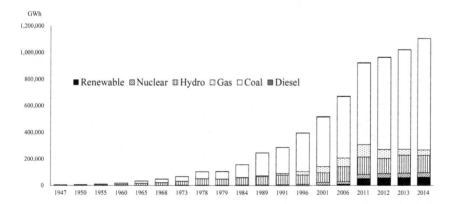

Figure 9.1 Mode wise growth of gross power generation (utilities only).

Source: Central Electricity Authority (2015).

which presents the evolution of modal power generation since Independence, it is readily apparent that India has developed its power capacity mainly by expanding its coal use. As of January 2022, the total installed capacity of the Indian power sector reached 393,389 MW, the third highest capacity in the world following that of China and the US. In terms of per-capita value, however, India trails after those countries in power sector development. Figure 9.2 shows per-capita GDP and per-capita power consumption in India and China, with comparisons of actual values in China with actual, projected, and estimated values in India. The actual values in China and India indicate that India lags far behind in both economic development and power consumption. Turning to the projected value proposed by the Planning Commission (2006), one sees that India's projected per-capita power consumption in 2031 falls short of the actual value in China in 2011. The estimated value, a fitted value from the simple regression results obtained using actual data from 1971 to 2011,[1] presents an even more disappointing scenario.

Several surveys of investors from around the world have indicated poor power infrastructure as the highest hurdle to investment in India. The difficulty of power outages can be an especially severe and direct obstacle. According to an estimate by the Federation of Indian Chambers of Commerce and Industry (FICCI) in 2013, the total cost of power outages in India was 68 billion dollars, or 0.4 per cent of GDP. Frequent power outages and voltage fluctuations compel industrial firms to invest in generators and stabilizers to mitigate their incidence and damage, although medium and small companies lack the funds to bear this expense. To them, the outages and fluctuations inflict damage

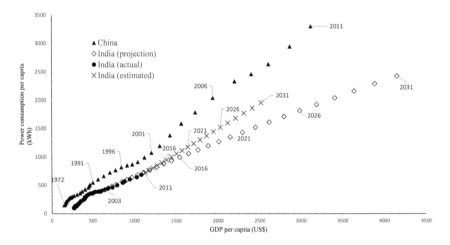

Figure 9.2 Power consumption and economic development in India and China.

Source: Original actual data are from World Development Indicator. Data on projected values are from the Planning Commission (2006).

Note: Estimated values are from calculations based on the actual trend from 1971 to 2011.

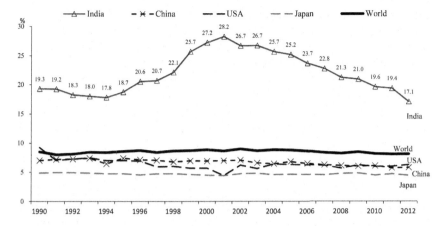

Figure 9.3 Electric power transmission and distribution losses (% of output).

Source: World Development Indicators.

directly to businesses. Allcott et al. (2014) demonstrate that power outages reduce the output of India's textile industry by about five percent and inflict especially heavy damage to plants without generators and to small plants with generators (because of scale economies in generator capacity).

Difficulties with transformers and distribution networks stemming from poor maintenance and investment can cause power outages. Figure 9.3 presents India's loss of electricity in the process of transmission and distribution along with related figures from China, the US, and Japan, and the world average. The Indian power sector incurs losses that are far greater than the world average. The poor quality of its transmission and distribution networks is readily apparent. Scheduled power cuts attributable to power shortages should be emphasized as a frequent cause. In Figure 9.4, a plot showing

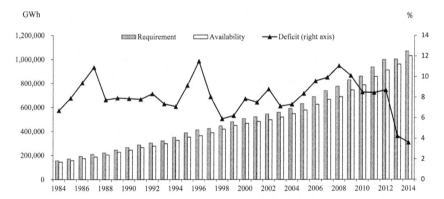

Figure 9.4 Power requirements and availability.

Source: See Figure 9.1.

the demand and supply balance from the years 1984–85 to 2014–15, it is clear that the gap separating requirement and availability remained narrow from the late 1990s to 2003, then widened to 11.07 per cent by fiscal 2008. The installed capacity was expanded during the same years but not sufficiently to cope with the high growth of power requirements. This narrowing trend in the 2000s turned in 2009–10 when the economic slowdown in India restrained the expansion of the power requirements, and several thermal power plants were launched under the Ultra Mega Power Projects promoted by the central government.

The interstate disparity of the problems described above must be explained. Figure 9.5 shows the state-level relation between per-capita GDP and per-capita power consumption from the fiscal year 2006–2012 in a manner similar to that shown in Figure 9.2. From this point, one can see that a huge gap separates leading states such as Delhi, Haryana, and Gujarat and lagging states such as Bihar and Uttar Pradesh in terms of per-capita electricity consumption and the level of economic development. Furthermore, the gap seems to have been growing. Addressing the differences among states on the power shortage problem (see Map 9.1), one might note that

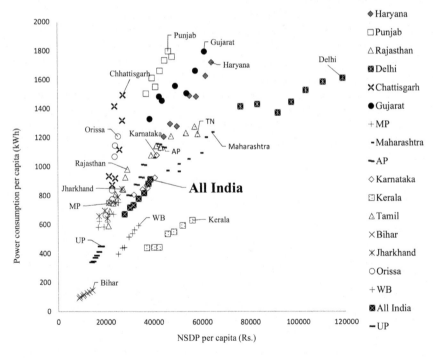

Figure 9.5 NSDP vs. electricity consumption per capita, 2006–2012.

Source: Original data is from Planning Commission (2014), CEA (2015), and EPW Research Foundation.

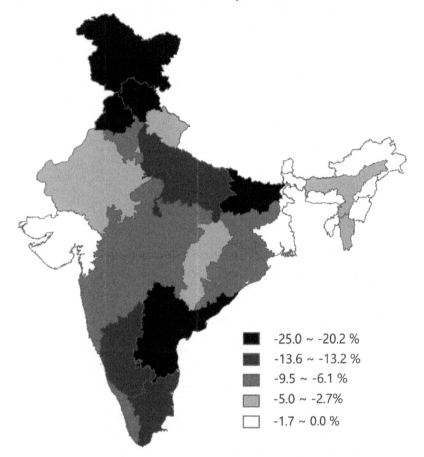

Map 9.1 Energy deficit in 2012.

Source: Data from Ministry of Power (2013).

Gujarat and West Bengal fare well, although the southern states suffer more severely than the other major states. It is noteworthy that in terms of quantity and quality, the Indian power sector is far behind the world average, although the severity of problems differs among states.

The Roots of the Problem

To examine the background factors linked to the challenges mentioned above, one should begin by pointing out the effect of the deteriorated financial status of the state power utilities. In Figure 9.6, which shows the commercial loss of state power utilities as a percentage of GDP, it is apparent that commercial loss rose rapidly in the late 1990s, reaching 1.4 per cent of GDP by 2000–2001. Later in the early 2000s, it receded again. Subsequently,

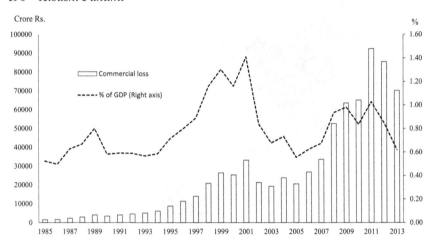

Figure 9.6 Commercial loss (without subsidy) of state power utilities.

Source: Calculated by the author from Power Finance Corporation (2008), Planning Commission (2012), (2014), and Reserve Bank of India (2015).

it expanded to its second-highest peak, 1.03 per cent of GDP, in 2011–2012. The tight fiscal constraints hamper investment in the establishment, operation, and maintenance of facilities, which in turn weakens the quality of the power supply service. The extremely high transmission and distribution losses (see Figure 9.3) are a core component of the huge commercial loss. Beyond the technical flaws stemming from a weak investment in transmission and distribution facilities, widening problems of electricity theft and non-payment aggravate the losses. India's average aggregate technical and commercial (AT&C) loss, which encompasses commercial losses and transmission and distribution losses together, reached 27 per cent in 2013. Although the situation has begun to recently improve, the problem persists, especially in rural areas. The very low cost recovery ratio also constrains the financing of power utilities. Figure 9.7 presents the major composition of the power supply cost and revenue and its changes over the three periods. The tariff revenue has grown too slowly to offset the rises in the cost for power purchase and generation, even after subsidies are received from state governments. The recovery ratio declined from 91 per cent in 2004 to 79 per cent in 2012, which directly worsened the financial status of the state power utilities.

As a more fundamental cause of the problem, one must mention political and economic factors. Before the implementation of the power sector reform, state governments strongly influenced important decisions made by the state power utilities on matters such as tariff-setting, investment approvals, financing, and recruitment. Commercial losses can also be offset by state subsidies. In the worst case, a bailout can be expected. Because of the intervention of state politics, an overall lack of accountability, and the

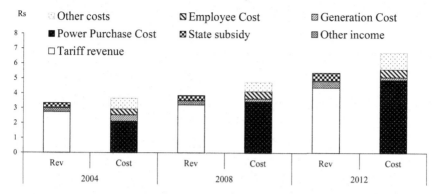

Figure 9.7 Composition of power supply cost and revenue per kilowatt-hour.

Source: Calculated by the author from PRC (2008, 2012, 2014).

Notes: Data of the utilities directly selling electricity to consumers only.
"Other costs" include costs for employees, O&M, interest, depreciation, and administration and general expenditures.

"moral hazard" stemming from the financial backing of state governments, the state power utilities have lacked the necessary incentive to perform well as commercial concerns.

The distorted tariff structure, under which agricultural users enjoy preferential electricity tariffs while industrial and commercial tariffs are set over cost and the surplus is used as a cross-subsidy to offset the deficit, has been criticized as a form of political patronage.[2] Since the main power source of the irrigation pump shifted from diesel to electricity, electricity became an important input for agriculture in the 1970s. After the 1970s, electric power policy became highly politicized. Power subsidies were widely adopted as a tool to win the votes of farmers and they can be recognized as a driver of social and economic development, especially in rural areas. Shah (2009) proposed that power subsidies helped promote the Green Revolution by reducing the cost of irrigation with electric pumps. Irrigation by tube wells serviced by electric pumps started spreading in the 1970s just as agriculture's share of electricity consumption began rising (see Figure 9.8). If financially troubled power utilities can provide a good service, then the tariff policy could be revaluated as an instrument of social policy to some degree, although the problem of fiscal sustainability remains. Fukumi (2016), however, has empirically showed that the financially degraded utilities failed to provide high-quality service even in the several states where they received huge subsidies to support their operations. Figure 9.9 shows a negative relation between the financial status of power utilities and the loss attributable to power outages at the state level, which implies a direct correlation between interstate disparity in the financial status of power utilities and the varying levels of quality in the power supply. We can therefore argue that

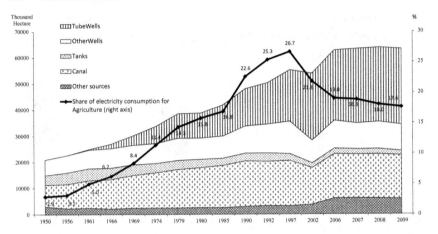

Figure 9.8 Net area irrigated from different sources of irrigation and the share of electricity consumption for agriculture.

Source: Indiastat, CEA (2015).

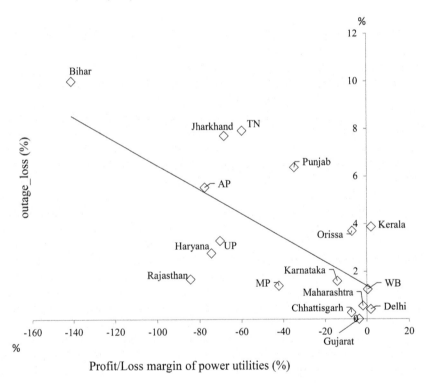

Profit/Loss margin of power utilities (%)

Figure 9.9 Financial status of utilities and commercial loss due to power outage.

Source: Fukumi (2016).

Note: Data of the utilities directly selling electricity to consumers only.

good-quality power would be difficult to supply without underlying commercial support, even though a subsidy policy might be requisite to some degree.

Governance Reform and Its Assessment

Targets to Be Achieved by Unbundling the SEBs and Establishing the SERCs

After the New Economic Policy was instituted in the early 1990s, India launched power sector reforms and implemented several measures to improve the situation of its power sector. The reforms began with efforts to promote the entry of independent power producers (IPPs), but the target shifted to financial reconstruction when it became apparent that the degraded financial status of the state power utilities was discouraging investment, especially in the distribution sector. Among the various measures taken, an important one was the unbundling of SEBs into generation, transmission, and distribution corporations.

Economically developed countries began to unbundle their power utilities in the 1980s with the aim of introducing competition in the generation sector by dismantling the single-buyer model. The primary objectives in India were to commercialize the power sector and to make the contributions of individual companies to overall commercial loss and profit more transparent, thereby compelling the management of power utilities to become more efficient. For utilities to corporatize, the Indian Company Act of 1956 required that their judicial status be converted from administrative bodies to companies. The Act sought to enable the transparent and independent management of utilities by bringing about fundamental changes in corporate governance.[3] The establishment of the SERCs was another important component of the reforms. Although the SERCs serve various functions, such as the issuance of licenses for distribution and intrastate transmission, the assurance of non-discriminatory open access, and so on,[4] their main function is to set tariffs. In recognition of where the political interventions on the power tariff issue had led before the reform, it was aimed to create a commission with the authority to decide on tariffs independently while maintaining a balance between subsidies, profitable tariffs, and quality of service.

Through initial arrangements by the World Bank, Orissa became the first state to unbundle its SEB and establish a SERC in 1996. Up to the end of the 1990s, the Orissa model spread rapidly by varying degrees to other states such as Haryana, Andhra Pradesh, and Rajasthan. Not long thereafter, the Electricity Act 2003 repealed all existing electricity laws and made electricity reform compulsory.[5] The Act has mandated the unbundling of the SEBs and the constitution of the state regulatory commissions in a time-bound manner. This has played an extremely important role in accelerating the reform process. All major states have fundamentally completed the requirements under the Act in the ten years since the Act was enforced, although exceptions can be found. Several states will need longer periods for implementation.[6]

To what extent has the reform of governance affected the power sector? Given the current deteriorated financial status of the power sector (Figure 9.6), it would be difficult to conclude that the unbundling of the SEBs and the establishment of the SERCs have had positive effects. Based on the cases presented by Haryana and Orissa, Ruet (2005) points out that the unbundling and corporatization were judicial changes. They have done little to diminish the strong influence of state government over the utilities. Similarly, doubt arises concerning the functions and independence of the SERCs. In one well-known case, the Congress Party offered free electricity to farmers after its return to power in 2004, although the former government increased the agricultural tariff and reduced the tariff distortion in the process of power sector reform. Dubash and Rao (2008) point out that electricity regulation was, in many ways, an extension of the state electricity department and previously established utilities, both through the selection of regulators and the appointment of employees. They suggest that, in spite of their strong power, the regulators might be unwilling to exercise that power on an independent commission basis in practice. In other words, these study results indicate that the quality of governance itself is sometimes limited by state-specific circumstances such as the political situation and economic structure.

Assessment of Governance Reform

The World Bank has attempted to evaluate the quality of corporate governance and regulatory governance quantitatively.[7] Using the guideline of the Department of Public Enterprises on (a) Board Composition, (b) Board Functioning, (c) Audit Committee, and (d) Government–Board relationship as a benchmark, it assesses aspects of corporate governance that can be expected to increase the internal and external accountability of utilities. The dataset includes various indexes such as "proportion of board members appointed as executive directors," "number of government directors," "the board size," and "existence of external auditors."[8] Regarding the quality of regulatory governance, two series of indexes are constructed using information about (a) the quality of institutional design of state-level regulations in terms of the Autonomy, Capacity, Transparency, and Accountability of the SERC and (b) the extent to which regulators have implemented mandates on tariff rationalization, protection of consumer rights, standards of performance, the progress of open access, and so on. Pargal and Mayer (2014) regressed these indexes to the variable of utility financial performance and found a positive relation, confirming the importance of corporate and regulatory governance.

Figure 9.10 presents an index of institutional design of regulation (*Regulatory_Governance*) constructed by aggregating the indexes on the

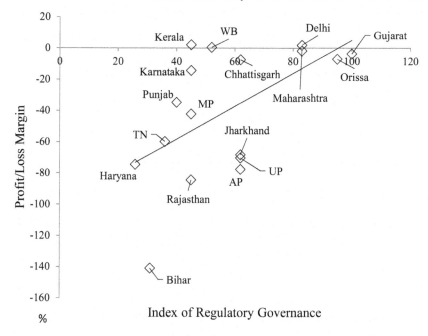

Figure 9.10 Regulatory governance and the financial status of utilities.

Source: Author's calculation using data from Pargal and Mayer(2014) and PFC (2014).

Note: Data of the utilities directly selling electricity to consumers only.

Autonomy, Capacity, and Transparency of the SERCs. Results show the state-level relation between the quality of regulatory governance and the financial status of the power utilities. A huge disparity is apparent among states in association with the quality of their regulatory governance. States with low-quality governance, such as Bihar, Haryana, and Tamil Nadu, produce huge commercial losses, whereas states with highly ranked governance, such as Gujarat, Orissa, Delhi, and Maharashtra, fare much better. A positive relation was found between better-designed regulatory governance and the sound financial performance of utilities.

Determinants of Blackouts in India

Empirical Variables

Figure 9.11 presents a summary of the background factors contributing to the poor quality of India's power supply based on the discussion above. The power deficit and low quality of infrastructure for distribution and transmission are identifiable as direct causes of the low quality of service (determinants (a) in Figure 9.11). These problems, however, also stem from the degraded financial status of the power utilities (determinants (b)),

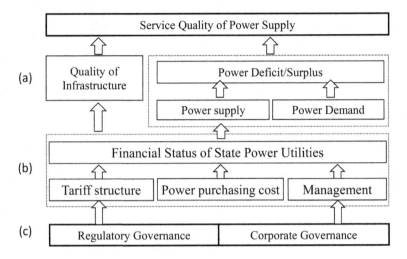

Figure 9.11 Determinants of the service quality in Indian power sector.

a condition that can be influenced by the quality of regulatory and corporate governance (determinants (c)).

Based on this brief sketch, we can assess the effects of regulatory and corporate governance on blackouts, including several factors that can affect blackouts as explanatory variables. As the dependent variable, we use establishment-level data for the quality of power supply in the 17 major states of India from The India 2014 Enterprise Survey Dataset published by the World Bank.[9] The survey assesses the quality of the power supply based on information related to estimated losses attributable to power outages as a percentage of total annual sales. These data are more subjective than precise because the survey respondents were only asked to "estimate" the losses resulting from power outages as percentages of their total annual sales. Nevertheless, this variable is used as a proxy for power supply quality on the assumption that it faithfully reflects the respondents' perceptions of the degree to which power outages disturb the operations of their establishments. Table 9.1 presents a data description of loss attributable to power outages (*Power_Outage*) state-by-state. The mean values for Gujarat, Chhattisgarh, and Delhi are less than 1 per cent, although that for Bihar exceeds 10 per cent. The data indicates that the establishments are unaffected by power outages in the states grouped as good performers in the preceding section, although the establishments in Bihar, the worst ranked state, suffer heavily.

Two state-level variables selected from various indexes are used as indexes of corporate and regulatory governance: the share of independent directors on the boards (*Corporate_Governance*) and the index of institutional design of regulation (*Regulatory_Governance*). Among the several indexes of corporate and regulatory governance provided by the World Bank, we employed these two variables because both variables were found to have significant

Table 9.1 Statewise description of the loss due to power outage

	Number of observations	Mean (%)	Standard deviation	Max (%)	Number of observations with value 0 %
Andhra Pradesh	548	5.55	6.87	60	62
Bihar	297	10.02	12.09	60	87
Chhattisgarh	280	0.28	0.87	5	244
Delhi	470	0.41	1.76	25	401
Gujarat	472	0.00	0.00	0	472
Haryana	298	2.78	3.59	30	49
Jharkhand	242	7.71	11.30	50	100
Karnataka	558	1.60	1.72	20	138
Kerala	408	3.88	4.44	20	138
Madhya Pradesh	329	1.41	2.65	20	189
Maharashtra	606	0.56	1.48	10	492
Orissa	203	3.70	4.19	30	19
Punjab	395	6.38	7.49	60	103
Rajasthan	281	1.69	3.01	20	138
Tamil Nadu	445	7.93	11.71	100	98
Uttar Pradesh	377	3.30	6.66	90	59
West Bengal	467	1.25	2.54	20	276
Total	6,676	3.20	6.52	100	3,065

Source: Calculated by the author from "The India 2014 Enterprise Survey Data set."

effects as explanatory variables in the regression reported by Pargal and Mayer (2014). We expect each to have a negative effect in our analysis based on two assumptions: (a) a higher share of independent directors not associated with utilities, government, or owners engenders more transparent management and better performance for utilities; and (b) SERCs with high rankings in terms of autonomy, capacity, transparency, and accountability function well, which raises the performance of the utilities.

Our other state-level controls include the financial status of power utilities in a state (*Profit_ Margin*), the aggregate technical and commercial losses (*AT&C_Loss*), and the electricity balance (*Electricity_Balance*). We expect the *Profit_Margin* to have a negative effect and the latter two variables to have positive effects. As firm-level controls, we used a dummy variable denoting whether the establishment is located in a megacity (*Megacity_Dummy*), the size of the establishment captured by the number of employees (*Firm_ Size*), a dummy variable denoting whether the establishment is located in an export-processing zone or industrial park (*EPZ_ Dummy*), and a dummy variable for the industry to which the establishment belongs. The descriptive statistics and correlation matrix of the variables included in the empirical model are given in Tables 9.2 and 9.3. Because the dependent variable has a value of zero for the number of establishments, we estimate this model using the maximum likelihood estimation of the Tobit model.

Table 9.2 Definitions of variables

Data level	Name	Definition	Type	Obs.	Mean	Max	Mini	S.D.	Source
Establishment	Power_Outage	Estimated loss as percentage of total annual sales due to power outage (%)	Numeric	6676	3.20	100	0	6.52	World Bank "The India 2014 Enterprise Survey Data set" (http://microdata.worldbank.org/index.php/catalog/2225)
	Firm_Size	The number of permanent, full-time workers end of last fiscal year	Numeric	7854	115.3	9999	2	364.3	
	EPZ_Dummy	Dummy for the establishment located in EPZ or industrial park (equal to zero if the establishment is located in either)	Binary	7859	0.57	1	0	0.50	
	Megacity_Dummy	Dummy for mega city (equal to zero if the establishment is located at the city with population over 1 million)	Binary	7859	0.45	1	0	0.50	
State	Corporate_Governance	The share of the independent director, who is not associated with utility, government, or owner	Numeric	11	13.1	33	0	14.0	World Bank "India Power Sector Review" (http://data.worldbank.org/data-catalog/india-power-sector-review)
	Regulatory_Governance	The index of institutional design of state-level regulation in terms of SERC Autonomy, Capacity, Transparency and Accountability	Numeric	17	57.3	100	26	22.0	
	Profit_Margin	The ratio of profit to the total revenue without subsidy from state governments. Taking average value of the utilities selling to the consumers directly in the state. (%)	Numeric	17	−0.35	0.02	−0.85	0.34	PFC (2014)
	AT&C_Loss	The ratio of profit to the total revenue with subsidy from state governments. Taking average value of the utilities selling to the consumers directly in the state. (%)	Numeric	17	27.7	54.6	10.5	12.9	PFC (2014)
	Electricity_Balance	Electricity balance = (Available electricity − Requirement electricity)/ Requirement electricity (%)	Numeric	17	−7.7	−0.2	−17.6	6.5	CEA (2013)

Notes:

The states employed here are Andhra Pradesh, Bihar, Chhattisgarh, Delhi, Gujarat, Haryana, Jharkhand, Karnataka, Kerala, Madhya Pradesh, Maharashtra, Orissa, Punjab, Rajasthan, Tamil Nadu, Uttar Pradesh, and West Bengal, while the index of corporate governance is not available for the six states, Bihar, Chhattisgarh, Jharkhand, Kerala, Rajasthan, and Uttar Pradesh.

The data on corporate and regulatory governance is the value of the year 2010–11, while other variables are the value of 2012–13.

Table 9.3 Correlation matrix

	Power_ Outage	Corporate_ Governance	Regulatory_ governance	Profit_ margin	AT&C_ loss	Electricity_ balance	Firm_ size	EPZ_ Dummy	Megacity_ dummy
Power_Outage	1.00								
Corporate_Governance	-0.27	1.00							
Regulatory_Governance	-0.25	0.37	1.00						
Profit_Margin	-0.34	0.43	0.59	1.00					
AT&C_Loss	-0.09	0.13	-0.14	0.17	1.00				
Electricity_Balance	-0.31	0.52	0.57	0.78	0.30	1.00			
Firm_Size	-0.02	-0.05	-0.11	-0.03	0.03	-0.06	1.00		
EPZ_Dummy	-0.06	-0.01	-0.05	0.02	-0.07	0.03	0.06	1.00	
Megacity_Dummy	-0.06	0.44	0.34	0.28	-0.17	0.33	-0.03	0.02	1.00

Estimation Results

Table 9.4 provides the maximum likelihood estimation results of the Tobit model on the effect of corporate governance. The first noteworthy finding is the negative and significant effect of the coefficients on *Corporate_Governance* at the 1 per cent level of significance in Eq. (1). This result implies that the share of independent directors has a strong effect on the quality of service. When using *Profit_Margin* or *Electricity_Balance* and *AT&C_loss* to control the effects of factors expected to be related more directly to power outages in Eqs. (2) and (3), it is apparent that *Corporate_Governance* has a significant effect with a negative sign. Assessing the effect of regulatory governance similarly, one obtains the results presented in Table 9.5. The three specifications present a negative and strong effect of the coefficients on *Regulatory_Governance* at a 1 per cent level of significance. All of these results are consistent with the discussion by Pargal and Mayer (2014), who found positive effects of corporate and regulatory governance on the financial performance of utilities. It would therefore be safe to infer that our empirical analysis supports an agenda of power sector reform calling for strengthened functions of the SERCs and tightened accountability of the power utilities.

Examining the estimation results for *Firm_Size, Megacity_Dummy, EPZ_Dummy,* and Industrial dummies, we cannot easily infer that these establishment-level variables have significant effects, given that their significance and the signs of their coefficients are inconsistent and dependent on the specifications. These results imply that, apart from the industrial characteristics, the characteristics of the states in which the enterprises are based tend to dominate the features of the establishments, such as their locations and the sizes of their firms. In other words, state-level efforts to improve have an important effect on the operation of private firms through the power supply.

Conclusion

This chapter explained an investigation into the effects of power sector reform on the quality of the power supply in India using indexes of corporate and regulatory governance provided by the World Bank. We demonstrated, by briefly sketching the difficulties faced in the Indian power sector and the concept of reform, that India can escape the vicious cycle by inputting commercial concerns into the sector through governance reforms, specifically by unbundling the SEBs and by establishing SERCs. Yet the effects of these reforms are limited by the influences of state-specific circumstances such as political situations and economic structures.

Based on that discussion, we used establishment-level data to investigate how the quality of corporate and regulatory governance affects power outages. Our estimates show that shortcomings in the quality of the corporate

Table 9.4 Effect of corporate governance

	Eq. (1)		Eq. (2)		Eq. (3)	
	Coefficient	Standard error	Coefficient	Standard error	Coefficient	Standard error
Corprate_Governance	−0.343	(0.035)***	−0.152	(0.031)***	−0.049	(0.029)*
Profit_Margin			−0.138	(0.01)***		
Electricity_Balance					−0.842	(0.06)***
AT&C_Loss					0.296	(0.047)***
Firm_Size	0.000	(0.001)	0.000	(0.001)	−0.001	(0.001)
Megacity_Dummy	0.051	(0.709)	−0.263	(0.686)	1.633	(0.706)**
EPZ_Dummy	−1.467	(0.661)**	−0.273	(0.644)	0.085	(0.635)
Industrial dummies						
Basic metals	−2.079	(1.574)	−0.069	(1.388)	0.966	(1.308)
Chemicals	−4.126	(1.585)***	−2.593	(1.465)*	−2.098	(1.357)
Electronics	−0.805	(1.566)	1.114	(1.395)	0.155	(1.288)
Fabricated metal products	−0.574	(1.56)	1.327	(1.472)	1.512	(1.388)
Food	3.077	(1.667)*	3.047	(1.514)**	4.036	(1.429)***
Furniture	−2.855	(2.584)	−0.027	(2.353)	−0.639	(2.382)
Garments	0.785	(1.737)	2.379	(1.622)	2.400	(1.534)
Leather	2.641	(2.083)	3.033	(2.044)	2.597	(1.766)
Machinery and equipment	−2.743	(1.665)	0.195	(1.501)	0.764	(1.441)
Non-metallic mineral products	0.049	(1.595)	−0.455	(1.47)	1.563	(1.308)

(*Continued*)

Table 9.4 Effect of corporate governance (Continued)

	Eq. (1)		Eq. (2)		Eq. (3)	
	Coefficient	Standard error	Coefficient	Standard error	Coefficient	Standard error
Paper	0.565	(2.329)	2.439	(2.222)	2.713	(2.077)
Plastics & rubber	−0.398	(1.572)	0.439	(1.441)	0.802	(1.322)
Precision instruments	−0.202	(2.529)	−0.539	(2.404)	−1.441	(2.191)
Publishing	−3.911	(1.878)**	−2.198	(1.763)	−3.054	(1.67)*
Recycling	5.842	(1.456)***	0.052	(1.326)	2.368	(1.241)*
Refined petroleum product	−4.376	(1.997)**	−1.675	(2.094)	−2.245	(1.783)
Textiles	3.401	(1.759)*	4.948	(1.688)***	4.936	(1.615)***
Tobacco	−1.140	(3.133)	−2.286	(3.232)	−2.061	(3.048)
Retail	−3.644	(1.594)**	−1.193	(1.48)	−2.134	(1.38)
Wholesale	−1.668	(1.651)	0.887	(1.52)	0.063	(1.385)
Construction section F	−5.615	(1.739)***	−2.673	(1.679)	−3.489	(1.579)**
Hotel and restaurants	−3.044	(1.601)*	−0.511	(1.485)	−1.771	(1.363)
IT	−4.019	(1.887)**	−1.405	(1.844)	−2.589	(1.689)
Services of motor vehicles	−7.328	(2.719)***	−3.652	(2.471)	−3.790	(2.408)
Transport Section I	−4.165	(1.655)***	−1.681	(1.529)	−2.585	(1.412)*
Transport machines	0.249	(1.804)	1.726	(1.71)	3.000	(1.628)*
Constant	5.054	(1.404)***	−3.479	(1.377)**	−5.665	(2.054)***
Number of observation	4,790		4790		4790	
Log pseudolikelihood	−538288		−521145		−516663	

Notes: Dependent variable: Power outage left-censored observations at outage loss <= 0: 2298 uncensored observations: 2492 right-censored observations: 0. "***", "**", and "*" denotes statistical significance at the 1%, 5%, and 10% levels correspondingly. Industrial dummy of wood is not included.

Table 9.5 Effect of regulatory governance

	Eq. (3)		Eq. (4)		Eq. (5)	
	Coefficient	Standard error	Coefficient	Standard error	Coefficient	Standard error
Regulatory_Governance	-0.244	(0.017)***	-0.167	(0.015)***	-0.144	(0.015)***
Profit_Margin			-0.096	(0.008)***		
Electricity_Balance					-0.504	(0.042)***
AT&C_Loss					0.045	(0.02)**
Firm_Size	-0.001	(0.001)*	-0.001	(0.001)**	-0.001	(0.001)***
Megacity_Dummy	1.739	(0.542)***	1.687	(0.541)***	1.869	(0.545)***
EPZ_Dummy	-0.673	(0.639)	-0.465	(0.606)	-0.202	(0.599)
Industrial dummies						
Basic metals	-1.795	(1.112)	-2.273	(1.026)**	-1.576	(1.065)
Chemicals	-2.024	(1.073)*	-3.040	(1.082)***	-3.254	(1.13)***
Electronics	-1.209	(1.055)	-1.726	(1.019)*	-2.374	(1.063)**
Fabricated metal products	-0.755	(1.049)	-1.339	(1.061)	-1.649	(1.111)
Food	2.644	(1.164)**	1.078	(1.091)	0.977	(1.135)
Furniture	-3.863	(1.885)**	-3.407	(1.866)*	-3.272	(1.872)*
Garments	0.349	(1.291)	-0.309	(1.292)	-0.899	(1.32)
Leather	-0.435	(1.442)	-0.662	(1.473)	-0.695	(1.469)
Machinery and equipment	-1.525	(1.159)	-1.712	(1.121)	-1.954	(1.171)*
Non-metallic mineral products	0.335	(1.08)	-1.990	(1.088)*	-1.002	(1.09)
Paper	1.654	(1.717)	0.688	(1.7)	0.434	(1.705)
Plastics & rubber	-0.122	(1.008)	-1.286	(1.013)	-1.369	(1.048)
Precision instruments	-0.963	(1.622)	-2.025	(1.636)	-2.761	(1.744)
Publishing	-3.820	(1.41)***	-4.201	(1.399)***	-5.257	(1.443)***
Recycling	3.634	(1.784)**	-1.021	(1.573)	0.995	(1.676)

(Continued)

Table 9.5 Effect of regulatory governance (Continued)

	Eq. (3)		Eq. (4)		Eq. (5)	
	Coefficient	*Standard error*	*Coefficient*	*Standard error*	*Coefficient*	*Standard error*
Refined petroleum product	12.809	(6.019)**	11.293	(5.504)**	13.069	(5.952)**
Textiles	2.713	(1.326)**	1.831	(1.321)	1.633	(1.332)
Tobacco	−6.656	(2.295)***	−6.908	(2.254)***	−6.638	(2.195)***
Retail	−4.317	(1.071)***	−4.170	(1.093)***	−5.022	(1.145)***
Wholesale	−4.498	(1.436)***	−3.949	(1.276)***	−4.016	(1.324)***
Construction Section F	−6.430	(1.424)***	−6.100	(1.42)***	−6.708	(1.405)***
Hotel and restaurants	−4.071	(1.069)***	−3.803	(1.069)***	−4.487	(1.101)***
IT	−5.648	(1.361)***	−5.083	(1.35)***	−5.389	(1.478)***
Services of motor vehicles	−4.945	(1.883)***	−5.197	(1.717)***	−5.495	(1.799)***
Transport Section I	−5.491	(1.168)***	−5.406	(1.141)***	−5.784	(1.172)***
Transport machines	−0.387	(1.31)	−1.046	(1.312)	−0.617	(1.334)
Constant	14.696	(1.139)***	7.462	(1.131)***	3.682	(1.322)***
Number of observation	6,671		6671		6671	
Log pseudolikelihood	−628273		−616174		−614179	

Notes: Dependent variable: Power outage left-censored observations at outage loss <= 0: 3060 uncensored observations: 3611 right-censored observations: 0. "***", "**", and "*" denotes statistical significance at the 1%, 5%, and 10% levels correspondingly. Industrial dummy of wood is not included.

governance of the utilities and regulatory governance of the SERCs have significant adverse effects on commercial loss attributable to power outages. We, therefore, conclude that the reform of corporate and regulatory governance is important to improve the power supply quality. In other words, by investigating the effect of corporate and regulatory governance on the quality of power supply at the firm level, we support the findings obtained at the state and utility level by Pargal and Mayer (2014).

To close this chapter, necessary improvements for this analysis must be pointed out. First, in spite of the various indexes of corporate and regulatory governance available, we use only two indexes based on the estimation results reported by Pargal and Mayer (2014). If one is to devise a more concrete prescription for improving the power supply quality, then it will be important to analyze the effects of other variables not covered here and to understand what institutions can function well. Second, although we have confirmed the importance of governance reform, the factors which can promote or retard the governance reform are left unexplored in our analysis. Several previous studies, such as those by Dubash and Rajan (2001) and Bhattacharyya (2007), suggest the importance of political factors including political leadership and political stability. The likely effects of economic structure are also noteworthy because a larger agricultural sector engenders stronger opposition to power sector reform, especially on tariff issues. Consequently, the effects of these state-specific circumstances should be explored. These matters are left as subjects for future study.

Notes

1 The "estimated" value is derived using the following procedures: (a) The gap between the actual value of per-capita power consumption and the projected value from 2004 through 2031 by the Planning Commission (2006) has been expanding year by year. We simply extend this trend and calculate the "estimated" value of power consumption per capita during 2012–2031. (b) On the assumption that power consumption promotes economic growth, we estimate the elasticity of GDP per capita with respect to per-capita power consumption using the actual value of GDP per capita and power consumption per capita during 1972–2011. (c) We estimate the value of GDP per capita from 2012–2031 using the estimated value of electricity consumption per capita and the elasticity of GDP per capita with respect to electricity consumption per capita.

2 According to Dubash and Rajan (2001), the electricity subsidy was first used as a tool for patronage in the election manifesto of the congress party during the Andhra Pradesh state assembly election in 1977, which committed to the adoption of a flat-rate tariff. This tariff was followed by similar moves in other states, such as the free electricity supply initiated by AIADMK in Tamil Nadu. At present, the tariff for agricultural consumers in Punjab and Tamil Nadu is set at zero. Industrial consumers are charged tariffs that are higher than the cost. Min and Golden (2014) found that the electricity losses in UP tend to increase in periods before the election, which suggests that political parties use electricity as a tool to win votes.

3 If based on the World Bank concept, measures to restructure balance sheets, enhance system information, restructure reporting, promote training, and invest in new capacities and maintenance could be included as components of corporatization (Ruet 2005).
4 Godbole (2002), Sharmaa et al. (2005), Singh (2006), and Dubash and Rao (2008) present additional details related to the responsibilities of the SERCs.
5 To promote reform, the Act also institutes rules promoting (a) the deregulation of licensing for the generation business, (b) open access in distribution, and (c) the power trading business. Bhattacharyya (2005), Planning Commission (2011), Tongia (2007), and Joseph (2010) present details related to the reforms and the Electricity Act of 2003.
6 Kerala SEB still operates as a vertically integrated utility. The power sectors in Jammu and Kashmir, Puducherry, Goa, Sikkim, Arunachal Pradesh, Manipur, Mizoram, Nagaland, and Tripura have not been reformed. They are still administered through government departments.
7 Pargal and Banerjee (2014) present an overview of the project by the World Bank.
8 Pargal and Mayer (2014) provide a list of indexes and definitions and demonstrate the interstate disparity among the same.
9 This survey of firm performance and various aspects of the business environment, such as access to finance, corruption, infrastructure, crime, and competition, address the manufacturing sectors and nine service sectors: construction, retail, wholesale, hotels, restaurants, transport, storage, communications, and IT. Formal companies with five or more employees were interviewed. The dataset and detailed information are available at the World Bank website (http://microdata.worldbank.org/index.php/catalog/2225).

References

Allcott, Hunt, Allan Collard-Wexler and Stephen D. O'Connell (2014) "How Do Electricity Shortages Affect Productivity? Evidence from India," *NBER Working Paper* No. 19977.
Bhattacharyya, Subhes C. (2005) "The Electricity Act 2003: Will It Transform the Indian Power Sector?," *Utilities Policy*, 13(3): 260–272.
Bhattacharyya, Subhes C. (2007) "Sustainability of Power Sector Reform in India: What Does Recent Experience Suggest?," *Journal of Cleaner Production*, 15(2): 235–246.
Central Electricity Authority (2015) *Growth of Electricity Sector in India from 1947–2015*, New Delhi: Ministry of Power, Government of India.
Dubash, Navroz K. and Rajan, S. C. (2001) "Power Politics Process of Power Sector Reform in India," *Economic and Political Weekly*, 36(35): 3367–3390.
Dubash, Navroz K. and D. Narasimha Rao (2008) "Regulatory Practice and Politics: Lessons from Independent Regulation in Indian Electricity," *Utilities Policy*, 16(4): 321–331.
Federation of Indian Chambers of Commerce & Industry (FICCI) (2013) *Power Transmission The real Bottleneck: An overview of the Indian power transmission sector, its challenges, and recommendations.*
Fukumi, A. (2016) "Power Sector Reform in India: Current Status and Issues," *School of Economics, University of Hyogo, Discussion Paper* No. 88.
Godbole, Madhav (2002) "Electricity Regulatory Commissions: The Jury Is Still Out," *Economic and Political Weekly*, 37(23): 2195–2200.

Joseph, Kelli L. (2010) "The Politics of Power: Electricity Reform in India," *Energy Policy*, 38(1): 503–511.

Min, Brian, and Miriam Golden (2014) "Electoral Cycles in Electricity Losses in India," *Energy Policy*, 65: 619–625.

Ministry of Power (2013) *Annual Report 2012–2013*, New Delhi: Ministry of Power, Government of India.

Pargal, Sheoli, and S. Ghosh Banerjee, 2014. *More Power to India: The Challenge of Electricity Distribution*, Washington, D.C.: World Bank Publications.

Pargal, Sheoli, and Kristy Mayer (2014) *Governance of Indian Power Sector Utilities: An Ongoing Journey*, Washington, D.C.: World Bank Publications.

Planning Commission (2006) *Integrated Energy Policy: Report of the Expert Committee*, New Delhi: Planning Commission, Government of India.

Planning Commission (2011), (2012), (2014) *Annual Report on the Working of State Power Utilities and Electricity Departments*, New Delhi: Planning Commission, Government of India.

Power Finance Corporation Limited (2008) *Report on the Performance of the State Power Utilities for the Years 2004–05 to 2006–07*, New Delhi: Power Finance Corporation Limited.

Power Finance Corporation Limited (2012) *The Performance of State Power Utilities for the Years 2008–09 to 2010–11*, New Delhi: Power Finance Corporation Limited.

Power Finance Corporation Limited (2014) *The Performance of State Power Utilities for the Years 2010–11 to 2012–13*, New Delhi: Power Finance Corporation Limited.

Reserve Bank of India (2015) *Handbook of Statistics on Indian Economy 2014–15*, Mumbai: Reserve Bank of India.

Ruet, Joel (2005) *Privatising Power Cuts?: Ownership and Reform of State Electricity Boards in India*, New Delhi: Academic Foundation.

Shah, Thshaar (2009) *Taming the Anarchy: Groundwater Governance in South Asia*, New Delhi: Routledge.

Sharma, D. Parameswara, P. S. Chandramohanan Nair, and R. Balasubramanian (2005) "Performance of Indian Power Sector during a Decade under Restructuring: A Critique," *Energy Policy*, 33(4): 563–576.

Singh, Anoop (2006) "Power Sector Reform in India: Current Issues and Prospects," *Energy Policy*, 34(16): 2480–2490.

Tongia, Rahul (2007) "The Political Economy of Indian Power Sector Reforms," in Victor, D. G. and Heller, T. C. eds. *The Political economy of Power Sector Reform: The Experience of Five Major Developing Countries*, New York: Cambridge University Press.

10 India in the World Economy
Inferences from Empirics of Economic Growth

Takahiro Sato

This study examines the growth experiences of India in relation to those of approximately one hundred countries during the last half-century. It also reveals hidden common factors that contribute to different growth performances based on an economic growth model. Utilizing a comparative perspective, this study exploits inferences drawn from the cross-national regression studies of historical development processes. India and China have grown rapidly over the past two decades. Because India and China are two of the largest developing countries, this study especially sets China's economic experiences as a reference to India's growth story and thereafter examines their respective paths.

Economic growth affects the well-being of people to a considerable degree. A country's income level must be regarded as an important determinant of its national well-being. A country with a growth rate of 7 per cent per year, which is India's current growth rate, doubles its income level every 10 years, whereas a country with a growth rate of 3.5 per cent per year, i.e., "the Hindu rate of growth", doubles its income level every 20 years. Persistent differences in growth rates generate vast differences in incomes in the long run.

This study is presented as the following. The first section presents the economic growth model as a key theoretical benchmark. It introduces the notions of "absolute convergence" and "conditional convergence" in the neoclassical growth model. The second section investigates India's growth experience from empirics of the neoclassical growth model. China's experience is set as a reference in this section. The last section summarizes the main results with conclusion.

The Economic Growth Model as a Theoretical Benchmark

This study uses the neoclassical growth model (Solow, 1956; Swan, 1956) as a theoretical framework.[1] As the property of the production function, the neoclassical growth model includes the assumptions of constant returns to scale, diminishing returns to each input and smooth substitution between inputs. Another crucially important aspect of the

DOI: 10.4324/9781003311898-11

neoclassical growth model is a constant-saving rate assumption. These two basic assumptions underpin the simple general-equilibrium model of economic growth.

The fundamental equation of the neoclassical growth model is given as

$$\dot{k} = sf(k) - nk,$$

where a dot over k denotes differentiation with respect to time, k is the capital–labor ratio, s is saving rate, f is the previously described neoclassical production function, and n is the population growth rate. This differential equation depends only on k. It is also noteworthy that the dynamics of k is the crucial factor determining the growth rate of per-capita income.

Figure 10.1 presents the dynamics of the neoclassical growth model. In Figure 10.1, the $sf(k)$ is a curve proportionate to the production function $f(k)$, and nk is a straight line from the origin. The dynamics of k results from the vertical gap separating $sf(k)$ and nk. We assume a poor country in the sense of small capital–labor ratio: k^{poor}. The vertical distance between $sf(k)$ and nk at $k = k^{poor}$ is positive, implying $\dot{k} > 0$, which means that the capital–labor ratio k increases toward the steady-state level of capital–labor ratio k^* over time. The steady-state k^* is determined at the crossing point of the $sf(k)$ curve and the nk straight line. Then, consider a rich country with k^{rich}. The vertical distance between $sf(k)$ and nk at $k = k^{rich}$ is positive, which implies that k increases toward k^* over time. Consequently, the neoclassical growth model predicts that any country converges to the same income level irrespective of whether the nation is poor or rich initially, which is designated as the absolute convergence hypothesis.

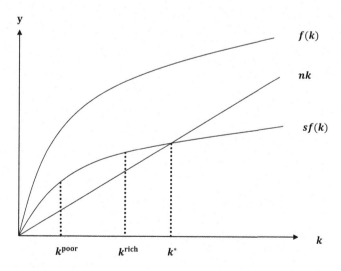

Figure 10.1 The dynamics of the neoclassical growth model.

By dividing both sides of the described above fundamental equation by k, the following growth-term equation is obtained.

$$\frac{\dot{k}}{k} = \frac{sf(k)}{k} - n$$

Specific examination of the growth rate of k is convenient; the growth rate of per-capita income is investigated in the next section. It is noteworthy that the growth rate of per-capita income is expressed as $S_k \dot{k}/k$, where S_k is the capital income share. In the Cobb–Douglas function, as one specification of the neoclassical production function, the capital income share is constant. Therefore, the growth rate of per-capita income exactly follows $\dot{k}/k$.

Figure 10.2 portrays the growth rate version of Figure 10.1. The growth rate of k is determined by the gap separating $sf(k)/k$ and n. It clearly illustrates that the growth rate of the poor country is higher than that of the rich country. The poor country catches up with the rich country. Over time, the growth rate converges to zero.

Contrary to the prediction of the absolute convergence hypothesis, the growth experiences in the real world are remarkably heterogeneous. Relaxation of the implicit assumptions of the neoclassical growth model on the same preference and technologies across countries generates a concept of conditional convergence. Panel A of Figure 10.3 presents the cases of different saving rates in poor and rich countries: $s^{poor} < s^{rich}$. In this case, the poor country's gap separating $sf(k)/k$ and n is less than the rich country's. Panel B shows the case of different population rates: $n^{poor} > n^{rich}$. Consequently, the growth rate of the rich is higher than that of the poor in both cases, contrary to the prediction of absolute convergence.

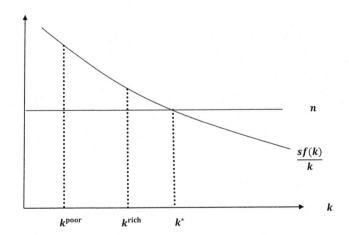

Figure 10.2 Absolute convergence in the neoclassical growth model.

Panel A: Different Saving Rates

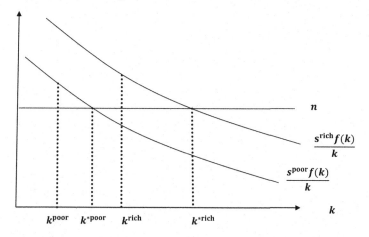

Panel B: Different Population Growth Rates

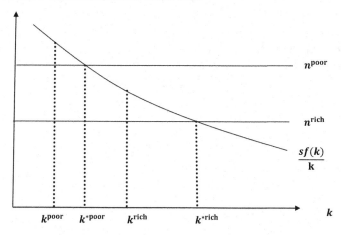

Figure 10.3 Conditional convergence in the neoclassical growth model. Panel A: Different saving rates. Panel B: Different population growth rates.

Taking account of the different steady-state positions in the countries, the result implies that a country grows faster when it is more distant from its own steady-state. In other words, a poor country tends to generate a higher growth rate once the determinants of the steady-state are controlled. This tendency is designated as a conditional convergence hypothesis. The concept of conditional convergence is consistent with the neoclassical growth model allowing heterogeneous technology and preference.

The Growth Experience of India from Inferences
of Growth Regression

Absolute versus Conditional Convergences

The existing empirical evidence for a panel dataset of a number of countries
supports the existence of conditional convergence. For given values of variables affecting the growth rate, growth is negatively related to the initial
level of real per-capita GDP. A higher initial level of per-capita GDP implies
a lower growth rate, all other things being equal. It is also noteworthy that
poor countries would not grow rapidly if they were to have low steady-state
positions. Rich countries would grow faster than poor countries if the rich
countries were further below their own respective steady-states. These
effects represent the general idea of conditional convergence. In contrast,
a concept of the absolute convergence implies that countries with the same
preference and technologies converge to the same steady-state. Therefore,
poor countries can catch up with rich countries unconditionally.

Figure 10.4 presents a scattered diagram of the growth rate and the initial
level of real per-capita GDP across approximately a hundred countries observed
during 1960–2010. The data of real per-capita GDP in constant 2005 US dollars
are generated using the World Bank's World Development Indicators (WDI) &
Global Development Finance (GDF), as shown in Table 10.1. The vertical axis
in Figure 10.4 shows observations of growth rates of per-capita GDP for

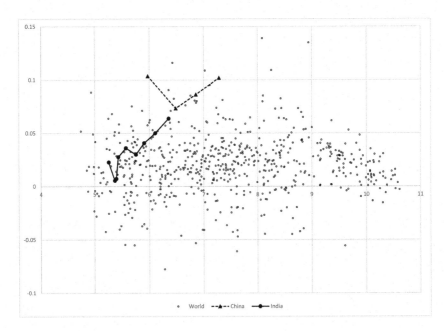

Figure 10.4 Simple correlation between the growth rate of per capita GDP and log
of initial per-capita GDP.

Table 10.1 Descriptive statistics and expected signs of growth regression

Variable	Mean	S.D.	Min	Max	Source	Expected sign
Annual growth rate of per capita GDP	0.020901	0.0277236	−0.077573	0.138937	WDI & GDF	−
Log of initial per capita GDP	7.409063	1.456383	4.744932	10.61152	WDI & GDF	Negative
Change in terms of trade	−0.0003132	0.0551926	−0.308356	0.309547	Barro and Lee (1994), WDI & GDF	Positive
Inflation rate	0.1200026	0.2157444	−0.043022	2.22353	WDI & GDF	Negative
Total fertility rate	4.068003	1.921397	1.14	8.27	WDI & GDF	Negative
Government consumption ratio	14.51339	5.396524	4.08	40.6	WDI & GDF	Negative
Investment ratio	22.33189	7.213002	4.84	66.5	WDI & GDF	Positive
External openness ratio	70.24896	48.26262	8.43	431	WDI & GDF	Positive
1/(life expectancy at birth)	0.0162308	0.0030151	0.012121	0.034602	WDI & GDF	Negative
Democracy index	6.067588	3.415694	0	10	Polity IV	?
Upper-level schooling years	1.949184	1.557857	0.043	8.056	Barro and Lee (2013)	Positive
Urban agglomerated population ratio	24.55164	18.27939	0	100	World Urbanization Prospects	?
Urban population ratio	47.6638	23.36899	2.294	100	World Urbanization Prospects	?

Notes:

Number of observations: 651.

A panel data covers observations for 23 in 1960–1965, 39 in 1965–1970, 59 in 1970–1975, 67 in 1975–1980, 48 in 1980–1985, 56 in 1985–1990, 59 in 1990–1995, 61 in 1995–2000, 120 in 2000–2005, and 119 in 2005–2010.

1960–1965, 1965–1970, 1970–1975, 1975–1980, 1980–1985, 1985–1990, 1990–1995, 1995–2000, 2000–2005, and 2005–2010. The horizontal axis shows corresponding values of the logarithm of per-capita GDP in 1960, 1965, 1970, 1975, 1980, 1985, 1990, 1995, 2000, and 2005. The relation between growth and initial GDP is almost imperceptible from the graph.

In fact, when no explanatory variable other than the initial GDP is applied for the regression (henceforth, parenthesis implies t statistics), the estimated coefficient of the log of initial GDP is positive but not statistically significant: 0.0005 (0.64).

$$\text{Growth Rate of GDP} = 0.017{***} + 0.0005 \log(\text{Initial GDP})$$
$$(3.08) \qquad (0.64)$$
$$\text{NOB} = 651, \text{Adj.}R^2 = -0.0009, F \text{ statistics} = 0.41$$

The regression result shows that no evidence exists of absolute convergence. However, it does not directly suggest rejection of the neoclassical growth model. The latter is consistent with the lack of absolute convergence when each country has its own steady-state because of differences in preferences and technology.

Figure 10.4 presents the historical trend of the GDP growth rate and the initial GDP in India and China. As shown in Table 10.2, the growth rate of India has increased from 2.25 per cent to 6.38 per cent from 1965–1970 to 2005–2010. Moreover, the per-capita GDP has risen from 5.26269 (193 US dollar) to 6.35957 (578 US dollar) during 1965–2005. India's growth pattern does not follow the convergence hypothesis. China's growth rate fell from 12.36 per cent to 7.32 per cent from 1990–95 to 1995–2000, but then it increased to 10.19 per cent during 2005–2010. It is readily apparent in this Figure that China's economic growth rate is the highest among the world after 1965. The per-capita GDP of China has risen from 5.971262 (392 US dollar) to 7.286192 (1460 US dollar) during 1990–2005. China has a higher growth rate and income level than India has.

Urbanization and Economic Growth

Table 10.1 presents variables used in growth regression analysis in the conditional sense. The regression analysis applies to a panel dataset of around one hundred countries during 1960–2010. The dataset includes a broad range of experiences from poor to rich countries for the last half-century. The covered countries were determined solely by data availability. The main strength of using a panel dataset is to expand the sample information. Not only cross-sectional but also time-series variations are exploited for a comparative study of the growth experience of India among numerous countries, with special reference to China.

The estimation of this study uses an ordinary least squares (OLS) method. The fixed effects technique addressing an unobserved time-invariant country-specific effect depends on time-series information within countries. Therefore, the fixed effects estimation excludes cross-sectional information, which is the main advantage of the comprehensive cross-national data. The OLS regression might be suitable for comparative analysis because it

Table 10.2 Data for China and India

Variable	Country	1965–1970	1970–1975	1975–1980	1980–1985	1985–1990	1990–1995	1995–2000	2000–2005	2005–2010
Annual growth rate of per capita GDP	China	0.0225	0.0055	0.0071	0.0276	0.0360	0.1036	0.0732	0.0862	0.1019
	India						0.0299	0.0408	0.0501	0.0638
Log of initial per capita GDP	China	5.26269	5.375278	5.402678	5.438079	5.575949	5.971262	6.489205	6.855409	7.286192
	India						5.755742	5.905362	6.109248	6.359574
Change in terms of trade	China	-0.027248	-0.012443	-0.063016	0.024671	0.011514	0.000000	-0.003961	-0.027393	-0.023844
	India						0.046022	-0.015392	0.009758	0.038045
Inflation rate	China	0.0622	0.1114	0.0388	0.0892	0.0746	0.1210	0.0174	0.0134	0.0280
	India						0.1000	0.0728	0.0390	0.0837
Total fertility rate	China	5.69	5.32	4.92	4.52	4.14	2.12	1.81	1.71	1.64
	India						3.76	3.35	2.99	2.74
Government consumption ratio	China	8.91	9.47	10.1	10.5	12.1	15.2	14.4	15.2	13.7
	India						11.5	11.8	11.8	10.9
Investment ratio	China	15.0	16.1	18.8	18.9	21.8	39.3	38.8	38.8	43.8
	India						23.5	25.1	26.6	35.9

(Continued)

Table 10.2 Data for China and India (*Continued*)

Variable	Country	1965–1970	1970–1975	1975–1980	1980–1985	1985–1990	1990–1995	1995–2000	2000–2005	2005–2010
External openness ratio	China	9.04	8.43	12.9	14.1	13.1	36.0	38.0	51.5	63.7
	India						17.8	22.8	29.6	45.9
1/(life expectancy at birth)	China	0.021231	0.019802	0.018587	0.017825	0.017361	0.014306	0.014124	0.013966	0.013774
	India						0.016978	0.016529	0.016051	0.015601
Democracy index	China	9.5	9.5	9.0	9.0	9.0	1.5	1.5	1.5	1.5
	India						9.0	9.5	9.5	9.5
Upper-level schooling years	China	0.211	0.273	0.522	0.785	0.957	1.398	1.854	2.298	2.706
	India						1.150	1.273	1.432	1.614
Urban agglomerated population ratio	China	9.97	10.63	11.41	12.29	13.06	14.19	17.74	23.64	27.32
	India						14.01	14.84	15.85	16.72
Urban population ratio	China	18.79	19.76	21.33	23.10	24.35	26.44	30.96	35.88	42.52
	India						25.55	26.61	27.67	29.24

can exploit the between-country dimension of panel data as well as within-country information.[2]

Because the research topics of this book are related to the fusion of rural areas and cities in the Indian socioeconomic historical context, we must first verify the relation between urbanization and growth. The dependent variable is the annual growth rate of real per-capita GDP over ten periods from 1960–1965 to 2005–2010. The regression shown in column 1 in Table 10.3 includes the conventional measurement of the urban population ratio as an explanatory variable.[3] Although the concept of the "urban area" in the conventional measurement of urban population varies across countries, the definition of urban agglomeration is uniform across countries. The estimated coefficient of this variable is 0.00008121233 (0.99), which is positive but not significantly different from zero. Turning to column 2 of Table 10.3, population of urban agglomerations with 300,000 inhabitants or more to the total population is included as an alternative proxy variable for urbanization. The result shows the non-significant positive estimated coefficient of the agglomerated urban area population ratio, 0.00008434908 (1.03), which implies that urban agglomeration does not raise the growth rate.

The regression results show that neither the urban population ratio nor the agglomerated urban population ratio is apparently a candidate as a determinant of economic growth.[4] The regression results in column 3 of Table 10.3 are used for the main analysis in this study.

Basic Growth Regression

When the other explanatory variables are given, the neoclassical model predicts a negative relation between the growth rate of GDP and the initial level of GDP. The estimated coefficient of the initial GDP, −0.00975309785 (−6.95), in column 3 of Table 10.3 is highly significant. It supports the conditional convergence prediction. The conditional rate of convergence is less than 1 per cent per year. The speed of convergence is slow in the sense that it would take 31 years for the economy to reach 50 per cent of the goal of the steady-state level of GDP. It would take 103 years to reach 90 per cent of the goal of the steady-state position.[5]

The partial relation between the growth rate and the initial GDP is shown in Figure 10.5. This is implied by the regression from column 3 of Table 10.3. The horizontal axis measures the log of the initial GDP for ten periods from 1960–65 to 2005–10 drawn from observations in the regression sample. The vertical axis shows the corresponding growth rate of GDP after removing the parts explained by all explanatory variables except for the log of initial GDP and the constant term. In other words, the contribution from a constant term and the initial level of GDP is excluded to compute the values of the GDP growth rate on the vertical axis in the scattered diagram. The negative relation between the unexplained part of the GDP growth rate and the initial GDP in Figure 10.5 shows the conditional convergence graphically.

Table 10.3 Regression for annual growth rate of per capita GDP

Independent variable	(1)	(2)	(3)
Log of initial per capita GDP	−0.010678665	−0.010478348	−0.009753098
	(6.25)***	(6.42)***	(6.95)***
Change in terms of trade	0.099725032	0.100014692	0.100387293
	(4.10)***	(4.14)***	(4.17)***
Inflation rate	−0.016248543	−0.016156654	−0.015365661
	(3.43)***	(3.44)***	(3.32)***
Total fertility rate	−0.006823	−0.006881247	−0.006765639
	(4.76)***	(4.78)***	(4.75)***
Government consumption ratio	−0.000667124	−0.000632891	−0.000664318
	(2.54)**	(2.45)**	(2.51)**
Investment ratio	0.000745331	0.000739132	0.000738823
	(2.98)***	(2.98)***	(2.96)***
External openness ratio	5.77231E-05	5.58079E-05	5.69362E-05
	(2.42)**	(2.36)**	(2.35)**
1/(life expectancy at birth)	−2.21803	−2.22951	−2.28121
	(3.01)***	(3.02)***	(3.05)***
Democracy index	−0.011100604	−0.010942424	−0.010946744
	(2.56)**	(2.53)**	(2.59)**
(Democracy index)^2	0.002190142	0.002151512	0.002176494
	(2.39)**	(2.34)**	(2.41)**
(Democracy index)^3/100	−0.012269806	−0.011975205	−0.012325218
	(2.19)**	(2.12)**	(2.23)**
Upper-level schooling years	−0.005846181	−0.005448386	−0.00504295
	(1.80)*	(1.78)*	(1.60)
(Upper-level schooling years)^2	0.000986954	0.000923958	0.000896137
	(2.39)**	(2.39)**	(2.25)**
Urban agglomerated population ratio		8.43491E-05	
		(1.03)	
Urban population ratio	8.12123E-05		
	(0.99)		
1965–1970 dummy	0.004384338	0.004394625	0.00421406
	(0.95)	(0.96)	(0.91)
1970–1975 dummy	−0.002581883	−0.002627022	−0.002890901
	(0.49)	(0.50)	(0.55)
1975–1980 dummy	−0.004942937	−0.005036779	−0.005341155
	(0.86)	(0.88)	(0.93)
1980–1985 dummy	−0.030577011	−0.030673538	−0.031098867
	(5.98)***	(6.04)***	(5.98)***
1985–1999 dummy	−0.019757402	−0.019840701	−0.020197373
	(3.07)***	(3.11)***	(3.10)***
1990–1995 dummy	−0.024792394	−0.024779299	−0.025009051
	(4.34)***	(4.36)***	(4.36)***
1995–2000 dummy	−0.022823731	−0.02272799	−0.022842623
	(3.86)***	(3.88)***	(3.86)***
2000–2005 dummy	−0.018111016	−0.017823258	−0.018236434
	(3.03)***	(3.03)***	(3.05)***
2005–2010 dummy	−0.026234225	−0.025882281	−0.026401349
	(4.06)***	(4.06)***	(4.09)***
Constant	0.18621079	0.185897317	0.1832629
	(7.35)***	(7.36)***	(7.46)***
Observations	651	651	651
Adj. R-squared	0.37	0.37	0.37

Notes: Cluster-robust t statistics in parentheses.

* significant at 10%; ** significant at 5%; *** significant at 1%.

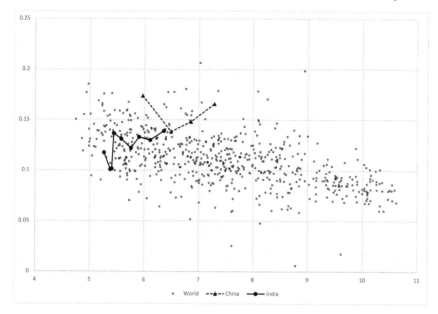

Figure 10.5 Partial relation between the growth rate of per-capita GDP and log of initial per-capita GDP.

In contrast, it is noteworthy that no simple correlation is apparent in Figure 10.4, implying that the absolute convergence hypothesis is rejected.

Figure 10.5 presents the common historical pattern of growth and initial GDP in India and China, as shown in Figure 10.4, which confirms that India's growth pattern does not follow the convergence hypothesis in the sense that the growth and income level simultaneously increased.

The regression includes average schooling years after secondary education, its square values, and the log of the inverted value of life expectancy at birth as explanatory variables. These variables are regarded as representing human capital. Results show a non-linear effect of schooling years on the growth rate given the initial level of GDP. The estimated coefficients of schooling years and its square are, respectively, -0.00504294983 (-1.60) and 0.0008961371 (2.25). The P value for F test of joint significance of schooling years and its square is 0.0178, which suggests that educational attainment has a statistically significant effect on economic growth. The estimated coefficients imply that schooling beyond three years raises the GDP growth rate in the range of the schooling year from 0.043 years as a minimum value to 8.054 years as a maximum value in the regression sample.[6]

Figure 10.6 portrays a partial relation between the growth rate and the schooling years after secondary education. This figure also presents the historical trend of schooling years after secondary education in India and China. As shown in Table 10.2, the schooling years of India have increased from 0.211 years to 1.614 years during 1965–2005. India's human capital

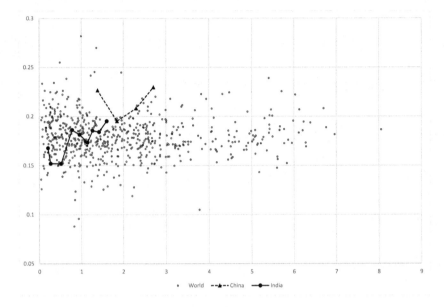

Figure 10.6 Partial relation between the growth rate of per-capita GDP and upper-
level schooling years.

accumulation has steadily grown. China's schooling years also increased
from 1.398 years to 2.706 years during 1990 to 2005. It is clearly evident in
this figure that China's human capital is higher than India's.

The result in column 3 of Table 10.3 presents the significant and negative
estimated coefficient of the log of inverted value of life expectancy, −2.28121
(−3.05), which suggests that life expectancy as a measure of the quality of
human capital or health capital raises the growth rate. Consequently, these
findings also support human capital as a key to economic growth.[7]

Figure 10.7 presents a partial relation between the growth rate and the
inverted value of life expectancy at birth. This figure also presents the
respective historical trends of the inverted value of life expectancy for India
and China. Table 10.2 shows that the life expectancy of India has increased
from 47.1 years (0.021231 in Table 10.2) to 64.1 years (0.015601) during 1965–
2005. India's health capital has steadily improved. China's life expectancy
also rose from 69.9 years (0.014306 in Table 10.2) to 72.6 years (0.013774)
from 1990 to 2005. It is readily apparent from this figure that China's health
level is better than India's.

The neoclassical growth model predicts that a higher rate of population
growth has a negative effect on the steady-state level of per-capita GDP. It
implies that given initial GDP, a total fertility rate representing population
growth reduces the GDP growth rate. Returning to column 3 of Table 10.3, the
significant negative estimated coefficient of the total fertility rate, −0.0067656385
(−4.75), supports the prediction of the neoclassical growth model.[8] The partial

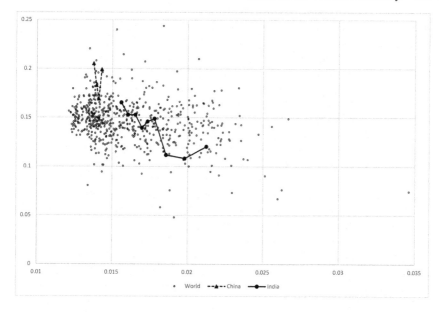

Figure 10.7 Partial relation between the growth rate of per-capita GDP and inverted value of life expectancy at birth.

relation between growth and fertility is shown in Figure 10.8. This figure also presents the historical trend of the total fertility rate in India and China. As shown in Table 10.2, the total fertility rate of India has decreased from 5.69 to 2.74 during 1965–2005. China's total fertility rate also decreased from 2.12 to 1.64 during 1990 to 2005, which suggests that China's total population is projected to decline in the long run. In fact, according to United Nation's World Population Prospects, India's population will become larger than China's from 2025.

The result in column 3 of Table 10.3 shows a significant and negative effect of government consumption to GDP on economic growth. The estimated coefficient is −0.00066431844 (−2.51). The government consumption ratio is regarded as the proxy variable for the magnitude of the waste of economic resources.[9] Figure 10.9 presents a partial relation between growth rate and the government consumption to GDP. This figure also illustrates the historical trend of government consumption relative to GDP in India and China. As Table 10.2 shows, the government consumption ratio of India has increased from 8.91 per cent in 1965 to 12.1 per cent in 1985. It subsequently fell gradually to 10.9 per cent in 2005. China's government consumption ratio has fluctuated between 13.7 per cent and 15.2 per cent during 1990–2005. China's government consumption level is higher than India's.

The neoclassical growth model predicts that a higher saving rate has a positive effect on the steady-state level of per-capita GDP. The same model includes the assumption that the saving rate is exogenous and equal to the

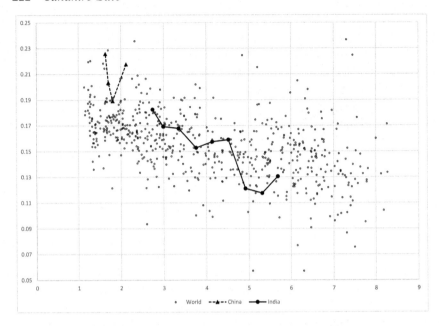

Figure 10.8 Partial relation between the growth rate of per-capita GDP and total fertility rate.

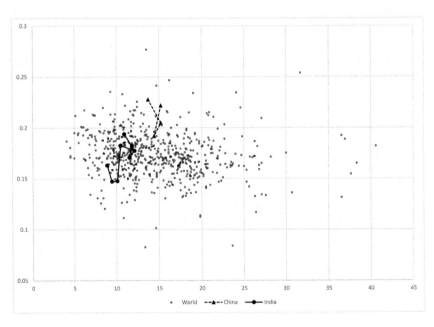

Figure 10.9 Partial relation between the growth rate of per-capita GDP and government consumption to GDP.

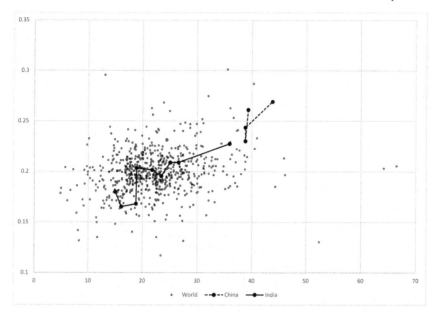

Figure 10.10 Partial relation between the growth rate of per-capita GDP and investment to GDP.

investment rate. In the open economy, the investment rate is a more appropriate explanatory variable than the savings rate. The neoclassical growth model implies that the initial GDP investment rate raises the growth rate of GDP. The result in column 3 of Table 10.3 presents a significant and positive effect of the investment rate on the per-capita GDP growth rate. The estimated coefficient is 0.00073882296 (2.96).[10] The partial relation between growth rate and investment rate is shown in Figure 10.10. This figure also presents the historical trend of the investment rate in India and China. As Table 10.2 shows, the investment rate of India has increased from 15.0 per cent to 35.9 per cent during 1965–2005. India's investment ratio has risen remarkably: its level in 2005 is in the highest class over the world. China's investment also rose from 39.3 per cent to 43.8 per cent during 1990–2005. It is plain from this figure that China's level of investment is higher than India's.

The inflation rate can be regarded as an indicator of macroeconomic stability. The estimation reported in column 3 of Table 10.3 presents the estimated coefficient of the inflation rate as −0.01536566114 (−3.32). It implies that inflation has a significant and negative effect on economic growth.[11]

The partial relation between the growth rate and the inflation rate is presented in Figure 10.11. Figure 10.11 has two panels because the inflation rates show remarkable variation. Evidence from the left panel of Figure 10.11 shows that inflation is harmful for growth, as indicated by the experience of

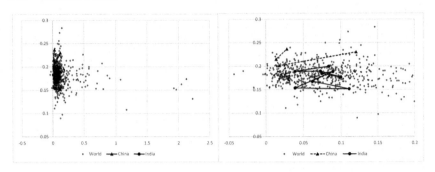

Figure 10.11 Partial relation between the growth rate of per-capita GDP and inflation rate.

countries with hyperinflation, which are shown as outliers. Evidence from the right panel, which shows a limited range of inflation rate from −5 per cent to 20 per cent, shows that no clear relation exists between inflation and growth. This figure also presents the historical trend of inflation rates in India and China. As Table 10.2 shows, the inflation rate of India has fluctuated in the range of 3.88 per cent in 1975–1980 and 11.14 per cent in 1970–1975 during 1965–2005. It is difficult to identify a clear relation between inflation and growth in India. China's inflation rate declined as a trend from 12.1 per cent to 2.8 per cent during 1990–2005. The range of China's inflation rate is wider than India's.

The regression results shown in column 3 of Table 10.3 present a significant positive coefficient for the change in terms of trade. The estimated coefficient of the change in terms of trade is 0.1003872931 (4.17). Improvement of the terms of trade has a positive effect on growth. The partial relation between the growth rate and the change in terms of trade is presented in Figure 10.12. India's terms of trade varied from −6.3 per cent in 1975–1980 to 4.6 per cent in 1990–1995 during the period from 1965–1970 to 2005–10. Figure 10.12 shows the positive relation between terms of trade and growth rate in India. In contrast, no such clear relation is apparent for China in Figure 10.12.

The ratio of exports plus imports to GDP is regarded as reflecting the degree of external openness. The regression in column 3 of Table 10.3 shows a significant positive coefficient for the external openness index. The estimated coefficient of external openness is 0.00005693621 (2.35).[12] The partial relation between growth rate and external openness is presented in Figure 10.13. Several countries have remarkably high values such as more than 300 per cent. Therefore, the figure is divided into a left panel for the entire world and a right panel limiting the sample countries to those with an openness index from 0 per cent to 100 per cent. This figure also presents the historical trend of external openness in India and China. As Table 10.2 shows, the external openness of India increased from 9.04 per cent to 45.9 per cent

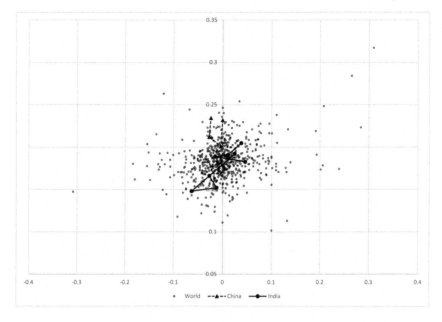

Figure 10.12 Partial relation between the growth rate of per-capita GDP and change in terms of trade.

during 1965–2005. India's openness ratio has risen remarkably, especially after 1990. China's openness ratio also rose from 36.0 per cent to 63.7 per cent during 1990–2005. China's openness is greater than India's.

The polity score drawn from the Center for Systemic Peace's Polity IV project measures the character of the governing authority based upon a scale stretching from dictatorship to democracy. It includes components that reflect the competitiveness of executive recruitment, openness of executive recruitment, constraints on chief executives, regulation of participation, and competitiveness of political participation. In this study, the

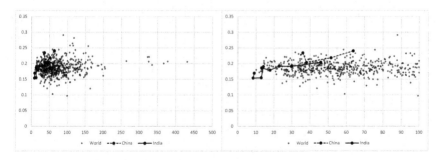

Figure 10.13 Partial relation between the growth rate of per-capita GDP and external openness ratio.

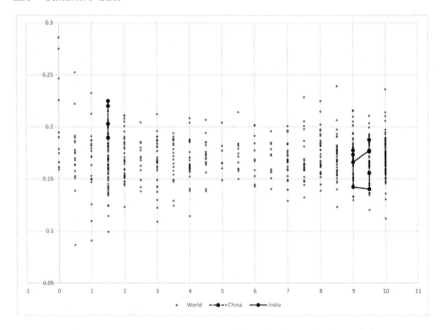

Figure 10.14 Partial relation between the growth rate of per-capita GDP and democracy index.

original score of −10 to +10 was revised to 0 to 10, with 0 denoting the worst and 10 denoting the best level of democracy.

The regression includes this democracy index, its own square, and its own cube. The results show a significant non-linear effect of democracy on economic growth. The estimated coefficients of the democracy index, its own square, and its own cube are, respectively, −0.010946744 (−2.59), 0.00217649398 (2.41), and −0.0123252181 (−2.23). The growth rate decreases as the democracy index increases from 0 toward 3.6. Then the growth rate increases as the democracy index rises from 3.6 to 8. Again, the growth rate declines as the democracy index goes up from 8 to 10. The maximum value of the growth rate is at 0 of the democracy index and the minimum value of growth rate is at 3.6 of the democracy index.[13] The partial relation between economic growth and the democracy index is presented in Figure 10.14. The growth rates of low democracy vary more than those of high democracy. A group of low-democracy countries includes both China, which is the country with the most growth and sub-Saharan African countries, which are growing less. To elucidate the complex relation between political regimes and economic development requires some caution regarding simple conclusions drawn from a point estimation of coefficients obtained by OLS. Consequently, a scatter diagram can provide useful graphical information about the democracy–growth relation.

The regression equation for the first percentile of the unexplained growth rate of per-capita GDP based on the democracy index and its square in the data shown in Figure 10.14 is the following.

$$\text{Unexplained Growth} = 0.0808*** + 0.0120*** \text{Democracy}$$
$$(11.08) \qquad (3.57)$$
$$-0.0007247** (\text{Democracy})^2$$
$$(-2.35)$$
$$\text{NOB} = 651, \text{ Pseudo } R^2 = 0.1550$$

The regression equation for the 99th percentile of the unexplained growth rate is shown below.

$$\text{Unexplained Growth} = 0.0808*** - 0.0221*** \text{Democracy}$$
$$(11.08) \qquad (-3.17)$$
$$+0.0018235*** (\text{Democracy})^2$$
$$(3.19)$$
$$\text{NOB} = 651, \text{ Pseudo} R^2 = 0.1801$$

These results tell a different story. Although the growth rate of the highest growing countries is determined in a U-shaped manner by democracy, the growth rate of the least growing countries is determined in an inverted U-shaped manner. This figure also presents the historical trend of the democracy index for India and China. As Table 10.2 shows, in contrast to other explanatory variables, the democracy index has not varied in either country. India's index was 9.0–9.5 during 1965–2005. China's index was 1.5 during 1990–2005. India's democracy index is remarkably higher than China's.

The regression includes a constant term and time dummies for the nine periods from 1965–1970 to 2005–2010. The reference period of time dummies is 1960–1965. The later six period dummies 1980–1985 to 2005–2010 are significant and negative. Results show that the overall growth rate of the world economy declined after 1980. Figure 10.15 presents the sample mean of growth rate obtained using the estimated constant term interacting with time dummies at the right axis and the sample mean of the growth rate at the left axis. Both growth rates peak in 1965–1970 and then reach troughs in 1980–1985. After 1985, both rates increase modestly. The growth rate of India grew steadily from 1980, remaining higher than the overall growth rate of the world economy from 1980. It is again noteworthy that China's growth rate is much higher than those of India and the world economy.

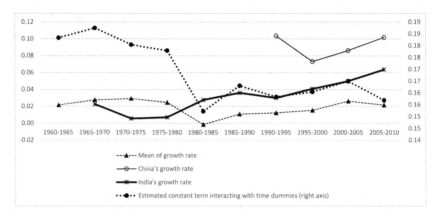

Figure 10.15 Economic growth rate during 1960–2010.

Robustness of Basic Growth Regression

The basic growth regression described in the previous section might be adversely affected by endogeneity bias, partly because of the possible correlation between the unobservable country-fixed effects and the explanatory variables. To address this issue, the fixed effects model is applied to eliminate the country-fixed effect. The regression results of columns 1–4 of Table 10.4 show that even controlling for the country-fixed effect, no evidence exists of a relation between urbanization and economic growth. Turning to column 5 of Table 10.4, the estimated coefficients of the schooling years are negative but not significant. However, the p value for the chi-squared test of joint significance of slope coefficients of schooling years and its square is 0.0276. That result confirms that human capital has a considerable effect on economic growth. All other main explanatory variables have significant coefficients with the same sign, as shown in column 3 of Table 10.3. Consequently, the results of fixed-effect regression are not at all inconsistent with those of basic growth regression.

Although they have the same sign, the degree of the estimated coefficient differs. For example, the overestimated variables in the basic regression compared with the fixed-effect regression are the square of schooling years, with 54 per cent more coefficient value, schooling years with 51 per cent more value, total fertility rate with 11 per cent more value, the cube of the democracy index with 9 per cent more value, the investment rate with 8 per cent more value, and the square of the democracy index with 3 per cent more value. The estimated coefficients of schooling years with non-linear effects imply that the schooling years beyond two years raise the GDP growth rate. The estimated coefficients of the democracy index imply that the growth rate decreases as the democracy index increases from 0 to 3.6; then the growth rate rises as the democracy index increases from 3.7 to 8.7. Again, the growth rate drops as the democracy index increases from 8 to 10.

Table 10.4 Fixed-effect regression for annual growth rate of per capita GDP

Independent variable	(1)	(2)	(3)	(4)	(5)
Log of initial per capita GDP	-0.045981672	-0.046280034	-0.046004265	-0.04619971	-0.011768485
	(8.13)***	(8.20)***	(8.16)***	(8.14)***	(7.87)***
Change in terms of trade	0.096436112	0.094969023	0.096373784	0.09540463	0.107774654
	(4.59)***	(4.69)***	(4.61)***	(4.71)***	(4.47)***
Inflation rate	-0.021996961	-0.02192844	-0.022006668	-0.021863992	-0.017810829
	(4.03)***	(4.13)***	(4.04)***	(4.10)***	(3.70)***
Total fertility rate	-0.003109308	-0.003165137	-0.003181183	-0.002723534	-0.006116146
	(1.47)	(1.62)	(1.74)*	(1.73)*	(4.17)***
Government consumption ratio	-0.001196826	-0.001202735	-0.001197987	-0.001196647	-0.000829771
	(3.28)***	(3.34)***	(3.27)***	(3.31)***	(3.12)***
Investment ratio	0.000768285	0.000772291	0.000768643	0.000771067	0.000683254
	(2.63)***	(2.62)***	(2.63)***	(2.63)***	(2.85)***
External openness ratio	0.000217042	0.00022419	0.000217139	0.000224142	6.51444E-05
	(3.35)***	(3.46)***	(3.35)***	(3.45)***	(2.40)**
1/(life expectancy at birth)	-2.31395	-2.55256	-2.31596	-2.52501	-2.7663
	(2.02)**	(2.36)**	(2.02)**	(2.35)**	(3.61)***
Democracy index	-0.014531634	-0.015429699	-0.014504884	-0.015595021	-0.011054152
	(2.46)**	(2.49)**	(2.43)**	(2.52)**	(2.54)**
(Democracy index)^2	0.002813827	0.002966593	0.002807123	0.00300495	0.002107156
	(2.24)**	(2.29)**	(2.21)**	(2.31)**	(2.29)**
(Democracy index)^3/100	-0.015584051	-0.016347366	-0.015539936	-0.016594793	-0.011312696
	(2.01)**	(2.06)**	(1.97)*	(2.08)**	(2.01)**
Upper-level schooling years	0.005089882	0.002536348	0.004711603	0.004455278	-0.003331301
	(1.08)	(0.64)	(1.74)*	(1.73)*	(1.04)
(Upper-level schooling years)^2	-5.43193E-05	0.000284868			0.000698279
	(0.09)	(0.51)			(1.75)*
Urban agglomerated population ratio		-0.00087614		-0.000872885	
		(1.64)		(1.61)	
Urban population ratio	-0.000456236		-0.000451489		
	(1.40)		(1.48)		
1965–1970 dummy	0.012094259	0.012572434	0.012098065	0.012501026	0.005550647
	(2.95)***	(3.00)***	(2.94)***	(2.98)***	(1.25)
1970–1975 dummy	0.011666789	0.012470965	0.011676902	0.012361632	-0.001032628
	(2.00)**	(2.05)**	(1.99)**	(2.02)**	(0.20)
1975–1980 dummy	0.013277846	0.014520038	0.01330016	0.014349644	-0.003467755
	(2.03)**	(2.10)**	(2.01)**	(2.05)**	(0.63)
1980–1985 dummy	-0.00916332	-0.007740405	-0.009136502	-0.007930204	-0.030162858
	(1.39)	(1.09)	(1.37)	(1.10)	(5.96)***
1985–1999 dummy	0.002254225	0.00344972	0.002295063	0.003178423	-0.020363597
	(0.29)	(0.44)	(0.29)	(0.40)	(3.22)***
1990–1995 dummy	-0.001086567	5.23258E-05	-0.00105	-0.000226362	-0.025988456
	(0.13)	(0.01)	(0.12)	(0.02)	(4.63)***
1995–2000 dummy	0.003769555	0.004716973	0.003795397	0.004483134	-0.023768752
	(0.43)	(0.51)	(0.43)	(0.47)	(4.12)***
2000–2005 dummy	0.012749927	0.013665617	0.012766768	0.013471548	-0.018413247
	(1.34)	(1.36)	(1.33)	(1.31)	(3.23)***
2005–2010 dummy	0.009155143	0.009812906	0.009154126	0.00970458	-0.026457555
	(0.85)	(0.87)	(0.86)	(0.85)	(4.24)***
Constant	0.4223924	0.431177353	0.423019395	0.426588767	0.204181477
	(7.74)***	(8.03)***	(7.86)***	(7.92)***	(8.31)***
Observations	651	651	651	651	651
Adj. R-squared	0.54	0.55	0.54	0.55	0.54
Number of countries	122	122	122	122	122

Notes: Cluster-robust t statistics in parentheses.

* significant at 10%; ** significant at 5%; *** significant at 1%.

The maximum value of the growth rate is at 0 of the democracy index; the minimum value of the growth rate is at 3.7 of the democracy index. These non-linear relations shown in the fixed-effect regression are not substantially different from those of the basic regression.

The underestimated variables in the basic regression relative to the fixed-effect regression are the government consumption ratio with 20 per cent less coefficient value, life expectancy at birth with 18 per cent less value, initial per-capita GDP with 17 per cent less value, inflation rate with 14 per cent less value, external openness ratio with 13 per cent less value, change in terms of trade with 7 per cent less value, and democracy index with 1 per cent less value. Consequently, endogeneity bias caused by the possible correlation between the unobservable country-fixed effects and the explanatory variables generates overestimation or underestimation of coefficients of the explanatory variable, more or less. The estimated coefficients from the fixed-effect regression and basic regression, however, do not differ substantially. The authors infer that the reliability of the results of basic growth regression becomes greater.

Concluding Remarks

Over the past few decades, the Indian economy has grown rapidly compared to the rest of the world's economies. This study has clarified patterns and features of long-term economic growth in India using growth regression analysis. The following main findings can be pointed out. First, the results of growth regression support the conditional convergence hypothesis. In contrast, both India's growth rate and income level have increased, breaking the convergence hypothesis. Second, growth regression shows health capital, investment ratio, and external openness contributing to economic growth. Results show that life expectancy at birth, the investment ratio, and the export–import ratio were improved in India. Third, the growth regression suggests that human capital has a non-linear effect on economic growth. It is noteworthy that schooling beyond three years raises the growth rate. Both schooling years and growth rates have increased in India. Fourth, it is supported by the growth regression that the total fertility rate has a negative effect on growth. It has also been observed in India that the growth rate increased as the total fertility rate declined. Fifth, the growth regression shows that government consumption reduces the growth rate. Contrary to the regression results, both India's growth rate and government consumption have risen. Sixth, according to results drawn from the growth regression, inflation has a negative effect on the growth rate. However, no clear relation is apparent between inflation and growth in India. Seventh, the growth regression results show that the improvement of terms of trade contributes to economic growth. The same was observed in India, where terms of trade fluctuated over time. Finally, growth regression results imply that democracy and economic growth have a non-linear complex relation and that the relation differs depending on the position of the distribution of growth rates: while in the highest group, the growth rate and democracy are U-shaped, in the lowest group, they are inverted U-shaped. No clear relation is apparent between democracy and growth in India, where the status of democracy has varied only slightly.

Economic growth is important. With one-third of India's total population living below the poverty line, long-term high economic growth will contribute to the improvement of the well-being of the populace. Our findings show that well-being itself, including factors such as life expectancy at birth and schooling years, has a beneficial effect on economic growth. A virtuous cycle of prosperity involving economic growth and well-being is more important for India.

Notes

1 See Barro and Sala-i-Martin (2004: Chapter 1) for more details of the neoclassical growth model.
2 According to Barro (1998), the fixed effect technique can exaggerate the measurement error bias, which tends to overestimate the coefficient of the initial GDP per capita from the exclusion of the cross-national information instead of eliminating the fixed-effect bias, which tends to underestimate the coefficient of the initial GDP per capita.
3 All explanatory variables other than urbanization variables were used much the same as those used by Barro and Sala-i-Martin (2004: Chapter 12). As shown later, this study replicates most of the results obtained by Barro and Sala-i-Martin (2004: Chapter 12) despite the differences in sample periods. Insightful arguments for growth regression which this study cannot refer are found in a study by Helpman (2004).
4 The same results were obtained by Bloom, Canning and Fink (2008).
5 $\log_e(2)/0.00975309785 = 31$, and $\log_e(10)/0.00975309785 = 103$. Barro and Sala-i-Martin (2004: p. 58) present details of the calculation of the convergence speed.
6 Similar results are also presented by Azariadis and Drazen (1990), Barro (1991), Easterly and Levine (1997), Krueger and Lindahl (2001), Bils and Klenow (2000), and Sachs and Warner (1995).
7 Similar results are also reported by Bloom, Canning and Sevilla (2004), Barro and Lee (1994), Bloom and Malaney (1998), and Bloom and Williamson (1998).
8 Similar results are also presented by Barro (1991, 1996, 1998).
9 Similar results are also presented by Barro (1991, 1996, 1998), Sachs and Warner (1995), and Acemoglu, Johnson and Robinson (2002).
10 Similar results are also presented by Barro (1991, 1996, 1998), Barro and Lee (1994), Sachs and Warner (1995), and Caselli, Esquivel and Lefort (1996).
11 Similar results are also available in reports by Barro (1998), Levine and Renelt (1992), Bruno and Easterly (1998), Motley (1998), Li and Zou (2002), and Fischer (1993).
12 Similar results were also reported by Harrison (1996), Sachs and Warner (1995), Wacziarg and Welch (2008), Levine and Renelt (1992), Frankel and Romer (1999), Dollar and Kraay (2003), and Alcalá and Ciccone (2004).
13 Earlier studies examined the relation between democracy, finding that growth can be positive, negative, or non-existent depending on the types of proxy variable employed for polity and model specification. Relevant studies are those

reported by Barro (1996, 1998), Alesina, Ozler, Roubini and Swagel (1996), Minier (1998), Dollar and Kraay (2003), Kormendi and Meguire (1985), Levine and Renelt (1992), Barro and Lee (1994), Sachs and Warner (1995), Barro (1991), Sala-i-Martin (1997a, 1997b), Acemoglu, Johnson and Robinson (2001), Feld and Voigt (2003), Easterly and Levine (2001), Alcalá and Ciccone (2004), and Rodrik, Subramanian and Trebbi (2004).

References

Acemoglu, D., Johnson, S. and Robinson, J. A. (2001) "The colonial origins of comparative development: An empirical investigation", *American Economic Review* 91 (5): 1369–1401.

Acemoglu, D., Johnson, S. and Robinson, J. A. (2002) "Reversal of fortune: Geography and institutions in the making of the modern world income distribution", *Quarterly Journal of Economics* 117 (4): 1231–1294.

Alcalá, F. and Ciccone, A. (2004) "Trade and productivity", *Quarterly Journal of Economics* 119 (2): 613–646.

Alesina, A., Ozler, S., Roubini, N. and Swagel P. (1996) "Political instability and economic growth", *Journal of Economic Growth* 1 (2): 189–211.

Azariadis, Costas and Drazen, A. (1990) "Threshold externalities in economic development", *Quarterly Journal of Economics* 105 (2): 501–526.

Barro, R. J. (1991) "Economic growth in a cross section of countries", *Quarterly Journal of Economics* 106 (2): 407–443.

Barro, R. J. (1996) "Democracy and growth", *Journal of Economic Growth* 1 (1): 1–27.

Barro, R. J. (1998) *Determinants of Economic Growth*, The MIT Press.

Barro, R. and Lee, J.-W. (1994) "Sources of economic growth", *Carnegie–Rochester Conference Series on Public Policy* 40: 1–57.

Barro, R. and Lee, J.-W. (2013) "A new data set of educational attainment in the world, 1950–2010", *Journal of Development Economics* 104: 184–198.

Barro, R. J. and Sala-i-Martin, X. (2004) *Economic Growth*, Second Edition, The MIT Press.

Bils, M. and Klenow, P. J. (2000) "Does schooling cause growth?", *American Economic Review* 90 (5): 1160–1183.

Bloom, D. E., Canning, D. and Fink, G. (2008) "Urbanization and the wealth of nations", *Science* 310: 772–775.

Bloom, D. E., Canning, D. and Sevilla, J. (2004) "The effect of health on economic growth: A production function approach", *World Development* 32 (1): 1–13.

Bloom, D. E. and Malaney, P. N. (1998) "Macroeconomic consequences of the Russian mortality crisis", *World Development* 26 (11): 2073–2085.

Bloom, D. E. and Williamson, J. G. (1998). "Demographic transitions and economic miracles in emerging Asia", *World Bank Economic Review* 12 (3): 419–455.

Bruno, M. and Easterly, W. (1998) "Inflation crises and long-run growth", *Journal of Monetary Economics* 41 (1): 3–26.

Caselli, F., Esquivel, G. and Lefort, F. (1996) "Reopening the convergence debate: A new look at cross country growth empirics", *Journal of Economic Growth* 1 (3): 363–389.

Dollar, D. and Kraay, A. (2003) "Institutions, trade and growth: Revisiting the evidence", *Journal of Monetary Economics* 50 (1): 133–162.

Easterly, W. and Levine, R. (1997) "Africa's growth tragedy: Policies and ethnic divisions", *Quarterly Journal of Economics* 112 (4): 1203–1250.

Easterly, W. and Levine, R. (2001) "It's not factor accumulation: Stylized facts and growth models", *World Bank Economic Review* 15: 177–219.

Feld, L. and Voigt, S. (2003) "Economic growth and judicial independence: Cross country evidence using a new set of indicators", *European Journal of Political Economy* 19 (3): 497–527.

Fischer, S. (1993) "The role of macroeconomic factors in growth", *Journal of Monetary Economics* 32 (3): 485–512.

Frankel, J. A. and Romer, D. (1999) "Does trade cause growth?", *American Economic Review* 89 (3): 379–399.

Harrison, A. E. (1996) "Openness and growth: A time-series, cross-national analysis for developing countries", *Journal of Development Economics* 48 (2): 419–447.

Helpman, E. (2004) *The Mystery of Economic Growth*, Harvard University Press.

Kormendi, R. and Meguire, P. (1985) "Macroeconomic determinants of growth: Cross country evidence", *Journal of Monetary Economics* 16 (2): 141–163.

Krueger, A. B. and Lindahl, M. (2001) "Education for growth: Why and for whom", *Journal of Economic Literature* 39 (4): 1101–1136.

Levine, R. and Renelt, D. (1992) "A sensitivity analysis of cross-national growth regressions", *American Economic Review* 82 (4): 942–963.

Li, H. and Zou, H. (2002) "Inflation, growth, and income distribution: A cross country study", *Annals of Economics and Finance* 3 (1): 85–101.

Minier, J. A. (1998) "Democracy and growth: alternative approaches", *Journal of Economic Growth* 3 (3): 241–266.

Rodrik, D., Subramanian, A. and Trebbi, F. (2004) "Institutions rule: The primacy of institutions over geography and integration in economic development", *Journal of Economic Growth* 9 (2): 131–165.

Sachs, J. and Warner, A. (1995) "Economic reform and the process of global integration", *Brookings Papers on Economic Activity* 1: 1–118.

Sala-i-Martin, X. (1997a) "I just ran 4 million regressions", National Bureau of Economic Research Working Paper No. 6252.

Sala-i-Martin, X. (1997b) "I just ran 2 million regressions", *American Economic Review* 87 (2): 178–183.

Solow, R. M. (1956) "A contribution to the theory of economic growth", *Quarterly Journal of Economics*, 70 (1): 65–94.

Swan, T. W. (1956) "Economic growth and capital accumulation", *Economic Record* 32 (2): 334–361.

Wacziarg, R. and Welch, K. H. (2008) "Trade liberalization and growth: New evidence", *World Bank Economic Review*, 22 (2): 187–231.

Index

Note: *Italicized* pages refer to figures, **bold** pages refer to tables and pages with "n" refers notes

monthly per-capita consumption expenditure (MPCE) **130**; Muthurajas 49–50; Pillai and Chettiyar 49, 51, 57; rice and wheat consumed in labour 107, **108**; urban and rural 115n4; wealthy 110

income: non-agrarian 53; and occupation 53–57; in rural areas 21; of worker and distribution **52**
independent power producers (IPPs) 193
India 2014 Enterprise Survey Dataset 196
Indian Company Act of 1956 193
Indian Constitution 185
Indian Dairy Corporation 131
Indian Ministry of Agriculture 44
Indian Ocean 11
Indian Technical Institute (ITI) 57, **58**
Indonesia 110, 114
industrial distribution of workers 70–73; *see also* distribution of workers
informal sector 3, 63; *see also* formal sector
in-migration 175–176; estimated *175*
innovation management, Amul and Mother Dairy 137–138
International Crops Research Institute for the Semi-Arid Tropics (ICRISAT) 28, 34
International Telecommunication Union 144
irrigation 13–15, 31, 33, 44, 191, *192*
Iruvelpattu 47

Jagir 7, **11**; demographic changes between 1801 and 1871 **12**
jajmani system 22n1
Japan Society for Promotion of Sciences (JSPS) 1, 6n1
Jawaharlal Nehru National Urban Renewal Mission 180–181
Jharkhand 96, 160n8, 165, 177

Kano, H. 23n5
Kapsos, S. 94n2
katcha houses 64
Key Village Development Program 131
Knatkovska, V. 65n3
Kolkata 5

Kroeze, C. 162
Kumar, H. 115n3
Kurosaki, T. 2, 25–45

labor/labour 30, *30*, 76; market 2, 62–63, 68, 74, 75, 77–79, 82, 86, 88; population and **69**; productivity 30, *31*; rural 90; withdrawal of adult women from 67, 94n2
land: conversion of 5; productivity *31*, *32*; tax 14; transfer 15; use 31, *32*, 33–34, 44
land development 9–10, 22; and population growth 13; and population increase 12; saturation of 13
landholding 20; changes by castes **19**; operational 141n4; ratio of the Chettiyars 15, *16*
landless laborers 121, 124
Lanjouw, P. 62
Lardinois, R. 22n4
Lhungdim, H. 158
liberalization: dairy industry development 134–137; economic 4, 67, 95, 117, 140; milk industry 131–139, 140; policy 1; trade 96, 114
life expectancy 1, 6, 219–220, *221*, 230–231
lifestyle change 4
literacy rates 1, 145
livestock *167*, 167–169, *169*
Livestock Census 167
long-term changes in crop specialization 29–33

Madhya Pradesh 28, 42, 96, 146–147, 165, 170
Madras Presidency 11, 13; changes in the irrigated extent of *14*
Mahatma Gandhi National Rural Employment Guarantee Act Programme (MGNREGA) 67, 72, 76, 88, 90, 124
Malaysia 110, 114
map: food regions *100*; in-migration, estimated *175*; nitrogen balance on farmland *170*; nitrogen fertilizer input *165*; nitrogen load from humans *181*; nitrogen load from livestock *169*; out-migration, estimated *174*; poultry *168*; spatial distribution *29*
market economy 11, 22
Mayer, K. 184–185, 194, 197, 205, 206n8

Printed in the United States
by Baker & Taylor Publisher Services